LIVING ON THE EDGE

AMAZING RELATIONSHIPS IN THE NATURAL WORLD

RODALE

JEFF CORWIN

Printed in the United States of America
Rodale Inc. makes every effort to use acid-free ∞, recycled paper ♻.

Photographs of Atta (leaf cutter) ants on pages 157, 215, and 216 are © 2003 by Marc A. Seid, Ph.D., Department of Biology, Boston University, and are used with permission.

Book design by Joanna Williams

Library of Congress Cataloging-in-Publication Data

Corwin, Jeff.
    Living on the edge : amazing relationships in the natural world / Jeff Corwin.
        p.   cm.
    Includes bibliographical references (p.   ).
    ISBN 1–57954–792–3 hardcover
    1. Desert biology—Sonoran Desert.   2. Savannas—Africa, Eastern.
    3. Rain forests—Costa Rica.   4. Llanos—Venezuela.   I. Title.
    QH104.5.S58C67   2003
    578.7—dc22   2003018603

Distributed to the book trade by St. Martin's Press

2   4   6   8   10   9   7   5   3   1   hardcover

Visit us on the Web at www.rodalestore.com, or call us toll-free at (800) 848-4735.

WE **INSPIRE** AND **ENABLE** PEOPLE TO IMPROVE
THEIR LIVES AND THE WORLD AROUND THEM

To my wonderful wife, Natasha:
thanks for always believing in me and for
your editorial brilliance as well

To my daughter, Maya Rose:
we are all mighty glad that you have
joined our pack

ACKNOWLEDGMENTS

There have been many individuals and organizations along the way that were greatly helpful with the development of this book. First, I would like to thank my parents, Marcy and Valerie Corwin, for their open-minded approach towards raising me. Had it not been for their parental skills, I probably would not be where I am today. In fact, I probably would be wealthier, better looking, and thinner. . . . Only kidding. I would also like to thank my sisters, Amy and Joy, for their relentless years of torment. Looks like I get the last laugh, which you gals can read all about (along with the rest of the world) in chapter five. I'm only kidding. . . . I also owe a great thanks to my late grandmothers, Louise and Charlotte. Their compassion for animals has had a very profound impact on all who knew them, including the critters! Thanks to Dr. John Jahoda of the biology department at Bridgewater State College for his excellent mentoring, and to the college as well for providing me with a first-class education. To Dr. Curt Griffin and Dr. Todd Fuller of the Department of Wildlife and Fisheries Conservation with the University of Massachusetts at Amherst. To my friend Fred Dodd, who first introduced me to the rainforests of Belize. To Pat (a.k.a. Martha) and Dan Ryan for providing me with shelter. To Ben Zuckerberg, for his hundreds of valuable hours of research. To Craig Ivanyi, curator of herpetology, ichthyology, and invertebrate zoology, and Shawnee Riplog-Peterson, curator of mammalogy and ornithology, both at the Arizona-Sonora Desert Museum. I would encourage anyone reading this book to visit this museum—it's a lot of fun, and the exhibits are excellent. Thanks to Lisa Bates of the Tucson Wildlife Center. To the South Shore Natural Science Center and the EcoZone. Thanks to Jud Cremata, Holly Williamson, and Dominique Boozer for research materials. To my friends Kevin Meagher and Tim Braine. To all my friends at Animal Planet. To my literary agent, Christi Cardenas. To Michael Ralbovsky and Joaney Gallagher of Rainforest Reptile Shows for all their help. To my editors, Stephanie Tade and Jennifer Kushnier, at Rodale. To Troy Juliar, for taking a chance on the idea. To Tea Cup—you were the light that burned twice as bright; and to Charlotte—I am so sorry that I never had the chance to see you after you lost all that weight before being eaten by the nasty coyote. Finally, a special thanks to the global community of field researchers, scientists, naturalists, and conservationists of both the past and present, whose research and discoveries within the realm of the natural world have provided me with the valuable and fascinating information needed to write this book.

CONTENTS

"I feel like I am in a bloody convection oven!" Jeff gasped when he stepped out onto the brittle and baked earth of the Sonoran Desert for the first time. There are seemingly few places on Earth more inhospitable than this vast arid landscape, but during the few weeks of spring rain it teems with newly awakened life keen on reproducing and prowling predators hungry to dominate the food chain.

"That's no boulder, that the monster's massive skull!" Jeff thought as he went nose to nose with a man-killing crocodile. Explore the vast frontier of this east African savannah, where the large grassy areas support some of the largest animals in the world, including elephants, giraffes, lions, and rhinoceros. Jeff brings you ringside in the dynamic contest of predator and prey and divulges perhaps the greatest predator of all.

"For the love of God, get 'em off!" Jeff cried as he failed to sidestep an approaching army of ants. Walk with him through this towering rainforest wonderland, laced with vines and trees that strangle, that is home to more species of plants, birds, and butterflies than in all of Europe. Chance upon a ghostly anteater, hear the deafening roar from a troop of monkeys, spot the tracks of a jungle cat, and learn what has drawn Jeff to the rainforest nearly 100 times.

"Dear God, man! Run . . . Run as fast as you can!" Jeff yelled as his crew was ambushed by a cranky giant river otter. In the center of the South American continent lies an immense prairie that exhibits utter extremes as each year, extensive fields of parched grasses are transformed to a glassy sea of flooded grassland. For the abundant and diverse plants and animals living here, the annual wet season brings with it an awesome display of animal and plant adaptability. Jeff demonstrates that the Llanos is one of our planet's most spectacular habitats.

FOREWORD

It was 1993, and the JASON Foundation for Education was planning its first expedition to the rainforests of the world. Although we had been to other exotic places before, including the Galapagos Islands and the Sea of Cortez, this was the first time I was leaving my watery world and entering a place I knew little about. It was clear that I needed to find scientists and naturalists who not only understood the ecological complexities of this important region of Earth, but who also had the natural gift of communication. I needed them to catch the imagination of the young students we were trying to reach—to excite and engage them in science while working in a hot humid world full of dangers, where I wanted the environment to be the story, not the dangers they would face working there.

It was at Bridgewater State University in Massachusetts where I first met Jeff. Bridgewater was becoming one of our newest receiving sites for our "live" telecasts, and they were getting ready to train their teachers in anticipation of receiving our programs from the rainforests of Belize. As soon as I arrived I met a young graduate student whom they thought would be ideal for our program.

What I remember most about that first encounter was Jeff's ever-present smile, boundless energy, and, most important, his passion for the creatures of the natural world. Equally important was his ability to take the complexities of the rainforests and explain them to those of us whose knowledge of the rainforest was meager at best. I knew right away that Jeff would prove to be an invaluable member of our team.

And I was right. Jeff took to the rainforest like a duck to water. The students who went with us on the expedition loved to be with Jeff, as did the hundreds of thousands of students and teachers watching at our downlink satellite sites around the world. I had my son Douglas with me on the expedition and he, like me, had never been in a rainforest. One night, Jeff and Douglas ventured deep into the jungle just as night was approaching.

The expression "total darkness" must have been coined by someone caught at night in a rainforest. When the sun goes down, the lights go off and every manner of creature comes to life. The sounds are deafening, and one's imagination goes into full gear. I waited up for Jeff and Douglas to return. They didn't. It was pouring rain, and coconut-sized fruits fell onto our tin roof with the sound of a bomb going off. I wanted to kill both of them for making me worry as much as I did.

But when I saw those two smiling faces emerge from the underbrush the next morning full of exciting stories about their nocturnal adventures, I, too, was drawn to their tales of adventure. To this very day, Douglas remembers that night, along with the sounds of wild pigs.

Since those early days with Jeff, I have watched his career mature and blossom. My youngest son Ben and daughter Emily Rose are his greatest fans, never wanting to miss *The Jeff Corwin Experience.*

Reading through this wonderful book, one quickly realizes that Jeff is much more than a great communicator. He is also a dedicated wildlife biologist who has deep concerns about the environmental health of our planet.

So I encourage the reader to jump into this book with both feet, and when you come out the other side, you will have a much better understanding of the fragile nature of the ecosystems of Earth as well as a much better appreciation of the valuable role Jeff Corwin plays in imparting that understanding to the next generation of global citizens who have the responsibility of insuring the future health of life on Earth.

—Dr. Robert D. Ballard
President, Institute for Exploration
Founder and Chief Scientist of the JASON Foundation for Education

THE
SONORAN DESERT
OF ARIZONA

onvection oven. I feel like I am in a bloody convection oven!" These were the first words I managed to squeak through fast-flaking lips upon stepping out onto the baked earth of the Sonoran Desert for the very first time. There are few places on Earth more inhospitable than this vast landscape of southern Arizona. It is a harsh place where shade is the ultimate luxury and the midday heat can render the horizon a blinding band of cataract white. The sun here is without mercy, and once this fiery orb has barely levitated above distant jagged peaks, the temperature can easily soar past 110°F. Water rarely finds its way here and when it does, it is less an elixir of life and more a force of destruction. What little scraps of life that have managed to take hold in the brittle earth are often washed away by the deluge of rain that is concentrated in the brief but powerful monsoon downpours of late summer.

The Sonoran Desert is a land of extremes. While daytime temperatures are often hotter than Pompeii on that fateful molten day, nighttime can be viciously frigid, allowing for a tongue-sticking frost to glaze every pebble. For much of the year the land lies parched beneath a few meager clouds until one day the sky blackens and then bursts with pummeling rains. It seems as though no life could exist here, and perhaps even the desolate terrain of Mars could provide a more inviting habitat than what the

Sonoran has to offer. In truth, this arid land is far from barren. For a few very brief moments during early spring and the rainy season of mid-to-late-summer, the desert explodes with life that lies dormant for most of the year. A diverse array of critters has adapted to the challenges of this ecosystem, and in the end all are equally resilient because this desert is infamous for her cruelty to the weak and the ill prepared.

So there I was, just three months shy of my twenty-eighth birthday and the most important decision of my life: marriage. I was never much of a planner and spontaneity to me was like white on rice. I met my future wife in an organic supermarket in Cambridge, Massachusetts. We went out for some Spanish tapas that evening, and sometime between paella and flan we decided to tie the knot. As the fateful day loomed closer, the reality of marital bondage struck me down worse than alligator breath. I decided that I needed to take stock of my metamorphosis toward absolute adulthood by going on a soul-searching sabbatical, a

last-minute vision quest to make sure that I wasn't being brash with my butchering of bachelorhood.

Now, don't get me wrong about the institution of marriage, because in theory I think it is a pretty good concept. It's just that I always thought that I would remain a permanent member of the bachelor club. I liked being single, so needless to say I was just as shocked as everyone around me when the marriage bug bit and the infection of potential monogamy took hold. Now with regard to actually being married . . . Although I went into the contract in a manner that was not, shall we say, kicking and screaming, but more with a whiny whimper—similar to that of a dog who reaches back to give himself a good cleaning the day after surgery, only to discover that his precious orbs of pride have mysteriously disappeared—I actually like being married. My wife and I have been married since 1995, and for the most part, our connubial life has been a great adventure.

You're probably thinking that I married a biologist, a veterinarian, or a zookeeper, but in truth, my wife's interest in wildlife has only resulted from her getting closer to what I do for a living. My wife is a scientist, but not in natural history; her specialty is literature. She studies European modernism, and she happens to be one of the most brilliant intellectuals I have ever met. She is the recipient of a very competitive research fellowship for her Ph.D. studies at a prestigious university in New England. She is also one of the kindest persons I know. To top it all off, she is drop-dead gorgeous! The best thing about being married to her is that she ended up becoming my best friend, and I am not just saying all this nice stuff because at this very moment she is looking over my shoulder, with one eyebrow suspiciously raised. I love you, honey!

So back to my premarital state. I decided that I would confront my fears in the lonely desert of the Southwest, specifically the Sonoran Desert of Arizona. I would go alone, outfitted only with a canteen, sunblock, and an assortment of barely edible protein bars. I departed for my odyssey in late April of 1995 to spend

Whoever said dry heat was better than humidity had never spent an afternoon beneath the Arizona sun. The humidity may indeed be nonexistent here, but so it is inside an incinerator.

nearly two weeks hiking across sweeps of sand and over steep, crumbling ledges in search of strange desert creatures, as well as some insight as to where my life was heading.

Upon arrival at Tucson International Airport, I walked out of the air-conditioned coolness and into a scorching wall of air, fiercer than any other temperature that I had ever experienced. Whoever said dry heat was better than humidity had never spent an afternoon beneath the Arizona sun. The humidity may indeed be nonexistent here, but so it is inside an incinerator, and both are about as equally pleasant. It was so hot that when I looked off toward the horizon, my eyes detected flickering waves of heated air dancing across an endless stretch of black tar. Instantly, my lips

THE ARIZONA DESTINY

The decision to explore the Sonoran Desert largely resulted from the embellished stories of youthful adventures shared with me by friends and colleagues. They, like myself, had an affinity for slimy and scaly critters. One friend in particular, Fred, told great tales of encounters with rattlesnakes as fat as a man's calf that sported rattles nearly as long as an ear of corn. He told me of secret patches of desert where if the moon is right, Gila monsters pour out of the ground. He hinted of ancient, sand-dusted roads near the border of Mexico, derelict routes tramped upon by weary miners and an occasional border-runner seeking fortune in the North. One neglected corridor in particular, running south from Tucson to Mexico, was not only treaded upon by the disenfranchised but was also a great haunt for colorful and cool serpents, like Mojave rattlers and Mexican black kings. Before I left for Arizona, Fred circled a little clump of hills on the map with his Sharpie, telling me, "You gotta go there. When I was in grad school at ASU, we'd go up there on weekends, and we'd find ridge-nosed rattlers and tricolor mountain king snakes by the dozens!" I was sold.

From the age of seven till nearly sixteen, I kept a tattered and ancient field guide to the amphibians and reptiles of the Southwest under my pillow. Each night before going to sleep, I would finger my way though this undisputed favorite. It seemed as though the pages were trained, merely upon my touch, to open to the well-worn chapters containing images and secrets of my favorite cold-blooded beasts. This book was not merely a field guide but more like a bible to me, and after years of devoted reading, I had managed to memorize endless amounts of natural history information on many of the species highlighted in that text. Most of these creatures shared one commonality: They all inhabited the daunting territory of the Sonoran Desert. And at the age of twenty-eight, after years of obsessing and daydreaming, I had the opportunity to see them face-to-face!

began to crack, as my forehead glazed with red, and it seemed like I couldn't smear the sunblock over my peaches-and-cream complexion fast enough.

I left New England with only two hundred bucks in my pocket and a debit card that was pretty much tapped out. I was not going to be packing and camping my way through the desert out of sport, but out of necessity. I couldn't afford to stay at any hotels, so for the most part, I would be sleeping in the backseat of a rented Japanese hatchback. Meals would be power bars, fruit cocktail from a can, and turkey jerky. Only on rare occasions would I treat myself to some roadside Mexican grub, or perhaps a plate of cheap Chinese.

The first afternoon I drove sixty miles into the desert, and when maneuvering around the many potholes that seemed hungry to swallow up my cheap rental became pretty much impossible, I decided to pull over and cover some ground on foot. Again, it was stiflingly hot, so with the intent of not overheating, I wore nothing but a T-shirt and shorts. Although I planned on crashing that night in the desert under the protective glow of a comforting moon, I brought just a single bed sheet, because a bulky sleeping bag would have been overkill. (When I am trying to fall asleep, nothing irritates me more than sweat slipping down folds of my skin until it saturates my sheets like a wet halo or worse

yet, my own miserable version of the Shroud of Turin.) I figured that if the daytime temperatures soared past the one hundred-degree mark, then surely the evening wouldn't be much cooler—after all, it was April. Boy, was I wrong!

After hours spent searching for critters that appeared to have gone AWOL, I decided at about 8:30 P.M. that it was time to hunker down and catch some shut-eye. I finally found a nice place to nest underneath a crumbling overhang of rock next to a dormant river wash. But I had a tough time settling in, since every time I came across a cozy little plot of desert to call my own, I would find a pile of smashed beer bottles or even worse, a collapsing pyramid of rusted cans riddled with bullet holes. Now here's the thing about Arizona that takes some getting used to. If you come across a remote street sign, an abandoned car part such as a tire rim or fender, a pile of unwanted tin receptacles—in fact, just about any form of discarded metal—you can pretty much bet that it has been shot up to the point of being barely recognizable. Now, that's not to say that your life here is in any more danger than anywhere else; it's just that some folks in Arizona like to pass the time by blowing off a little gunpowder.

So there I was, flapping out my bed sheet, kicking away the occasional sharp stone or prickly stick that could potentially impede a good night's sleep. At first, the temperature was quite pleasant. I eased down upon a firm but comfortable bed of sand that had been warmed up nicely from a full day of sun exposure, and then curled myself up within the folds of sheet like it was a cocoon.

Once I got used to the random coyote howling and a hooting owl, I quickly fell asleep. Then, about an hour into my slumber, came a nightmare. First, the wretched dream consisted of being plunged naked into the Arctic waters after a nasty shipwreck. Then, the nightmare transformed into a scene where I was locked out of my parents' house in the dead of February, unable to call up to them to let me in, with my feet frozen to the earth, my testicles pulled up past my kidneys. That's when, thankfully, I finally

woke up. The temperature had dropped to just above freezing, and my bladder was about to empty itself in a last-ditch effort to keep my body from succumbing to the cold.

I was absolutely miserable as I gathered my belongings and made what felt like a final death march to my crappy rental, hidden somewhere east out of the desert and nearly five miles down the road. After a good two hours of searching, I finally found my car, which seemed a lot less crappy to me now that it was the only barrier standing between me and a bad bout of hypothermia. I nearly cried with relief when I stumbled onto it, and I piled into the backseat as fast as I could. I then cranked up the engine to get a little warm air flowing before anxiously sliding into my entire wardrobe for extra insulation against the frigid night. The Michelin Man is probably more svelte than I was that night after bulking up with numerous layers of clothing. The next day I went to Target and bought a sleeping bag.

If that first night's frosty ordeal was any indication of how the rest of my

Sonoran adventure was going to go, then I was in a whole heap of trouble.

I spent nearly two weeks flipping over every rock I could physically lift. My back was starting to strain, and I had developed a very raw blister patch in the crook of my thumb from repeatedly using my snake hook (a.k.a. modified golf club) as a wedge for jacking up intriguing clumps of debris that had the potential of being good serpent concealers. No log was left unrolled, and every dark crevice, including all burrow-like cavities I came across, had been illuminated. I searched from sunrise till late morning, then broke for grub and a nap till late afternoon. I resumed my reptilian quest from sunset till near to midnight. I traveled from Organ Pipe Cactus National Monument to Gila Bend, from Saguaro National Park to Mexico. In the end, I must have covered six hundred miles of terrain. If my goal was to see every species of Southwestern cactus, or to develop a melanoma-inducing sunburn, then my mission would have been a great success. But I was there to see wild lizards, snakes, and desert tortoises, creatures that turned out to be more elusive than I had ever imagined. I was good at finding snakes—heck, my grandmother said I could sniff them out of a stone wall, and that I was nearly psychic when it came to finding these critters. Yet this was not to be the case in Arizona. There would be no Gila monsters flowing from their subterranean dens, and the eerie rasping shudder of a rattlesnake's rattle kept silent wherever I searched. Tortoises never ventured from their lairs into the light for me, and tricolor king snakes remained shadowed beyond my reach.

In the end, the only worthwhile snake I found during my premarital trek was a measly bull snake teetering on the verge of starvation. Despite many hours of searching, Arizona had turned out to be a big bust, leaving me with an unsavory sense of dejection that ran throughout my fast-deflating confidence. Still, although I didn't get to see the critters that had served as the foundation for the fantasies of my youth, I did get something good out of the anticlimactic trek. I learned that I didn't need a vision quest to find out if I was ready for marriage because when life got tough, I got wimpy and missed my fiancée. Yes, the Sonoran Desert turned out to be a letdown, but even so, I decided to give it a second chance.

THE PRODIGAL SON RETURNS

Two years later I returned to the defiant desert of Arizona, but this time I ventured there in midsummer at the onset of the monsoon rains. My second experience in this vast stretch of arid wilderness was the complete reversal of my first. This time I observed many of the creatures that had previously evaded discovery. The summer rains saturated the thirsty earth, replenishing vacant streambeds, reviving a great plethora of dormant life. Finally, the Sonoran had been restored in my imagination and provided me with living proof of its stature as one of the greatest ecosystems, unique to the North American continent. My second journey, along with the additional treks I've since made to this severe but strangely beautiful country, surpassed all of my expectations. For me, the

Sonoran Desert has transformed from a place of disillusionment where failure and frustration ran rampant, to one of my favorite regions on Earth. She has taught me that timing is everything, and if you arrive just a wee bit early or a tad too late, you'll miss one of the greatest natural spectacles that the good Earth has to offer. In order to ensure that you have an opportunity to experience the magic hour when the wildlife of the Sonoran reaches its zenith, I am going to take you there at the height of the monsoon season.

It's just about sunset during an early July day. The sky has blackened with ominous clouds that seem unnaturally close to the ground. Frequently throughout the afternoon, they have exploded in short bursts, generously wetting the terra firma. Across from a swollen stream that has been washed over with foamy water browned heavy with sediment, a small puddle has formed. Fissures running across the crust of soil have begun to soften and swell as if they were healing wounds. The reflection of the fat sun shines boldly across the growing pool, except where it has been sharply split by the soothing shadow of a colossal saguaro. With a tall, beehive-like hairdo for a top and two prickly arms twisted in opposite directions, the cactus resembles an oversized Gumby.

In its shadow, at the edge of the forming pool, slumbers a small slippery creature, buried nearly two feet deep in the earth. It has been waiting patiently for the water to come, and as the refreshing fluid seeps into the earth, the animal awakens and begins to squirm. Like an Egyptian mummy revived by a reading from the *Book of the Dead*, the little beast writhes around in its encrusted capsule until it is freed. Quickly, the slimy creature moves upwards, until it erupts out of the darkness and into the glow of the last light. Soon others just like it break free from their coffins of mud. Like the first wave of a great army, they make their way to the waterhole, and upon jumping into the muddy liquid they begin to sing. The reproductive battle has begun!

They are Couch's spadefoot toads (*Scaphiopus couchii*), one of my favorite Southwestern amphibians! With blotchy green skin, a pug-like muzzle, and cute bugging eyes, the face of a spadefoot is sort of the amphibian version of a cross between Yoda and Marty Feldman. Even though they have soft and pudgy bodies not much longer than my thumb, I can't think of a tougher, more durable frog in all of North America. These rugged critters owe their names to the miniature shovel-like wedges of rigid skin pro-

Spadefoot toads are not toads at all but are actually true frogs. Most true toads belong to the Bufonidae family and have dry, bumpy skin.

Couch's spadefoot toad has only two things on its mind as it emerges from its dormant state: dinner and sex!

truding from the ball of each heel. Spade-foot toads are master excavators, and when the monsoon rains have all but dried up, these frogs dig into the earth by swirling their legs around and around, eggbeater-style. Within moments, the spadefoot can burrow two to three feet deep, until it is safely beyond reach of the sun's sweltering rays. Still, the soil is often chalk dry, forcing the spadefoot to deal with parched prospects, and for many species of amphibians a lack of moisture is often a death sentence.

Many amphibians—for example, most species of frogs and salamanders—have lungs that are not efficient enough to get all the necessary oxygen they need to sustain life, so they make up for this deficit by breathing through their skin. This is called cutaneous respiration, and in order for oxygen to pass through the barrier of skin and into the bloodstream, the outside of the creature needs to remain moist. For most frogs, desiccation means death.

Spadefoots have developed an ingenious means for dealing with the threat of dehydration: Their skin can transform into a tightly sealed sarcophagus. When environmental conditions are deadly dry, the skin of the spadefoot functions almost like a womb, keeping the vulnerable frog moist and protected. Basically, the top layer of the skin bubbles out from the frog's body until it hardens into a crisp, black sack that prevents much of the valuable body moisture from escaping. Once encased in its protective cocoon, the spadefoot toad becomes inactive as if fossilized. Amazingly, this hardy creature can stay in a dormant state for nearly two years, reemerging only when the conditions are ideal for survival and reproduction. This is why I could not find one of the mysterious critters during my first expedition to the Sonoran Desert—I was there at the wrong time of year. I could not find a single one, despite the fact that there were probably hundreds of them sleeping peacefully out of reach beneath my feet. Although they skunked me the first time, upon my return I had a chance to witness tons of them during their mating season, all huddled up, rubbing and squirming in one big slimy orgy!

An increase of moisture in the arid soil is of course the alarm clock that wakes the spadefoot up from its Rip Van Winkle

Notice the spade-like black callus at the base of the frog's heel, used for excavation.

state. And now that the spadefoots are conscious, the first thing to hit them is hunger. The first frog out has already made it to the edge of the pool. Above his head is a dragonfly perched at the tip of a creosote branch that was beaten down by the fierce rains of the afternoon. The frog freezes up as he locks in on the dragonfly. But before the spadefoot can get a decent fix on it, the giant bug levitates above the branch and then races off.

Hanging upside down along the spine of a lonely strand of grass, two other dragonflies are eagerly having sex. The male has locked onto the female and together they hover in the air and swirl a bit, eventually returning to their point of takeoff. Despite their acrobatic flight pattern, he never lets go of his nimble mate, until he has completed his task of injecting her with millions of years of genetic history. Moments after copulation he flies off, never to see her again. That's when the other dragonfly, the one that nearly became frog bait, makes his move.

After the first suitor is well out of sight, the precocious dragonfly swoops in, making a beeline towards the female. He violently grabs onto her and, like a Black Hawk helicopter, he zips her up into the air. He rips her away from the grass blade with such jarring force that her head and abdomen slam against each other, causing her to fold inward to the point of nearly snapping in two. Then, without warning, he freefalls at neck-breaking speed towards the fast-approaching puddle of coffee-colored water beneath them. Just before they kamikaze themselves to a watery grave, he pulls back and then rolls their flailing bodies upward, until they spiral into a perfect 360-degree spin. As he spins and whips her around and about,

the centrifugal force causes most of the liquid in her body to rush toward the back end of her abdomen, including the sperm implanted in her by the previous mate. With one final loop-de-loop, the vent at the end of her abdomen opens up and all the sperm from her recent tryst spews out of her body and into oblivion. He slips in faster than a jackrabbit on a blind date, and after implanting his seed, he finally releases her. She freefalls for just a few seconds and then, after regaining composure, she rockets off toward the horizon.

The victorious male returns to the bent creosote branch to catch his breath and take stock of his conquest. He looks up to see another pair of mating dragonflies passing overhead. Just as he is about to make his move, a crushing pain suddenly wraps around his thorax. He struggles to free himself from the mashing squeeze, but his resistance is futile. The more he struggles, the higher the crunching sensation travels until finally it reaches the fragile tissues of his neck. As the four transparent wings collapse around the dragonfly's shimmering orbs, a smoky darkness taints his kaleidoscopic vision until all goes black. After two or three gulps, the crumpling body of the dragonfly slides rapidly past the spadefoot's gullet and into its eager belly. Patience paid off for the hungry frog, while the dragonfly's sexual piracy came with the ultimate price.

So in the end, what is the lesson? Is it "cheat, cheat, never beat"? Well, not exactly. Yes, the dragonfly did pay for his sexual exploits with his life, but in the end, he found the quickest, easiest, and cheapest method to ensure that his genes make it to the next generation, while simultaneously eliminating the potential of any rival sperm from the competition. So he's not going to be around to see the kids grow up, but truth be told, he probably had reached the end of his lifespan, and with regard to parenting skills, he would have been a deadbeat dad.

The spadefoot has exchanged one appetite for another, and like the dragonfly he just devoured, he's ready to get some action. The horny spadefoot is not alone; others just like him, with a need to breed, have begun to gather at the pool. The competition has become tough, as dozens of amorous spadefoots have begun to croon like lonely tomcats beneath the glow of a robust moon. They inflate the air sacks beneath their chins so tightly that the skin stretches to near transparency, like a chewing gum bubble on the verge of bursting. Upon exhalation, a melodious shrill flows from the passionate muzzle of each male trying to draw in a potential mate. But there is more than just love in the air; there is danger as well. Lovesick females are not the only critters attracted to the songs of the sentimental spadefoots; there are predators looming in the darkness of night. Flesh-eating creatures have discovered the chaotic chorus of singing spadefoots, and they have begun to move in for an easy meal.

Not far from the pool rest the collapsed remains of a barrel cactus (*Ferocactus wislizeni*). The thorn-covered corpse lies on its side, partially crushed by its own weight. The innards of the cactus rotted out years ago, leaving behind a fibrous exoskeleton. Over time, a miniature slope of sand has blown its way into the hollow cavity, while the evidence of half-eaten seeds, dried scat, and a purposefully arranged pile of debris allude to a multitude of small creatures that have come

---

Imagine an aroma a thousand times more intense and palpable than a field of lavender under a July sun; that's what it is like to have a Jacobson's organ.

---

and gone. Something stirs beneath a dried-up tuft of twisted vegetation. A long legless torso begins to rise through the withered strands of once hearty plants. As the ancient bits of vegetation give way, a scaly back levitates above the matter and is soon followed by two perfectly round, lidless eyes. The entire head erupts out of the pile, revealing an unnaturally large and somewhat awkward-looking snout. The tip of the creature's muzzle curls up sharply and is very beak-like. Plump jowls hang off its broad head, and its lips seem more fish than reptile.

As the rest of the creature's long and robust body peels away from the debris, a black tongue, shiny like oil, slips out between the lips, flickers a bit, and then quickly retracts. The tongue snaps out and back in like a rubber band a couple more times, liberally coating its slick surface with a blanket of invisible molecules. Then the serpent finally folds it backwards, until it is hidden behind a fortress of razor-sharp teeth, uniform in shape. Once inside the moist orifice, the glistening forked tips of flesh needle their way into a narrow pit positioned along the roof of the mouth. This pit, containing highly sensitive tissue, is called the Jacobson's organ, and it provides the reptile with the remarkable ability to analyze the chemistry of its surrounding environment. This miraculous structure allows the creature to literally taste its way out of danger, taste its way home, and taste its way to its next meal.

Imagine an aroma a thousand times more intense and palpable than a field of lavender under a July sun; that's what it is like to have a Jacobson's organ. The creature has picked up a chemical trail that leads out of the cactus and towards the pool. This barely detectable trail, comprised of a million microscopic particles, made its way from the communing spadefoots and on to the predator's quivering tongue. For a few moments, the creature savors the scent of the frogs, but a mouthful of molecules is not enough. Slowly, it crawls out of the hollow cactus, allowing only its tongue to guide it to the possible quarry gathering at the pool. The hungry serpent has carved out an existence at the very edge of its range. As a species, it usually occupies grassier, more prairie-like habitats where life can be less volatile, but this hardy individual has managed to thrive along the outskirts of its territory, living a gambler's life by capitalizing on the seasonal jackpot of potential prey. The essence of spadefoot grows more concentrated as the predator draws closer. Soon, the hungry creature will strike and there will be bloodshed. An appetite is about to be satisfied as a horde of spadefoots is about to be sacrificed.

The predator on the prowl just happens to be one of my favorite snakes, the Mexican hognose (*Heterodon nasicus kennerlyi*). Now, I know I tend to throw around the word "favorite" quite regularly, but it's true. The hognose is an extraordinary serpent, uniquely designed to hunt a very specific prey. Hognose snakes are specialists when it comes to the kill, and they dine almost exclusively on frogs and, especially, toads—but will occasionally partake of small rodents and lizards. The thing about toads is that they tend to be rather nasty to the palate, and in some cases downright deadly! But poisonous prey is not a hindrance for the hognose; in fact, the more toxic the toad, the better the meal. Although the spadefoot's skin does produce a medley of rather weak toxins, which may keep a few predators at bay, when it comes to the hognose, a bit of glandular poison just adds more punch to the meal. The other great attribute of hognose snakes is that they tend to have pretty dramatic personalities when it comes to defense. For the most part they are all piss and vinegar, but when push comes to shove, they tend to put on a pretty great show. Old-timers often refer to the hog-

The Mexican hognose snake, also called a puff adder, prefers a bold Chianti with its spadefoot.

nose snake as the puff adder, and as you soon shall see, when it comes to keeping itself out of the food chain, the hognose has a first-class act.

I had a hognose snake as a pet when I was growing up. Her name was Gilda, and she was wonderful. If I dozed off in my hammock with her coiled on my belly, I could always count on her being there when I awoke. Anyone who believes that snakes are empty of personality and character has never met a hognose. I was lucky: Gilda easily took to eating mice (my mother did not feel so very fortunate, however, living in a house inhabited by dozens of insatiable snakes and countless numbers of mice on death row), but for most hognose snakes, captivity is a death sentence. Most captive hognose snakes, if not given a proper diet of toads, would rather die of starvation than consent to eating anything else. Fifty years ago hognose snakes where pretty common throughout North America, but today this is no longer the case. Because of habitat loss, a drop in overall toad populations (due to an increase in pollution and a decrease in wetlands), and excessive collecting for the pet trade, these wonderfully odd serpents have all but disappeared. It will be a great loss to the natural history of North America if the hognose snake should fall victim to extinction.

All right, I'll hop off my soapbox now and get back to the pool churning with frogs, some of which are about to become a late-night snack. A swirling cloud of mud has enveloped any last bit of clarity as the pool, not much bigger than a driveway puddle, begins to reach its spadefoot saturation point. They kick and frolic, hop in for a dip, then out for a snack. Bloated males proudly sing out like deflating bagpipes and there is a lot of chasing going on. The first spadefoot to make it on the scene has started to grow weary from hours of unrewarded shrilling. Just sec-

onds before wading back into the shadows at the edge of the pool, dejected by his inability to attract a mate, he captures the eye of a plump female. She likes what she sees and makes her interest known by casually floating over in his direction. He perks up, and soon he is bobbing around her, trying to keep her attention. Then he makes his move. Jumping on her from behind, the suitor manages to wrap his stumpy arms around her torso until his thumbs lock together. The lucky spadefoot has finally grabbed himself a mate, and he will do everything in his power to hold on to her. Jealousy spreads quickly amongst the unattached bachelors in the pool, and they are quick to have a go at him. From all directions they paw at him, trying to force him to release his conquest. He holds on tight, even when one of the other males confuses him for a female and hops on for a ride. A threesome is not his style, so he manages to fling the competition off his back.

Two pairs of webbed feet simultaneously kick toward the edge of the pool, piggyback-style. Upon retreating to a more tranquil area, the male's arms begin to convulse. He closes his eyes in concentration as his arms clamp down tightly around the base of the female's ribcage. This ancient form of amphibian sex is known as amplexus, and many frog species have been doing it for nearly 200 million years. As the male squeezes down on the female, her vent (also called the cloaca) begins to dilate. Suddenly, a strand containing hundreds of pebble-sized dots, spherical in shape and brown in color, come shooting out of her. As she releases her eggs he covers them with a white cloud of sperm. Fertilization is almost instantaneous, and after the eggs have been deposited, the parental contribution of both male and female abruptly ends. He quickly unlocks his grasp, allowing the female to slip away. There is no exchange of phone numbers or embarrassing walk of shame, for that matter. It's just plain and simple biology, without any baggage—a behavior that ensures that a future generation of spadefoots is established.

As the male swims back to the center of the pool, his former flame catches her breath and prepares to move on. Now empty of eggs, she hops out of the pool, then squeezes her body under a protective pile of stones. All is calm, until one of the stones close to her side begins to move. She does not notice the gap forming between her and the stone as an invader begins to carve out a bit of space for an attack. Ever so quietly, the bed of pebbles begins to give way, until a scale-studded snout gingerly breaks through. The frog is fast asleep and does not detect the slick tongue, forked at the tip, which flickers with excitement to her side. Soon, the entire head of the intruder is revealed. It is the Mexican hognose snake, enticed by the aroma of the female spadefoot hovering in the air like steam wafting off a freshly baked pie. The snake uses its stumpy, upturned muzzle to dig its way to the plump frog.

The snake stretches out to the sleeping spadefoot, and just as he is about to strike, she awakens. The frightened frog leaps straight up, slamming her head against the rocky ceiling. Her recoiling limbs barely clear the swipe of jagged teeth. Although the spadefoot's hasty jump jolted her out of harm's way, she would not be so lucky upon her descent. The nimble legs of the spadefoot desperately pull back from the snapping jaws of the serpent, but her terrified reaction fails to place her beyond the determined reach of the hognose. With one quick jerk she is pulled down to the ground. The panicking spadefoot looks back with dread at the gnawing jaws that are quickly sliding up her thrashing legs. Despite all her struggling, she is about to be swallowed alive, and she is powerless to stop it.

Like a warm, wet sock the mouth of the hognose slides up the spadefoot's legs until its snout reaches the pelvic girdle. As the snake gobbles his way up to the soft belly, the spadefoot quickly inflates her torso in hopes of becoming too plump to swallow. The snake struggles to open his mouth wide enough to envelop the expanding belly. By ballooning herself up, the spadefoot has created an obstacle in the serpent's esophagus. Even though the spadefoot is clogging the snake's throat, the hognose is still able to breathe through a flexible tube, called the epiglotis, that extends up and beyond the shaft of the tongue. Both predator and prey stop for a moment to take a breath. Suddenly, the spadefoot starts to put up a great fight, pulling herself out from the pins-and-needles grasp of the serpent's teeth. Just as the frog nearly frees herself, the hognose lurches forward, pushing his expanding mouth up to the writhing creature's ribcage. A snake can open its mouth up to seven times wider than at its resting state, but even at this level of expansion, the hognose just can't seem to get his chops past the spadefoot's abdomen. And yet, the hognose has one more trick up its sleeve.

Two long fangs, located at the rear of the upper jaw, slowly slide out from a slimy sheath of folded gum tissue. The snake yawns as wide as it can, until its fangs are perpendicular to the sides of the spadefoot's bloated belly. Then, the jowls bite down on the frog until each fang pierces into the drum-tight skin. There is a muffled pop, and then a wet, bubbly hiss as the frog begins to deflate beneath the predator's crushing bite. The hapless frog will continue to resist until it is well within the serpent's belly. The teeth of the snake act like individual hooks that pull the frog downwards past the jaws until the lips finally close behind the still-struggling prey. Alone in the muggy darkness, the spadefoot's little heart continues to pump steadily. The strong heart will beat long after the caustic juices of the snake's stomach corrode through skin, flesh, and bone. Forever trapped and forgotten, the spadefoot is being digested alive. The hognose has a very hearty appetite, and before the night is over, at least half a dozen more spadefoots will follow the fate of the first. After being fattened up with spadefoots, the hognose will retreat back to the shelter of the dilapidated cactus to sleep it off.

A NEW DAWN

In the first light of daybreak, the panorama of tall saguaro cacti glows like amber. Even though the sun has just barely revealed itself, the early morning temperature quickly rises past the level of human comfort. Most of the nightlife has taken shelter to avoid the risk of being scorched by the unforgiving sun. With the exception of a few stragglers, the spadefoots have retreated away from the pool in search of moist shade beneath whatever scrap of debris they can lay claim to.

Each female spadefoot can lay up to five hundred eggs, and during the night nearly ten thousand eggs were deposited into the shallow pool. Individual eggs in each cluster are suspended in a clear, gelatinous mass made up of proteins, quick to sop up water upon being squirted out of the female's vent. Although the eggs are vulnerable and the odds are against most of them, a few will survive. The temperature in the water is spiking, yet the eggs are hanging on. Predators like water bugs, insect larvae, and fungi are killing many but not all. Amazingly, the eggs have already begun developing into tadpoles. It takes only fifteen hours for a spadefoot egg to progress into a tadpole. Miraculously, a tadpole can metamorphose into a fully formed spadefoot toad in a little more than nine days. Among amphibians, spadefoots are record breakers when it comes to reproduction. The desert allows the spadefoot just the briefest window of time for one generation to bring in the next, so a leisurely approach to reproduction is not an option.

Across from the pool, on the opposite side of the creek wash, there is a swirl of gravelly earth not much bigger than a dinner plate. In the center of this groomed radius rest minarets of neatly stacked pebbles with a number of raisin-sized crevices at their base. It is a colony of harvester ants (*Pogonomyrmex maricopa*), busy with diligent workers, either returning from a shift of scavenging seeds and bits of plant material for food or heading out to do the same. Deep in the nest, there are thousands more waiting for their turn to contribute to the colony.

The hustle and bustle of the colony has caught the curiosity of a cactus wren (*Campylorhynchus brunneicapillus*), who's eager to snatch up a couple of ants for a quick meal. She flies from her nest, tucked within an arsenal of spines beneath a twisted bower of cactus called teddy-bear cholla. Not only is her nest

The cactus wren is one tough little bird. Pity the fool who bothers with her brood.

built near the cactus, but it is constructed of it as well. As they say—it's all about location, location, location, and this little parcel of real estate is pretty much predator-proof. In order to further reduce the opportunity for predators such as hawks, coyotes, or bull snakes to snatch one of her offspring, the cactus wren has gone through the trouble of building decoy nests scattered around her property to throw them off track. Any bird looking for a considerate neighbor best not build next to a cactus wren, because this ornery avian will fly on over and rip the competitor's nest to shreds.

She is pretty large, as wrens go, with a fairly ordinary shape. Her plumage can hardly be called dramatic, basically a lot of brown and white, and a creamy breast with a few black flecks. Her drab wings and tail feathers are broken up with a number of brownish bars. Her eyes are sharp, and her shiny beak is somewhat sickle in shape. What I find most intriguing about the cactus wren is that at first glance it comes across as quite ordinary, but when you delve into its natural history, you discover a very resilient bird, surviving in one of the harshest habitats on Earth. Cactus wrens are not picky eaters and will consume just about anything, including all matter of cactus seeds, fruit, wasps, spiders, grasshoppers, and, on rare occasions, small animals like frogs and lizards. And of course, when given the chance, they'll eat ants.

Our wren flutters down to the edge of the harvester colony, hops around a bit, then begins snatching up ants, one after the other. Here is the thing about har-

vester ants, though: When push comes to shove, and the colony is in jeopardy, these tiny terrors can be downright nasty. The cactus wren may be in the mood for a little snack, but these harvester ants switch into battle mode at once, and are just about to test this bird's appetite.

Hundreds of harvester ants begin to swarm from the outlets in the center of the nest, rushing at the wren from all sides. At first, the wren appears ecstatic at the hoards of ants charging her; it makes picking them off much easier. Her attitude changes dramatically, however, when the ants that she is trying to capture leap onto her legs and quickly disappear into her plumage. Within a nanosecond, the now frantic wren is covered with a squirming blanket of ants that begin to bite her in unison. Together, they deliver an excruciating wallop. Their strong mandibles cut deep into the bird's skin; at the same time, they manage to inject the attacker with a potent sting. Instantly, the cactus wren has lost interest in feeding and sets off to flee. The bird hops back a couple of yards beyond the reach of the expanding mob of shimmering ants and begins rolling around in the dust, desperately trying to shed her assailants. As the panicking wren writhes in the dirt, a young coyote (*Canis latrans*) discovers an enticing treat beneath an overhang of teddy-bear cholla.

Instinct commands the four helpless hatchlings within the nest, a wispy mass of woven grass and cacti, to sit absolutely still so as not to draw the attention of the predator peering at them through a broken blind of cactus spines. But it is too late; even though the hungry coyote can't make out what is hidden beneath the swirl of dried vegetation, it can smell and hear the very edible contents of the nest. Extracting the morsels of warm flesh from the natural basket of prickly cactus presents a serious challenge, though. The coyote lacks experience in this sort of situation, as he reaches out and gingerly paws at the nest. He yelps and pulls back; his only reward is a painful poke in the pads. Finally, the

famished canine sticks his muzzle into the thicket of quills, hoping to snap up the four helpless wrens, frozen in fear. Again, he yelps out a piercing squeal, quickly withdrawing his head with only a mouthful of nasty cactus spines to show for his effort. To make matters worse, a large chunk of cholla has broken away from the central stock and is firmly attached to the pathetic coyote's eyelid.

No pathetic pooch, the desert coyote knows when to hold 'em, knows when to fold 'em, knows when to walk away, knows when to run.

The coyote squeals in agony as it throws its head back and forth in an attempt to dislodge the determined cactus, but no matter how vigorous the swing, the snarl of cholla will not budge. Out of desperation, the wretched creature grinds its head into the dirt, but this makes matters worse. The cactus is no longer dangling from the eyelid; it is firmly lodged in skin and hair. Now the eyelid has been pinned closed, and the entire ear on the left side of the coyote's head has been folded into the prickly mess. It will take only patience on behalf of the coyote before this clinging clump of cactus detaches itself from the tangle of fur and flesh. Still

BEWARE THE CHOLLA

Mind you, coyotes are no wimps, because having a cholla cactus latch on to you is serious business. I have had a cholla stick to me many times, and not only does this nasty stuff cause excruciating pain, it is damn near impossible to dislodge. It seems the more you work at pulling the spines out, the deeper they dig in. I once had a nasty one attached around my ankle, and a couple of the spines had managed to puncture straight through my Achilles tendon. When cholla spines penetrate your skin, aside from the immediate pain, they also cause stinging and itching, which last long after you manage to pull the thorns out—or should I say "if."

I am actually getting goosebumps writing about the stuff. Ah heck, I'd rather tangle with a pissed-off Mojave rattler than deal with a clinging bunch of cholla cactus. As thorny plants go, it's gnarly stuff. A friend of mine, Glen, got nailed by a fist-sized piece of the obnoxious jumping cholla (*Opuntia bigelovii*) on his hand. It took me nearly an hour to pull it all out. All his fingers had been pinned to each other, and he had shed his share of tears before I managed to tease out all the spines. Glen would probably say it was the dryness in the air, but I am telling you, that cholla got this boy all watery-eyed. Just barely grazing certain kinds of this cactus—like the jumping cholla—will cause it to almost leap onto you. Messing with this malicious plant ranks right up there with getting a root canal.

hungry, the coyote timidly slumps away from the nest, but the situation is not a total loss. Against the coyote's will, it has now taken on the role of dispersing teddy-bear cholla cactus throughout the Sonoran ecosystem. Soon after the coyote's departure, the disheveled cactus wren returns to her nest, completely oblivious of the calamity that nearly befell her brood.

Back at the harvester nest, the ants have been recouping after the attack. Casualties have been unceremoniously discarded, as a new team of recruits falls into place. Throughout the entire battle, an unbroken chain of workers continued to venture from the nest and forage for food. Harvester ants are the quintessential "social inveterates." There are no individuals; all work as one for the good of the colony. Independent thought does not compute, and every reaction results from millions of years of evolutionary hardwiring. There are no commendations for sacrifice, no reward for the contributions made by every ant toward the betterment of the species. No one stops to ponder or chitchat, and all communication is expressed through odor. Chemistry is the language of the harvester ant, and the unique smells, called pheromones, produced by each member of the colony serve as the means of communication. They are insular in their view of the world and care only about the colony, if instinct allows them to care at all, although the greater ecosystem does benefit from their presence. Every time the ants forage for food, seeds are scattered and dropped, thus distributing and promoting plant species throughout the Sonoran community. Perhaps the greatest contribution made by the ants is that they are a valuable source of protein for many creatures. Despite the arsenal of defenses put forth by the colony, harvester ants are regularly consumed by a diverse array of critters, everything from insects to lizards, birds to mammals. There is even an ancient Native American recipe for harvester ant porridge.

Although I haven't developed a taste for harvester ants, there are creatures out there that eat them almost exclusively.

DON'T TRY THIS AT HOME

A few years ago, I decided to eat some harvester ants. It was one of the worst, most painful meals of my life. At the time, I was conducting research on weird stuff, usually insect in origin, that serves as a legitimate and nutritious food source consumed by indigenous peoples around the world. I came across a recipe for harvester ant gruel that had been invented by the Native Americans a few centuries ago. I didn't have time to make the dish, so I thought what the heck, I'll eat them directly from the nest alfresco. I have seen tribal people of Africa huddled around an earthy tower blooming with termites, greedily gobbling down the critters as if they were Beluga caviar. God knows, I've eaten termites on a number of occasions, so why would a meal of live harvester ants be any different? Well, for one thing, most termites don't have giant mandibles that inject a stinging acidic secretion into the tissue of whatever they are attacking.

I filled my mouth with around two dozen live ants, and as I began to chew, yet again, came to the realization that I am an idiot. It felt like I was chewing on a mouthful of glass shards and battery acid. No matter how much I chewed, the damn ants would not die, and they were ruthlessly attacking any bit of flesh that they could latch onto. Even the decapitated ants were still reflexively chomping away. I had ant heads with their pinching mandibles stuck under my tongue, lodged deep in my gums; they were even jammed in back of my tonsils. For weeks afterward I was flossing out necrotic bits of ants from my teeth.

Just a few feet from the nest, tucked between two slabs of stone, sits a lizard. It has observed the dramatic battle that unfolded between the cactus wren and the harvester ants. Now that the bird has retreated, the prehistoric-looking animal moves in for the attack. There are few lizards that are as weird and as wonderful as the desert horned lizard (*Phrynosoma platyrhinos*), or, as it is affectionately known by many, the horny toad—a title that is somewhat deceiving, considering that they are not amphibians but reptiles. Wrapping around the back of its head is a crest of spines. The rounded face of the horny toad terminates at a narrow muzzle. A multitude of differently formed scales, varying from flat to pointed, are studded across a disc-shaped torso that appears to be unnaturally flush to the ground. The tail is small and narrow, but well protected by dozens of prickly scales. Horny toads are very finicky eaters, and for the most part, they will partake only of ants. Some studies have suggested that the health of horny toads declines if they don't eat ants. One theory proposes that these picky lizards need the formic acid produced by the ants to survive.

When I look at a horny toad in the palm of my hand, I see a creature more reminiscent of a miniature triceratops than a lizard.

With an eye set on feasting, the horny toad skirts over to the edge of the ant colony and quickly transforms from a cuddly lizard into a voracious monster. Again, the soldiers pour out of the colony and rapidly form a defensive wall. The warriors are armed with thrashing mandibles as well as probing stingers that will be used to deliver their chemical assault against the giant reptile looming over the perimeter of the colony. The scuffle with the cactus wren was child's play compared to what the ravenous horny toad is about to unleash. In a single sitting, a horny toad, measuring about half the size of my hand, can suck up a whopping two hundred ants! To the ants, the lizard smells of destruction, an odor they have become familiar with. The horny toad sees the fast-approaching battalion of ants, but he does not retreat. He waits for the ants to get within inches of his armored body and then—wham!

Ants are pinched off, one after the other, at an alarming rate. The horny toad is able to press its face tightly to the

The horny toad might more properly be called the Hoover of the harvester ant world.

ground, one of the benefits of having a flattish mug, and instantly tweeze away the quivering ants. The lizard greedily scoffs up dozens of ants in seconds. Powerful jaws instantly pin the struggling ants as the predator's flexible and sticky tongue pushes forward, flush with the lips, and adheres to the prey. Chemical weapons are launched as fierce mandibles thrash back and forth, but resistance only seems to fuel the horny toad's relentless hunger for more ants. The ants have now covered the entire body of the bold lizard, attacking every bit of tissue they can latch on to. When they go for the eyes, the undeterred reptile just snaps

them shut and eats away in the darkness. There is nothing the ants can do but wait until the horny toad has filled its stomach. Like the hognose, the horny toad is a specialist when it comes to diet, fully prepared to deal with the obstacles put forth by prey.

As the lizard feasts on an endless buffet of ants, the unfortunate coyote has managed to free himself of the clinging cactus and has doubled back in the direction of the muddy pool. He, too, has an appetite to satisfy, and now that he no longer has to contend with the clawing grasp of teddy-bear cholla, he returns to the hunt. Once again, he follows the creek bed, now dry. As the coyote saunters along the twisting wash, he sees something laying flat on the ground, tucked beneath a tufted bow of grass. At first, it appears to be a tawny-colored stone, but a band of hot air wafts against it, causing a layer of small hairs to flutter. The breeze drifts down to the coyote, bringing with it a familiar and welcome odor: the scent of black-tailed jackrabbit (*Lepus californicus*). The canine's ears, slightly scabbed from cactus spines, perk up. The coyote drops his muzzle below his shoulders as his piercing eyes fix on the napping rabbit. Stepping as softly as possible, the nimble hunter sneaks forward, quiet as the sharp shadow tracing alongside him against a wall of brittle earth. His footsteps quicken, getting closer to his prey, but then he hesitates and locks up.

The jackrabbit snaps up from a deep slumber; it is uneasy and senses danger. Fearing that the slightest movement—a gulp of breath or a twitch of an eye— would reveal his presence, the coyote freezes his ribcage while locking his eyelids open against the dry air. The coyote would dearly love to blink a little wet relief over his eyeballs but he can't; he knows he is just seconds from snatching a meal, and he can't afford to jeopardize the hunt. The jackrabbit is now alert and sitting up. Tower-like ears stand erect as he glares up the creek bed with great concentration, but sees nothing. Creeping gingerly, seemingly on his toes, with legs shifting ever so slightly, the coyote appears to levitate towards the potential quarry

ahead. Now they are within two yards of each other: the prey perched nervously against a mound of grass, the predator lurching forward, seconds from making a kill. Then it happens.

The coyote bursts into a mad dash toward the jackrabbit. Springing up with great force, the jackrabbit bounces out from the blind of sagebrush and onto the crumbling ledge of soil running along the creek bed. The coyote chases the fleeing target up and over the steep embankment. In full charge, the coyote quickly gains on his prey, but then the jackrabbit pulls a fast one. Just when it seems that the pursuing coyote is about to take out the jackrabbit, the latter leaps two yards off the ground, allowing the coyote to fly past it. The coyote spins around and backtracks to the jackrabbit, but the jackrabbit changes its frantic hurtles from a straight line to a zigzag pattern. A crisscrossing streak of billowing dust grows quickly between the two sprinting creatures, with the coyote starting to fall behind. As the jackrabbit runs faster, the coyote begins to lose steam, until eventually the race is over, and the swift-footed target finds itself well out of harm's way. Exhausted and panting, the hapless coyote has failed yet again to secure a meal. To make matters worse, he has also burned a significant amount of valuable calories in the attempt. With his head hung low, the gloomy canine stumbles back into the dry creek bed and resumes his hunger-fueled pilgrimage.

Now that the coast is clear, the black-tailed jackrabbit leaps into a pile of fallen mesquite to catch its breath. He pants a bit, but is quick to recover. The near-death experience is all but forgotten, so the jackrabbit does what jackrabbits do best, which is of course . . . eating. Before even ripping into a bit of grass, the creature's jaws have already begun to chew in anticipation. He tugs at the fibrous vegetation until his eyes catch a mound of jackrabbit scat. After giving the pile a quick sniff, the rabbit digs in. It seems as though the jackrabbit prefers its own crap to fresh fodder. Well, truth be told, all rabbits, whether cottontails, jacks, or hares, belong to the group of mammals called lagomorphs, and what all lagomorphs have in common is that they will enthusiastically consume their own crap. Why? Thing is, rabbits don't have a very efficient digestive tract, so much of what they eat passes through them undigested. Consuming their own feces allows the lagomorphs to extract valuable nutrients that otherwise would be wasted. Thus, the somewhat indecorous behavior of rabbits scoffing down scat increases their survival by promoting an efficient use of energy.

While eating its own waste may help the black-tailed jackrabbit conserve energy, failure to keep tabs on what's transpiring beyond the pile of poop may cost this lagomorph far more than it can afford. As the jackrabbit focuses on its meal, a shadow flashes over the huddled creature. A lofty branch of mesquite bowing to the front of the jackrabbit nods ever so slightly beneath the weight of a large bird, which has just landed upon it. Regally perched on the branch, dried shiny and gray from decades of weathering, sits a Harris's hawk (*Parabuteo unicinctus*). It is a very solid bird that stands nearly two feet tall, with a three-and-a-half-foot wingspan. The hawk's plumage is dark brown with white tips at the ends of its tail feathers. Large black eyes shimmer against a yellow featherless mask. A ruthlessly sharp beak curls from the proud face. Hanging off the stilt-like yellow legs are long talons, sharp enough to punch through leather. The jackrabbit looks up to see the assassin glaring down at it. If the jackrabbit is smart, it will hunker down within the tangle of mesquite and sit it out. The Harris's hawk will probably grow tired of waiting and move on, sparing the lagomorph's life. But here is the thing about black-tailed jackrabbits: Intelligence is an attribute they tend to lack.

The bold hawk hops down to a lower branch and then starts to whistle out a high-pitched shriek. The jackrabbit perks up as the raptor continues the taunting. The great bird leans forward with wings fanned outward, and then squeals out an unnerving screech. The terrified jackrabbit decides to make a run for it. It dives under an overhang of mesquite and then bounces nearly six feet up and over a tumble of desiccated paloverde. The Harris's hawk has barely even budged, flaunting its menacing presence. As the jackrabbit stares at

The black-tailed jackrabbit could not escape death at the claws of the Harris's hawk.

the killer bird, waiting for the attack, a hovering shadow swiftly crosses the cowering creature. A swooshing sound cuts through the air behind the jackrabbit, causing it to spin around and look up to the sky. It is another Harris's hawk, swooping in like a kamikaze. The jackrabbit instantly flips to the left and dashes off in a mad series of leaps, like a gazelle. Gliding in quickly from behind are the two Harris's hawks; they screech boldly into the wind, jeering at the fleeing jackrabbit.

Springing forward as fast as it can, the jackrabbit hones in its sensitive ears like satellite dishes on the two predators closing in from behind. Then, diving in from out of nowhere is a third Harris's hawk. The raptor comes streaking in with wings flailed outward and stretched talons ready to rip. The jackrabbit desperately leaps up but there is no place for him to go. The two creatures collide. Dust clouds around the impact, like smoke at a car wreck, as tufts of fur fly into the air. Each talon digs deeply into the jackrabbit's twisted body, and even though it is lethally pinned, the creature struggles to regain its footing. Like meat hooks, the talons pierce through the rabbit's jaw and nostrils, puncturing the throat and left eyeball. The jackrabbit lets out a bone-chilling scream. To me, there are few sounds more disturbing than a rabbit squealing in terror. The Harris's hawk has latched on with confidence to the jack-rabbit's pathetic body, which jerks and flops, until finally all is still.

The two other Harris's hawks are quick to join their cohort. There is no squabbling over who eats first. The most dominant hawk gets the first few bites, then the rest of the carcass is shared. A highly social bird of prey, the Harris's hawk is unique in its hunting abilities; its sophisticated cooperative hunting strategies are equal to the killing skills of highly intelligent carnivores, like wolves, lions, and hyenas. The bird's complex social structure is not limited to just hunting. Harris's hawks live in unique family units, sort of like the raptor version of a kibbutz. Heck, they even have nannies to help rear the offspring. While other raptor species prefer to go it alone, Harris's hawks are gregarious creatures whose cooperation and reciprocity form the foundations for survival. In the infrastructure of Harris's hawk society, selfishness is not tolerated.

Back at the pool, there is new life! Tadpoles have begun busting out of the thousands of eggs left there the night before. Their little bodies aren't much bigger than the sharpened point of a lead pencil. They flutter and sink, kick up and float. Some are still jiggling free from the translucent layer of jelly enveloping vacant eggs sacks, while others are flapping about in search of some algae to nibble on. The water temperature has risen to fish-killing levels, yet the tiny spadefoot larvae are thriving. The tadpoles will grow at an astonishing rate, but many challenges lie ahead before they become actual frogs.

Towering above the pool is a massive saguaro cactus (*Carnegiea gigantea*). It stands nearly twenty feet tall and is as thick as a telephone pole. It is void of any leaves, which would just be more costly tissue to support. To survive in the Sonoran Desert, an organism must be frugal with regard to energy expenditure; efficiency is often the key to survival. The green pigment called chlorophyll, used to convert sunlight into life-sustaining energy and normally limited to the top layer of leaves of other plant species, is instead spread across the entire surface of the

Many birds and animals rely on the giant saguaro cactus as food and/or shelter.

saguaro. The outer husk-like coating of the saguaro is pretty impenetrable, but its true defense consists of the thousands of needle-sharp spines running the entire length of the cactus along vertical ridges. Despite an array of formidable defenses, there are many creatures that take full advantage of the saguaro. An extensive range of critters depends upon this keystone species of cactus for survival. Animals like birds, bats, snakes, and rats all use the saguaro as either food or shelter, or both.

A hole, no wider than a soda can, is nestled against the spiny exterior of the saguaro, just beneath one of its massive arms. Wrapping around the perfectly rounded hole is a calloused lip about half an inch wide. The fist-sized opening leads to a narrow cavity that sinks in six or seven inches, until it begins to slope down toward the roots. The depth of the cavity is similar to the length of my arm and the width is just a bit wider that my wrist. The cavity is lined with a layer of the same callous material, brown in color and flaky to the touch, lining the outer edge of the entrance. Tucked at the bottom of the cavity are three small and scruffy chicks. They keenly lift up their heads upon hearing a familiar and welcoming rustle at the entrance. Bobbing their over-sized heads back and forth, the awkward hatchlings clumsily flap their near-naked wings in anticipation of the visitor. They begin whispering a muted peep as a larger bird gently slides on top of them. She is a Gila woodpecker (*Melanerpes uropygialis*), a moderately sized avian that is fairly attractive in appearance. Her head is pale gray with a whitish forehead, and a slate-colored bill, strong and sharp, jets off her face. Her back and tail are barred black and white, while her breast and belly have a warm tinge of gold scattered across a fluffy bed of gray. The Gila woodpecker, along with her mate, constructed the nest last February, and now they have three healthy hatchlings to show for their effort.

After hollowing out a nest in the saguaro, Gila woodpeckers let the cavity season for a few months—until at least the following spring. They can't nest in it immediately, because the slushy green pulp that makes up the center of the cactus produces a gooey secretion. This sappy material is what will eventually harden into the scar tissue lining the walls of the nest and surrounding the edge of the entrance. To keep the impact of the sun to a minimum, nests are usually constructed facing north. Long after the pair of Gila woodpeckers has abandoned the nest, other bird species, including miniature owls, flycatchers, wrens, warblers, martins, and kestrels, will serve as tenants for generations to come. With luck, almost a hundred years of birds will call this saguaro home.

The bulbous heads of the hatchlings feverishly sway from left to right as the mother lowers her bill and regurgitates a steamy mash of unidentifiable insects, grubs, and fruit pulp. The ravenous chicks gobble down the protein-rich mush and then impatiently beg for more. Without protest, she scuttles up toward the light, perches for a moment to let her eyes adjust to the brightness, and then swoops off in search of prey.

As late afternoon sinks in, the harsh white light fades to a warm glow, and the temperature drops to a very pleasant eighty-five degrees. Behind the saguaro is a ridge of sand twisted by years of wind. The dune slopes down to a rubble of pebbles and sharp stones; there are a few sprigs of grass shooting out from the spaces between the stones. Squatting solidly at the edge, where the sand slides into the rock, grows a twisted snarl of prickly pear cactus (*Opuntia humifusa*). The knot of cacti is a bit over a yard tall and wide. The thicket of prickly pear runs around two to three yards parallel to the small dune. The bristly clump consists of at least three different individual cacti. Each cactus has a primary stock with dozens of paddle-shaped segments (think Ping-Pong). Sprouting from the stock and from some of the paddles is a plentiful selection of oval-shaped fruit, the ripest of which are luxuriant in texture and rubyred in color. Scattered over the entire surface of each prickly pear are thousands of minute bundles packed tight with irritating spines.

Just a few yards from the prickly pear

cacti is a circular entrance on the ground. It is almost wide enough to stick your head into, but I don't recommend it. The opposite side of the entrance, where light never shines, houses a deep tunnel that runs many yards into the earth. It would take you days to crawl to the end of this tunnel, only to discover additional passages snaking off in different directions, picking up where the first one ends. This is the Sonoran underworld, a dwelling-place of strange and mysterious creatures who seek darkness rather than light. As the sun sinks past a chiseled terrain, and the sky grows red before fading to blackness, the creatures hidden within the subterranean passageways are beginning to stir. One of them in particular is making its way to the top. The heavy beast slowly follows an underground route to the entrance, one painstaking step after the next. The creature wheezes with each labored stride, but eventually it manages to reach the opening.

Meanwhile, with the sun nearly set, the young coyote has yet to rustle up any grub worth swallowing. As it fumbles past the cactus wren's nest, the desperate beast briefly glances over but is quick to move on, his lesson learned. The wren is sitting contentedly with her brood; she glances up to see the Gila woodpecker return to its nest cavity within the shaft of the saguaro. The woodpecker perches for a moment and then falls in, her bill stuffed with a squirming ball of insects. The horny toad, too, has withdrawn to its hideout underneath a stack of flat stones, his belly stuffed with harvester ants. The lizard firmly lays his flat, disc-shaped torso on the warm earth. As the temperature continues to drop, the horny toad will use the expanded surface area of its belly to absorb the warmth that passively radiates up into its body. Like most other reptiles, the horny toad generates very little body heat on its own, depending on the surrounding environment to supplement him with warmth. Without the proper heat needed to get the digestive juices flowing, a belly full of food could easily rot, causing illness or even death. While the horny toad dozes off, the hungry coyote continues its progress.

Nearly ten minutes have passed, and the subterranean dweller has just managed to clear the entrance of its burrow. It stops for a few minutes to stretch out its neck, making sure there is no ambush ahead, and then exits. This ancient creature is a desert tortoise (*Gopherus agassizii*). It has a dome-shaped shell, called a carapace, that rests on four elephantine legs. This is a turtle designed for a terrestrial life, and a watery habitat would be as alien to the desert tortoise as a rainforest to a penguin. This tortoise has no webbing between the toes; his legs are built not for propulsion, but for carrying a heavy load, and are rather column-like in structure. He moves extremely slowly, as if life has never had any urgency. Indeed, his metabolism just barely creeps along, so there is never any need to scoff down a meal. In addition, because the tortoise is an herbivore, there is no need to dash after prey. The tortoise's helmet-like carapace provides an ideal defense, so few predators will tangle with him.

Much like grandpa and his motor home, the desert tortoise carries his water supply with him.

The greatest challenge to a desert tortoise is water conservation. Surprisingly, the lethargic reptile uses its bladder as a natural water tank, giving the tortoise the luxury of going for months without a drink. Another major obstacle faced by the desert tortoise is heat exposure. The

tortoise solves the problem of murderous temperatures by escaping to its subterranean refuge, which may extend thirty feet into the earth. If need be, the creature can spend ninety-eight percent of the year sequestered deep in its lair, venturing above ground only during the milder periods. Many creatures freeload in the tunnels and dens excavated by this sluggish yet industrious tortoise, and its survival has a direct impact on dozens of other life-forms. As with the saguaro cactus, the undemanding and slow desert tortoise plays the vital role of keystone species.

Just before sunset and just after sunrise, when temperatures linger at their mildest, is the time when the desert tortoise prefers to forage. It has taken him an hour to crawl up the long, underground corridor, but when the sluggish beast reaches the warm light, he starts to pick up speed (think of a bowling ball rolling up a greased hill). He is on a mission to find his favorite food—the prickly pear fruit—and the tortoise knows exactly where to go. Finally, he arrives at the thicket of prickly pear cacti. After scan-

ning the area in search of the ripest fruit, he unravels the wrinkly skin around his neck as he extends his head out a good eight inches from the lip of the carapace. The tortoise releases a slow wheeze from deep within his lungs, and his mouth begins to chomp robotically long before his beak actually makes contact with the succulent prickly pear. He gorges on the fruit, mashing it up and squirting its juices. His face, red with pulp, looks bloody; drool weeps off his chin and flows down his neck. The fiberglass-like spines of the fruit do not bother the tortoise; they, along with the hundreds of tiny seeds, will pass through the reptile's gut undigested. In fact, much of what this creature eats passes through relatively intact. The desert tortoise has been cursed with an inefficient digestive system, but his inability to digest all the plant matter translates into another valuable role he plays: disperser of seeds.

Fifteen minutes later, the tortoise, his hunger now satisfied, makes the pilgrimage back to his burrow in the nearly extinguished light. He passes a crescent-shaped opening, similar to the entrance that leads to his own den. In fact, he excavated it nearly ten years ago but, for whatever reason, had abandoned it. As he slowly eclipses the entrance, eerie shrieks come echoing up from the bowels of the den. There are squatters rustling within, and they are coming to life just as the ancient architect of this forgotten dwelling makes his way home. The hissing chatter grows louder, and a diminutive owl pops into view. This bird, not much larger than a robin, is a burrowing owl (*Athene cunicularia*). Although quite capable of digging out their own dens, burrowing owls are opportunists, and if a gopher, a desert tortoise, or a badger should decide to move uptown, these adaptable little owls are more than happy to take over. Burrowing owls have unusually long legs, which are ideal both for digging and for pouncing on prey. These brazen little hunters possess striking eyes of bright yellow. As this burrowing owl flutters off, six precocious chicks, all fluffy with down, come shuffling to the entrance. They will wait there anxiously for the return of their parent.

While the mother owl is hunting, the now-desperate coyote continues to search for his meal. His head, low to the ground, swings back and forth like a blind man's cane. As the coyote's nostrils draw in quick puffs of air in hopes of picking up a trail leading to something edible, the

As their name implies, burrowing owls are quite capable of digging out their own dens. But they are more than happy to be squatters, too.

horny toad, resting amid the warm rocks, suddenly becomes uneasy. The ability of reptiles to detect the presence of an intruder is uncanny, and this stout lizard is no exception. The horny toad begins to sandwich its way further between two flat stones. The coyote detects the reptile's scent, and his salivary glands start wetting his chops in true Pavlovian style. When the horny toad is mere seconds away from being safely tucked in, an eager paw frantically jams into the pile of stones and flicks the horny toad out into the open. Landing flat on its back, the startled lizard quickly flips over on its belly and scuttles toward the rock-strewn shelter.

The horny toad nearly manages to slip back into the crevice but the coyote's paw is quick to slam down in front of the entrance, blocking the lizard's only escape route. Then, a cage of wet tongue and sharp teeth scoops up the reptile. Instead of biting down and crushing the horny toad, the coyote cautiously slithers its tongue over and around the thorny mass. Although the texture is unfamiliar to the predator, the lizard seems edible enough, so the ravenous carnivore decides to wolf down the sinewy, scale-covered snack. Just as the horny toad begins to slide down the slimy throat, reeking of rotten eggs, the lower end of the beleaguered lizard starts to gyrate. The spikes running along the sides of the reptile's belly slash against the pulpy flesh of coyote's throat. The flabbergasted hunter opens up his maw and reflexively gags out the slime-coated lizard. Upon hitting the dust, the horny toad nonchalantly shakes itself off and abruptly assumes a defensive posture. Angled face-to-face with the coyote, the resilient reptile flattens its lower back, while simultaneously raising up its torso. Then, as the coyote moves in for the kill, the horny toad clenches all its muscles from the anus to the neck, causing pressure to build around its sinus region. The lizard pushes with all its might, and gobs of a viscous liquid, bloody in color, instantly pool around the lower lids of its eyes.

As the coyote's snuffling nostrils press up close to the stubborn lizard, it happens. With every last bit of energy it can muster, the horny toad tenses up again, and a stream of bloody droplets suddenly comes spurting out of its eyes and into the face of the coyote! Stunned by the lizard's stigmatic display, the coyote pulls back. He shakes it off and maneuvers in for another attack, but the reptilian defensive strike happens again. The horny toad squirts out a second stream of corporeal goop, this time nailing the coyote directly in the eyes. The coyote is absolutely repulsed by the liquid; the injected substance causes his eyes to itch and ooze. The nasty, chest-ripping xenomorph from the *Alien* flicks has nothing on this horny toad. Heck, it could even give Ripley (a.k.a. Sigourney Weaver) a run for her money.

Once again, the coyote has been out-witted, and he decides that a mouthful of splintery bones and tonsil-pricking scales just isn't worth it. He abruptly does an about-face and skulks off as the horny toad, no worse for wear, creeps back into its shelter. There's nothing more humbling for a top dog in the food chain than to get an ass-whupping, especially if the victor happens to be one of the lowest links. The coyote drags on with his tail lit-

erally between his legs; he just doesn't have the stamina to lift it. At this point, it is only hunger that drives him. The dejected coyote stops at the murky puddle to take a drink. Here, he unknowingly manages to consume a few calories by sucking down half a dozen wriggling tadpoles. After shaking off a few dribbles of drool, the famished canine heads off, still hoping for better luck elsewhere.

The spadefoot tadpoles have no sorrow for the brethren needlessly lost to the thirst of a lonesome coyote. Truth be told, the selfish larvae will fare much better minus the competition for space, food, and oxygen. Only a single day has passed since the tadpoles came squirting into the world, and they are developing at an amazing rate. The offspring are growing at an exponential level, and while some frog species may take an entire spring and summer to mature, members of this spirited species possess the potential of transforming into adults in a fraction of that time. Still, these tadpoles are not growing fast enough, since the monsoon rains will soon begin to slow, while the relentless

A distant relative to spiders, the bark scorpion has some of the most toxic venom of all North American scorpions. Trust me on this one.

sun will only become more brutal. There will be greater challenges to overcome than predators, before any of the spade-foot spawn can get out of the pool alive.

Now that night has settled in, many monstrous invertebrates, looking to capitalize on those more vulnerable, have arrived at the scene. A two-inch long bark scorpion (*Centruroides sculpturatus*) crawls out from underneath a hollow of withered wood. The scorpion is straw in color and has hundreds of bristly hairs projecting from the back of his exoskeleton. With its lobster-like claws, called

pedipalps, spread out and ready to grasp, the bark scorpion roams the desert floor in search of something—whether animal or insect—to devour.

All is quiet. Then, as the scorpion clears the ridge of a large stone, a waft of warm air swooshes in from above. Landing directly in front of the scorpion is the burrowing owl. She has just departed her brood of squawking babes in search of some protein-rich fodder to bring back to the nest. She stands there, bold and erect, her keen, moon-like eyes fixed sharply on the scorpion. Spotting the predator, the scorpion rotates in the opposite direction and begins to creep off. Just as eight prickly legs start to disappear over the edge of the rock, the owl launches into the air and then promptly descends upon the escaping scorpion.

The barb-like talons on her left foot are quick to pierce the cephalothorax, the first body segment connecting the invertebrate's head and torso, while the talons on her right foot confidently pin down the scorpion's tail. A glimmering globule of clear venom, potent enough to drop a hundred burrowing owls, forms at the tip of the stinger. The hook-shaped syringe is stretched out straight from the scorpion's body but is powerless to stop the predator pouncing from above. Reaching up over its head, the desperate scorpion pinches the clutching talons in hope of tweezing the owl off its back. With a twist of her finely honed beak, the owl severs the nerves leading from the brain to the rest of the scorpion's body, and the struggling victim quickly goes limp. With a few more scorpions to join this one, the clan of burrowing owls will eat well tonight.

The bark scorpion, which has remained virtually unchanged during the past 400 million years, possesses one of the strongest, most toxic venoms of all North American species of scorpion, yet there are numerous predators that have developed the ability to prey upon it with minimal risk. But as the burrowing owl shall soon discover, there are other creatures dwelling in the Sonoran night who take the scorpion's formula for defense to the next level. The hunter returns to her dark and dusty warren, eager to present the limp trophy to her offspring. The famished babes will squabble and brawl over the paltry ration. The venomous arachnid will not be enough for this brood, and tonight their greed will give way to sacrifice, as one very unlucky owlet unwillingly satisfies the voracious appetites of its siblings.

The mother owl quickly shuffles down the narrow shaft leading to the burrow, as her six ravenous babes shoot up from the other end, eager to meet her halfway. The hatchlings span a week apart in age, with the youngest owlet falling seven days behind the oldest. Although the fluffy runt is half the size of its oldest sibling, she is busting with gumption and endures all of the challenges that come with her humble stature. Although the mother is a skilled hunter and invests much energy into her family, their existence in the Sonoran Desert has been exceptionally grueling. Normally, there would be two parents working to raise the clan, but the father has been absent for three days and will never again be reunited with his family. Perhaps he has served as a snack for a predator, such as a great horned owl or a bobcat, or even a large gopher snake, or maybe he has succumbed to a defensive and deadly wallop delivered to him from some sort of venomous prey. The reason for his disappearance carries little significance; what truly matters is that his mate is forced to work twice as hard. Without him playing the important role of co-nurturer and protector, the chances of all his offspring surviving to adulthood have been dramatically reduced.

The six precocious babes immediately discover the tattered scorpion, draped within the clamped beak of their mother as if it were nothing more than a limp noodle. The famished owlets reconnect to the maternal core of the mother-hunter by chirping out infantile squeaks. Any initial defensive posturing displayed by the owl, as she spots the chaotic and shivering wall of white fluff, is purely instinctive. It disappears instantly upon recognizing the cries of her brood. She lowers her head until one of the owlets reaches up and snatches the dead scorpion from her beak.

Immediately, the others grab onto the prey, pulling it in every possible direction. Caught up in a grisly game of tug-of-war, the scorpion is being drawn and quartered, as the chicks stretch it to near ripping. Despite her fight to take her fair share of the prize, the youngest and most delicate owlet is dragged toward the direction of her greedy siblings as they try to pull the scorpion from her grasp. As the scorpion is being pulled back and forth, the largest owlet yanks the pathetic invertebrate upwards, causing it to rip apart quickly. The five larger owlets fall back, each with nothing more than a meager beakful of scrawny legs, while the tiniest sibling stumbles away with the lion's share of the kill. For just a second the little owlet freezes up in disbelief of her good fortune, before she hastily begins the great task of gobbling down the generous serving of scorpion corpse.

As she struggles to wrap her beak around the bulky wad of crunchy exoskeleton and slimy flesh, the others move in to yank back the mutilated ration of

"I TOLD YOU I COULD DO IT"

Conquering a feisty scorpion is no small task. I have captured many scorpion species in my day, from mildly venomous and tame as kittens, to the fiercest ones, capable of causing a Bedouin nomad of North Africa to beg for a quick and merciful death after being stung. I remember the first and only time I was stung by a scorpion. I was twenty-two, working at a serpentarium in Greece. A buddy of mine and I were collecting specimens for an exhibition on one of the remote Aegean islands, when I came across a scorpion tucked underneath a slab of volcanic rock. I couldn't wait to amaze my pal by showing him how good I was at snatching scorpions freehand. There was one tiny hitch, however: The only time I had ever worked with scorpions before was at the long end of a pair of forceps. Well, he didn't need to know that. Boy, was he going to be impressed!

Since we didn't have any forceps, I came up with the brilliant idea of bundling my shirt into a makeshift potholder that I would use to deftly scoop up the scorpion. My hand resembled a badly wrapped turban as I reached down and began sandwiching the poison-packed critter between what I thought were well-padded digits. My friend looked on with his lower jaw hanging in disbelief, probably thinking, "Now I know why they invented birth control," as my insulated fingers began to gingerly close around the body of the writhing scorpion. Just as I intended to announce triumphantly, "Tah-dah! I told you I could do it," a brain-splitting, scrotum-kicking pain instantly shot through my entire body. It throbbed out of my index finger like lightning, and when I closed my eyes in agony, an intense, white web pulsed across my clamped lids.

Although most of my hand was tucked under a thick layer of crumpled T-shirt, it appeared that my index finger had stuck out of the sleeve opening and made direct contact with the scorpion's stinger. The pain was excruciating, and my ego had shrunk to an all-time low. After glancing down at the scorpion, my friend, Eraklis, informed me that there were two species of scorpion that lived on the islands, one harmless and one life-threatening. He then suggested, with a smirk across his face, that although he didn't know the difference between the two, in about half an hour we'd know which species it was that nailed me. The lesson was well learned, and ever since that fateful day on Santorini, I have made an effort to identify a scorpion before handling it.

scorpion. They hook into the prey with their greedy beaks but the little owlet refuses to submit to her bullying kin. After all, she has fought for the scorpion fair and square, and has earned this protein-rich reward. She squeaks and squeals in frustration, as the others pull back the scorpion and her along with it. Mother looks down at the discouraging spectacle, but does not interfere. It is not her place to settle scores and mediate the quarrel; Nature just doesn't work that way when it comes to burrowing owls. The wrenching and heaving resume again, until finally, the macerated clump is ripped away from the littlest owlet. The vanquishers hoard their conquest, while the youngest one looks back at them, dejected and helpless. As they begin to gag down bits of mush from within their squabbling circle, the plucky little owlet hops forward hoping for her own piece, not much really, just enough to fill her empty gut. The owlets smear gobs of scorpion across their chomping beaks while slurping down slimy strings of ooze; they are so consumed by their gluttony, that they don't

even detect the sneaky fluff ball, moving in for a little scrap. She carefully stretches her neck forward into the swirl of pecking beaks, and while she gingerly tweezes away a tiny morsel of flesh, the eldest and strongest sibling suddenly takes notice. A shriek rings out, as a talon-wielding foot angrily stomps down. A quick but brutal blow is delivered to the torso of the little owlet, causing her to drop the pinch of meat from her startled beak and retreat.

Ejected from the elite ring of sustenance, the little owlet wants back in; she is famished and desperately desires a share of the kill. She lifts herself up and tries to hobble back to the disappearing pile of food, but something is wrong, terribly wrong. The muscles on the left part of her body begin to seize up. She gasps for air but is unable to fill her desperate lungs. As she draws in a labored breath, a wheezing trail of wet air starts to bubble out from her chest. A glob of pink foam hanging from her fuzzy breast grows with each breath, while a wave of weakness rushes through her body. One of the thrusting talons from the eldest owlet has punctured her ribcage, piercing the left lung. Unable to remain standing, she falls back onto her haunch with legs spread wide and talons quivering. The weakness is overtaking her fast, while her breath grows more faint, and then she folds onto her side with her eyes fixed on the indifferent ring of five owlets. Their frenzied gorging of the scorpion kill is uninterrupted; not even the struggles of their injured sister will cause them to look back. They just don't care. Life in the wild can be cruel, and unfortunately for the little owlet, her own life has just run its course. After a few more sluggish beats, her heart grows silent. A cold tingle envelops her body, while the image of the cluster of bobbing owlets turns fuzzy, until all goes black. Her siblings pounce on their freshly departed sister and rip her apart. The cannibalism may seem cruel, but energy is a precious commodity, and nothing is wasted. The mother turns away from her offspring. Instinct pushes her up the tunnel and into the night's air. There is more prey to be captured before the night is finished to fill the still-wanting bellies of her five owlets.

Although still hungry, the chicks in the owl's brood have at least some food in their tiny stomachs—albeit a scorpion and their sister—which is more than one can say for the hapless coyote. He continues his hunt still, but time is running out. He is young, just over a year in age and very inexperienced. The coyote is alone in the world, with only hunger as his companion. The longer he goes on without a meal, the weaker he grows, and thus the less likely he is to score a successful hunt. Alas, it is a bitter pill, one of life's many catch-22's. It's like trying to join the Screen Actors Guild (SAG) to get a part in a flick: You won't be allowed to take the gig unless you are a member. At the same time, SAG won't let you become a member until you have had a genuine role in a SAG-certified film. The only difference between a hungry coyote and a hungry actor is that the latter just waits tables to make ends meet, while the former has no choice but to perish, if its failure continues much longer. The coyote ambles up to the prickly pear thicket, unaware of the plump owlets hiding just a few feet away.

Although the coyote would prefer to be tearing into muscle and bone, he settles for a thorny mouthful of prickly pear fruit. Begrudgingly, he gnaws and swallows the thistly pulp, then returns to the dry creek wash, where he resumes his haunt of the meandering corridor of shifting sand. Trudging along, the famished coyote spots a small serpent with a golden hue gliding up a slope of sand like a silk ribbon caught up in a gentle breeze. Scampering in for a closer look, the coyote discovers a delicate-looking rattlesnake, called a sidewinder (*Crotalus cerastes*). Instinct tells him that this creature is not to be messed with. When push comes to shove, sidewinders can pack a nasty bite. As with other rattlesnakes, they belong to the diverse group of serpents known as vipers. With long opposable fangs, capable of delivering copious doses of tissue-corrosive venom, sidewinders are snakes to be respected. Despite their ability to deliver a devastating bite, they prefer to reserve their hemotoxic venom for prey. When given the chance, these nimble snakes, like all other rattlesnake species, often choose to warn obtrusive invaders by nervously shivering their rattles, rather than biting.

When they hear the unmistakable hissing shudder of a spastically vibrating rattle, most predators choose to go the other way. The coyote wisely backs off a few feet, then pushes on, making sure to sidestep around the sidewinder. As he passes by, the snake lunges out with a strike. It has no intention of injecting the coyote with its liquid death; the snake just wants to affirm who is boss. The heat-sensing pits underneath the sidewinder's nostrils help it to thermally track all warm-blooded creatures moving around it. As the aura of radiating heat fades off, the sidewinder relaxes for a bit, then side-slithers up the sandy incline and out of the wash.

I always take great pleasure in observing a sidewinder slide uphill along a shifting bed of sand. The way they move is almost miraculous. If you have ever tried to run up a sand dune, then you know how grueling it is as your legs wobble and sink in their inefficient bid to climb. It can almost feel as if the sand is swallowing you up! Moving across the sand comes easy to sidewinders, however. They actually throw themselves over the sand by hurdling one end forward, soon followed by the next, while moving along their side. Watching a sidewinder glide over the sand, I am reminded of a magic carpet. By having just a fraction of its body surface touch the sand at any one time as it moves, the sidewinder reduces friction and sinking. Another benefit to getting around sidewinder-style is that if the sand is too hot, the snake avoids being scorched by gliding across the sand without making much physical contact with it.

Meanwhile, the mother owl continues to search for more food. There is another strange, lobster-like creature lurking about in the darkness, and as with the scorpion, this armored hunter wields a pair of powerful, cockroach-crushing pincers. Alas, its future is sealed, as it is quickly discovered by the burrowing owl flying overhead.

The agile sidewinder prefers to warn obtrusive trespassers by quivering its rattle, rather than biting them.

The cephalothorax and pedipalps of this creature are more robust, compared to the recently sacrificed scorpion. Unlike the scorpion, though, this creepy bug appears not to have a stinging tail. The owl loops a few more times overhead, and then rolls into a freefalling dive toward the target. The brazen bird flutters to the ground just inches behind the intended prey. Resembling an excited yogi, the owl's head slides like mercury across flexible vertebrae, while its nimble body prances from side to side. Suddenly, the stealthy bird is on top of its prey, trapping the creature beneath a grate of stiletto-sharp talons. As the beak draws closer to the cephalothorax, ready to splice through brittle exoskeleton and into pulpy flesh, the pinned creature struggles to poke its plump abdomen between two talons and toward the owl's face. Thrashing back and forth at the end of the insect's oval rump is a hair-thin whip that is not wielded as a weapon, but instead serves as a sensory organ that is hypersensitive to the touch. The filamentous tail desperately flickers in the darkness, hesitantly bouncing off an approaching wall of feathers, all too aware of its impending doom.

The wispy feeler reaches out and touches the captor's beak just as it begins to close around the optical region at the front of the cephalothorax. Without warning, the tail whips forward, flush against the creature's back, seconds before an intense mist sprays out of small slits located at the base of the tail. The pungent vapor quickly wafts up to the owl's face, triggering the startled hunter to double back and release its captive. The sharp, mucous-inducing sting is so intense, that the burrowing owl is unable to open its eyelids, and when finally, after a minute, it is able to tolerate a slight squint, the moonlight reveals that its cunning victim has vanished.

This crafty invertebrate was no mere bark scorpion, but a chemically armed look-alike called a vinegaroon (*Mastigoproctus giganteus*). Instead of jabbing a stinger into the flesh of its enemies, the vinegaroon shoots out a concentrated cloud of acetic acid (a.k.a. vinegar)! That's right: The vinegaroon keeps out of harm's way by temporarily blinding, gagging, and repelling potential predators with the caustic fumes of its acidic bomb.

After a few more minutes, the humbled owl ruffles away any lingering molecules of the odoriferous assault and then flies off. Although she is not wounded, the hunter has been dazed by the rancid attack and will return to the burrow exhausted, with only a meager scorpion to show for an entire evening's hunt.

The burrowing owl is not the only creature fluttering about in the Sonoran night. Hidden behind an arsenal of cactus spines is a delicate but somewhat ordinary-looking flower that has allowed its petals to open wide under a black heaven. It is the moon and not the sun that summons weary petals to stretch open against its barbarous spines, an invitation to partake of luscious and sweet nectar, intended not for a bee or a butterfly, but for a bat! Hundreds of plant species, from the deserts of the Southwestern United States through the rainforests of Central and South America, are dependent on bats for pollination and seed dispersal. These noc-

The vinegaroon blinds, gags, and ultimately repels potential predators with its noxious secret bomb.

turnal creatures habitually get a bad rep for being malevolent harbingers of some nocturnal devilry. All too often the only recognition we are willing to dole out to this ecologically important and very highly evolved mammalian group is for the gobbling up of an occasional mosquito by insectivorous bats. Globally, bats play an integral role in promoting biodiversity and balance throughout many ecosystems, as thousands of plant and animal species are dependent upon these misunderstood creatures for survival. If you are partial to papayas, mangos, figs, and tequila (from agave cacti), then thank a bat! Personally, I am smitten with bats, and they are welcome in my belfry anytime. By the way,

---

I have sniffed many a cactus flower, and although I've never detected any foul stench, I have pricked myself in the eyeball while trying to stick my face in close for a nice, deep whiff.

---

the old yarn about a bat getting all tangled up in your Aunt Gertrude's beehive hairdo is an absolute fabrication. Now, I'm not calling Auntie Gertie a liar; I merely suggest that perhaps she should cut back on the cough syrup and give some slack to the beleaguered chiropterans of the world.

Only an hour has passed since the tiara of tender petals has unraveled from its powdery core, and already a flock of thirty bats, ravenous for a nectar-induced fix, have begun to swoop and spiral around the bristly emergent. The bats swarm around the solitary cactus, hungry for the rich nectar of its oddly positioned flowers or perhaps for a quick nibble from its pendulums of zesty fruit. They are lesser long-nosed bats (*Leptonycteris curasoae yerbabuenae*), delicate and nimble flyers that are akin to hummingbirds with regard to agility and appetite. They are the quintessential specialists, designed in shape and behavior to capitalize on a particular resource that many other creatures do not have access to. Throughout the spring and summer months, many species of cactus, like agave, cardon, saguaro, and organ pipe, entice the bat with their nutritious and tasty offerings. As with many other species of moderately sized bats, called microchiropterans, lesser long-nosed bats are graceful in flight and are equipped with their own sophisticated system of internal radar, called echolocation. Under the veil of darkness, these agile flyers navigate masterfully through the crisp atmosphere by emitting high-frequency sound waves that are detected by their sensitive, satellite-like ears after bouncing off myriad fast-approaching obstacles.

The cacti's chief reward for their tribute to the nectivorous microchiropterans is a chance to secure a future for the cohort of prickly progeny. The bats serve as taxis, transporting precious pollen from one flower to the next. Many plant species dependent upon bats for either pollination or seed dispersal have evolved some fascinating adaptations to lure in these finicky flyers. One very nifty characteristic is the ability to flower at night or to produce fruits that reach their optimal ripeness during the nocturnal hours. If bats are the primary vector for moving pollen and distributing seeds, it is important for the plant to produce flowers and fruit that are strategically located for easy access. Some are cauliflorous, meaning they grow along branches, stems, and the trunk—like the papaya, for example. Other species—for instance, mangoes—produce pendular blossoms and fruits that dangle from elongated stocks, hung far from entangling branches. Since pigments aren't very detectable at night, many of these flowers often lack in vibrancy, because there's no sense in wasting energy to look all nice and comely if no one can see you in the first place. To attract bats, a number of plant species produce blossoms that have pungent, if not downright putrid, odors that bats seem to find pleasing to the muzzle. I have sniffed many a cactus flower, and although I've never detected any foul stench per se, I have, on more than one occasion, pricked myself in the eyeball while trying to stick my face in close for a nice, deep whiff. Alas, it appears that bats are far more adept at sneaking up on a cactus flower than I, never mind that they do it on the wing and during the pitch black of night.

The first bat moves in, hovering just an inch away from the flower, as well as the fierce spines sprouting behind it. The wings beat at a dizzying rate, like those of a hummingbird, keeping the bat stationary. Then it plunges its narrow muzzle deep into the flower's funnel-shaped ring of folded petals, called the corolla. Sliding rapidly in and out from the bat's slender jaws is a remarkably long tongue. The thin and slick tongue is three inches in length, nearly as long as the bat's head and body! This limber and lengthy tongue extracts a generous stream of nectar that flows from the flower and down the creature's gullet. This lesser long-nosed bat, which weighs in at about eight ounces (think a stingy handful of raisins), will feed like this throughout the night, visiting, for just an instant, many a cactus flower scattered across the desert. Eventually, well before sunrise, this gregarious critter will rejoin the great colony made up of more than 70,000 individual bats. Together, they work as one, drinking in Nature's mead while simultaneously infusing countless cacti with the necessary elements to complete the formula for future life.

Once again the great fireball climbs above a glowing heap of stones, as it has done more than 3.5 million times before. Revealed beneath the sun's amber sheen is the pathetic coyote, curled up into a scruffy ball on a scrape of dusty rock. His body contains barely enough energy to shiver, never mind cry out, yet he musters up a lonely howl, which resonates crackly and dry from the depths of his throat. He wails again and again into the still air, as his forlorn cry echoes out to a distant canyon unanswered. Hunger has tortured the lonesome coyote throughout much of the night, and the illumination of morning reveals his wretched state to a buzzard circling high above. This eater of the dead looks down upon the haggard pup, but does not break from its effortless volplaning just yet. The clever raptor will bide its time until death finally comes, dropping the sorry coyote flat to the earth for the last time. Not far from where the coyote stoops is the pool where 10,000 spadefoot tadpoles began their life just a few days ago. It appears that before visiting the coyote, Death came calling again on the tadpoles, as it had done many times before, ever since they managed to burst free from their gelatinous spheres.

Death has taken on many manifestations at the fast-shrinking pool of squirming murk. She has shown herself as a predator—a ferocious water bug, complete with gizzard-ripping sickles for limbs, and a transient wading bird, eager to fill its crop with a slimy ball of undulating protein. She has visited the spawn as a wave of vapor-busting heat, transforming the shallows of the pool into a near-boiling soup of coagulating carcasses. But perhaps her greatest apparition is in the form of disease, routinely touching the mass of tadpoles with wisps of bacteria and fungus, which spread quickly, like oil upon water, striking down the weak by the hundreds with just a single bloom. Death, in all her glory, has thinned out the once robust population of spadefoot tadpoles to just a few hundred individuals, ensuring that only the strongest, most fit tadpoles will survive.

In just under a week, pudgy limbs have begun to sprout from bulbous bodies as the tadpoles' tails, once so important for propulsion, have started to shrink. The gill slits, saddling the jowls of each surviving tadpole, have started to seal up like healing wounds, and a fresh pair of lungs quickly sprouts within the embrace of a rapidly hardening ribcage. In just a few a more days the tadpoles will be full-fledged frogs, but for many the completion of metamorphosis will not come soon enough to free them from Death's last hurrah.

Despite the tadpoles' rapid, almost miraculous, rate of growth, the desert is catching up. Rain has failed to return and reconstitute the pool, while each day provides nearly eleven hours of incessant sun. The pool has shrunk by nearly two-thirds from its original size, and the depth has slipped from six inches to just over an inch. The quantity of oxygen has dropped to a nearly infinitesimal level, while the mid-afternoon temperature of the pool spikes high enough to nearly poach an egg. The surviving tadpoles present a desperate scene, as they wriggle against the bodies of both the living and the decomposing, their heads bobbing up, frantic for breath. The tadpoles are packed so tightly that they appear to outweigh what little water remains. There is not enough water and oxygen to support the remaining offspring, and life-sustaining nourishment in the form of algae and detritus has all but disappeared.

There is only one survival strategy remaining that could potentially whittle out a little breathing room for the remaining tadpoles, while simultaneously providing an abundant stream of growth-infusing protein. It is a behavior that will not only

---

Cannibalism is the new edict for life in this muddy pit, and the craving to devour thy neighbor will not be satisfied until the last survivors remain.

---

decrease competition for valuable real estate, but will also provide the fittest tadpoles with that extra edge needed to free themselves from the mire of their creation. The only way out is for the strongest to devour the weakest, and the boldest tadpoles consume their neighbors. In the end, the hunger for survival has fostered cannibalism, a crude but very resourceful tactic that serves as the ultimate test for survival. The water level has dropped to the point at which the tadpoles are unable to completely submerge themselves, and the stress among the trapped spawn is be-

ginning to peak. The tadpoles are no longer capable of escaping the sun's unforgiving glare, which causes their thin, almost translucent skin to blister and crack.

Finally it happens: One tadpole rips into another by fastening his O-shaped lips onto plump skin and pulling away chunks of flesh. Brand-new limbs are jerked off and gobbled down before ever having the chance to set foot upon terra firma. Streams of intestine are yanked taut by ravenous tadpoles, as if caught up in a grotesque game of tug-of-war. A feeding frenzy this is not, for the cannibalism now unfolding between the larval spadefoots is deceptively nonchalant. The water does not bubble and froth with gobs of flesh, for this is a subtle slaughter. A bobbing tadpole does not even realize that he is being preyed upon by his neighbors as he is tugged, prodded, and pushed, until finally they open him up from underneath. The victim continues to gasp for bubbles of air as his body is mutilated by the unremitting stream of nipping mouths, striking at him from all sides. Cannibalism is the new edict for life in this muddy pit, and the craving to devour thy neighbor will not be satisfied until the last survivors remain.

As the siblicide at the pool continues, a pack of eight collared peccaries (*Tayassu tajacu*) cautiously rambles though a column of cacti and into the gully of scrub and crumbled rock. Upon discovering a plentiful patch of prickly pear cactus laden with ripe fruit, the peccaries instantly transform from cautious to curious, as they begin feasting on the succulent and sweet harvest. The troop of bumbling peccaries is so preoccupied with foraging for grub, the animals are completely oblivious to the presence of the hungry coyote, hunkered down on his rock. They furiously tear into the patch of cactus, filling their jowls with soft wet fruit, gobbling down just about any part of the bristly plant that they can stuff past their washboard-tough palates. There is nothing happier than a peccary filling its gut! Peccaries just love to eat, and do it just about whenever they can. For the most part they are herbivores, rutting around through the earth in search of tu-

bers, roots, bulbs, and rhizomes. In the Southwest, they are masters at cactus browsing, with prickly pear ranking as a delicacy, spines and all. More than twenty percent of the prickly pear cactus growing throughout the Sonoran Desert each year will be devoured by peccaries! Many cactus species, like prickly pear, barrel, and saguaro, depend on them for seed dispersal, since these rapacious consumers act as nonstop pastry bags, continuously squeezing out globs of scat, which is packed with a future generation of cacti. Lucky for the hungry peccaries, the weary coyote has not detected them either, at least not yet.

Known throughout the Southwest as javelinas, collared peccaries are hardy and adaptive creatures, capable of thriving in harsh expanses of desert habitat, which for most of the other ungulate, or hoofed, species is off-limits. As a species, peccaries are not limited to the deserts of the Southwest; in fact, they can be found inhabiting a diverse array of habitats throughout the New World, from grassland savannahs to lush tropical rainforests.

Found in Texas, New Mexico, Arizona, and Central America, the javelina (say an *h*, not a *j*) is the only native, pig-like wild animal in the U.S. It gets its name from the Spanish word for javelin because of its razor-sharp tusks.

Javelinas are no ordinary pigs. They are smart, svelte, and convivial creatures with personalities ranging from cute and cuddly to downright ornery. I have frequently encountered packs of peccary while out hiking both in Arizona and in Central America. The normal reaction of a pack of wild peccaries upon discovering my awkward shape shambling onto the scene is to scamper instantly into the bush until well out of sight. On a few occa-sions, though, they have sent me scram-bling up a tree, seeking refuge.

There are few wild moments that I can recall more terrifying than being charged by a peccary. Again, the first strategy for a peccary is to flee the scene of danger, but if it feels cornered, a trapped peccary will swiftly turn from flight to fight. I have heard the grating resonance of an angry peccary grinding its saber-like tusks prior to an attack. The sound hits the ears like a fingernail file being pulled through clenched teeth, causing the hairs on the back of the neck to prickle. A pissed-off peccary is not to be messed with, since its long exposed teeth, normally used for tilling up grub from the earth, can easily shred the flesh of an oncoming predator. In all other cases, a peccary would rather eat.

After reducing the patch of prickly pear cactus to a few stubby clumps, the pack of eight peccaries divides up into two groups in search of additional fodder to gulp down. The smaller group, containing an adult sow with two piglets, stumbles onto the exoskeleton of a barrel cactus, half-buried in the sand. Peccaries have an acute sense of smell, and if there is anything edible hidden beneath a layer of earth, they will sniff it out. The smallest of the two piglets detects a peculiar odor coming from inside the hollow of the desiccated cactus. Cautiously, the little javelina probes the opening of the cactus with its muzzle, attempting to find the origin of the aroma. Deliberate sniffs of air puff in and out of its wet snout,

until the piglet finally hones in on the curious stench. After a few seconds of rooting warily through an inch or two of sand and debris, the peccary jolts its head out of the cactus hollow.

Startled by its discovery, the pug-sized peccary pulls back as a legless creature, clearly incensed with the meddling intruder, emerges from the darkness. It is none other than the Mexican hognose snake, with his belly still fat from a previous feast of spadefoot toads. He would prefer to lethargically lay low during the digestion process, rather than deal with an invasive trespasser. The quill-like hairs sprouting from the young peccary's back perk up, as it squeals out an abrupt, high-pitched grunt. Foraging not far from the piglet is the sow, who, upon hearing the distress call coming from her babe, quickly moves in. The hognose snake is now dangerously trapped between mother and offspring, but the situation for the vulnerable reptile becomes even more desperate when the other piglet joins the arena. Although not armed with potent venom, the hognose snake possesses a rather remark-

(continued on page 64)

A PACK OF
PERILOUS PECCARIES

My most vivid encounter with these creatures occurred in Central America while searching for frogs in a rice paddy. I had been cooped up in a thatched hut for three days because of heavy rain hammering down from the heavens practically nonstop. Finally, boredom got the best of me, so I heaved myself out of a hammock, strapped on my headlamp, and exited the musty hut, hungry for a little adventure. If adventure was the payoff for the evening, I was just about to hit the mother lode.

The rain pelted down with such vengeance that I became sopped within seconds of stepping into the night air. Streams of watery fingers danced across the lens of my headlamp, causing my field-of-view to be little more than a mishmash of distorted shapes. After two hours of practically feeling my way through the jungle, I finally made it to the rice paddy, where, as I knew, thousands of copulating tree frogs were gathered for their biannual orgy. The crumbling banks of the rice paddy were overflowing with murky water, while the constant pitter-pat of rain blended with a great chorus of singing tree frogs. I slid down the mushy bank until I sank hip deep in water and mud. It took a lot of effort and balance for me to wallow through the muck, as each step required me to free my feet from the powerful vacuum of mud pulling them down.

Everywhere I looked I saw mating frogs, locked in passionate embrace, totally oblivious to the giant Peeping Tom peering down at them. The rain caused the circle of light from my headlamp to wobble, making it difficult for my eyes to focus on the frogs. As I struggled to get a decent view of the action, a menacing snort bellowed out from behind me. My heart nearly seized as my body froze. Slowly, I turned around, wincing. The origin of the fearsome snarl was exactly what I did not want to see. The creature standing on the ridge of mud that ran along the perimeter of the rice paddy was none other than an angry peccary.

Whatever I had done to tick it off, I still do not know, but whatever it was must have been pretty significant, because that cantankerous pig wanted a piece of my hide. My heart pounded away while I stared up at the bank, trying to get a good look at the beast. All I could see, however, was the devilish gleam in its eyes. How could this situation get any worse? I was mired past my navel in the mud, with a ticked-off peccary in front of me, waiting to teach me who's the boss. Well, guess what? It did. The pair of eyes glowing red as embers was soon joined by others. At least ten additional peccaries, like sentries scoping out the enemy, took to the ridges around the rice paddy. Although I knew that it was highly unlikely that the peccaries would dive into the deep pottage of mud to come after me, I was still quite terrified. They snorted and gnashed their teeth from all sides of the rice paddy, as my eyes jerked back and forth, trying to get a fix on the stealthy creatures.

Nearly half an hour of the peccary posturing had passed, when I finally made the decision to make a hasty exit. Slowly, I backed up to the only corner where no peccaries were present, all the while keeping my eyes locked on the multiple pairs of glowing orbits. Never losing track of the pacing pack of peccaries, I leaned back against the corner as I wedged my arms into the wet earth until I was able to lift my butt onto the ridge. Under the strain of wobbly knees, I slowly rose to my feet. Just as I was about to make a run for it, I heard the snapping of twigs and a series of muffled grunts, accompanied by the patter of hooves splattering through mud. Before I could mutter out the briefest expletive most appropriate for the moment, one of the creatures had rushed towards me and then paused just a few feet away from me. Let me tell you, the phrase "lazy and/or slow as a fat pig" does not apply to a wild peccary. It is a lean, mean, and nimble machine, capable of startlingly fast sprints.

I stood there petrified, unable to make a peep. Not only was I completely mute, I was also physically and emotionally powerless to defend myself. Amazingly, the peccary did not attack. Instead, he chose to discharge a few more snarls before turning about, and then confidently, along with his mates, sauntering off into the forest. Had the grunting gang chosen to attack, I probably would have had the tar ripped out of me. I will never know what it was that ignited the peccary's temper. My best guess is that he thought I was a threat, and wanted to remind me who was in charge. As I anxiously waddled back to the camp, I couldn't tell what had contributed the most to the wetness of my shorts, the relentless rain or my nervous bladder. Still, it is important to remember that an angry peccary is usually an exception to the rule, since they normally are peaceful creatures. When threatened, however, they are very capable of an aggressive defense as a last resort.

able defense that is ideal for keeping aggressors from getting too close, as the curious javelinas shall soon discover.

Plant matter is what normally goes into the belly of a javelina, but these creatures will rarely pass up an opportunity to partake of a little protein. Given the chance, they will readily devour grubs hidden beneath a rotten log, a clutch of bird's eggs from a ground nest, or even an unlucky reptile flushed out into the open.

The sow is hesitant at first, but since she does not hear the unsettling rustle of vibrating rattle associated with dangerous snakes, she decides to get a closer look. She sticks her wet snout flush against the hognose while drawing up a deep sniff. The frightened snake buries its head beneath the twists of its tightly coiled body, as it lets out a menacing hiss. Still undaunted by the posturing serpent, the sow presses her muzzle hard against the spiraling snake and takes another whiff. Soon, the javelina will clamp down on the hognose and violently thrash it about, causing vertebrae to snap and nerves to sever. But seconds prior to becoming

nothing more than a limp and pathetic trophy dangling from the sow's compressing jaws, the hognose hurls out a defense that the javelinas won't soon forget.

Two curled-up snouts meet, one belonging to the javelina, the other, the hognose snake. No longer willing to lie down and meekly submit to the giant monster, the hognose will fight to the very end. He launches his defense by standing tall and proud, with nearly one third of his body towering above the ground. The two piglets dart to safety behind their mother's rump, as she stumbles back and assesses the serpent's strategy. Believing that there is no more to come from the hognose, she moves in once again, but this time for the kill. Just as her jaws are about to close around the neck of the hognose, the serpent defiantly rises up once again, but this time it does something astonishing. The snake dramatically unfolds an ominous hood that stretches wide from both sides of its upper neck. The hood seems to triple the size of the serpent's head, instantly transforming the hognose from potential snack into menacing adversary.

With hood spread wide, the hognose comes across as though he were a deadly cobra, and he even lets out a series of fierce hisses. He has captured the sow's attention, and her reaction to his threatening display will ultimately depend on how well he performs.

Although fooled at first, the sow is no longer amused by the serpent's spectacular display. After just a few moments of hesitation, she lunges forward and grabs the hognose by the nape. She snaps her head down towards the ground, whipping the hognose against the compacted dirt. Dust billows up around the helpless snake, which appears to have been mortally wounded from the force of the violent hurtle. Waves of twitching flesh writhe up the snake's twisted torso, which has landed belly down in the dirt. Then, the hognose rotates belly side up, perhaps in one final and defiant reflex expressed by his rapidly deteriorating nervous system. The mouth is warped open in a brutal gape, as bloody mucus bubbles inflate from the esophagus and then burst against his protruding fangs. The forked tongue hangs ragged from the left corner of the jaw as the snake draws in a few more labored breaths before finally becoming still.

The last bit of protest to the attack comes when the snake's twitching anal vent dilates and releases a stream of rank musk. The putrid stench wafting up from the cloaca of the lifeless hognose is so foul that it repels even the gluttonous javelinas. The three pigs fall back a few yards from the stinking serpent. Agitated by the snake's instant inedibility, the sow rambles back and forth while her two piglets huddle close behind. She continues to sashay around the stinking corpse, as if hoping that the squalid odor will soon fade so they can make a meal of the snake. The curious piglet that initially discovered the hidden hognose loses interest in the grisly affair and wanders off to a nearby patch of prickly pear cactus, while mother and sibling stay back, transfixed by the malodorous snake.

Upon arriving at the cactus patch, the wandering piglet is so focused on plucking up mouthfuls of succulent fruit that it fails to notice a blurred ball of tawny pelage hovering atop a rock just a few yards away. It is the coyote, famished and beat, which gazes down at the young javelina. The immature javelina is oblivious to the canine's presence, and without mother nearby to provide a speedy defense, it is in very real danger of slipping into the food chain.

The scrawny coyote is shaking with anticipation, and although he is very weak, the thrill of predation sends a wave of adrenaline through his sunken veins, fortifying him with the energy needed for what might very well be his last chance to play the role of predator. If the coyote pursues the piglet and fails to take it down, he will exhaust his last remaining bit of energy, needed to sustain life. Moreover, the vulnerable coyote may receive a mortal wound, delivered by the sow, should she attempt to rescue her offspring. Either of these scenarios will ultimately spell death for the coyote, but he has nothing to lose. If he lets this rare opportunity to fill his belly and refortify his constitution pass, he will die.

At first the coyote hesitates, but then quickly gathers his wits before sliding down the backside of the rock opposite to where the young javelina feasts. He lands silently on the desert floor with only a slight puff of dust marking his arrival. The nimble coyote huddles down to the ground, with his head sunk low beneath his shoulders. He is both anxious and excited as he begins to crawl slowly toward the javelina. Squatting down with belly fur dusting the ground and limbs bent awkwardly back causes his muscles to cramp and shiver. But the coyote is determined, and he stays on course. For nearly ten minutes he gradually creeps toward the piglet until he is but a yard away from pouncing. His heart is beating hard, his limbs are shaking but he does not falter, just one more step . . . Snap! The worst has just happened: One of his paws has landed on a twig that is quick to crack beneath his weight. The hunter halts, just as his quarry spins into an about-face. The two creatures face each other. Eyes locked, both hearts pounding, the prey nervously glares ahead, attempting to get a fix on the stalker, while the predator stares back at what might be his last chance to procure survival.

The coyote is so disciplined in its ability to stay still that when an irritating fly perches in the corner of his eye and drinks up a string of gooey mucus, the stoic canine refuses to blink. The piglet, on the other hand, nervously grunts and sniffs, the coarse hairs scattered across his rump standing on end. The naive javelina knows that there is something out there, watching and waiting, yet it sees nothing peculiar. The youngster observes only a brown, bushy clump positioned next to other familiar shapes. Although the javelina sees nothing out of the ordinary, his snout has inhaled a pungent odor of danger. Then suddenly, the coyote leaps out from the fuzzy background, as if it has spontaneously materialized from the surrounding rock and vegetation. He lunges forward, sending the piglet springing into the air to avoid capture. The javelina squeals in terror as jagged jaws latch onto its fleshy hindquarters and then yank the flailing beast down. The panicked shrills of fright coming from the struggling javelina are deafening, but a ferocious vigor is surging through every cell of the coyote's body. Now that he has grasped the prey, he will never let it go.

In order to survive, the coyote must take this chance. He must be quick and cunning, and above all, he must be successful.

The sow abandons the hognose and instantly races toward the unmistakable calls of distress coming from her babe, while the other piglet instinctively seeks refuge in the hollow of an old mesquite stump. She arrives to see her offspring being violently mauled by the jaws of the hunter. The sow charges, but her babe weighs only eight pounds and is an easy load for the coyote to carry. The coyote dashes off with the dead piglet dangling from his mouth, but soon the sow is gaining on him. Then, the chubby swag slips from the coyote's jaws and tumbles backwards, folding into a veil of dust. Instinct tells the exhausted coyote to leave the trophy behind and flee the scene, but he doesn't. Instead, he spins around and races into the wall of dust.

The sow and coyote zip past each other, and while she twirls in reverse upon seeing him flash by, he races toward the piglet. Again she is gaining, but it is the hunger for survival that fuels the sprinting coyote. He approaches the fallen booty at maximum velocity and manages to scoop it up without skipping a single step. The coyote's heart is about to burst and his legs are pounding the earth like never before. He charges forward anyway, until the pursuing sow begins to lose steam. As the coyote races ahead, the sow starts to fall back. Finally the sow comes to a stop. She is utterly exhausted and is no longer able to make chase. She stands there with spirits broken and heaving for breath, watching the snatcher of her babe vanish into the horizon. All he leaves behind is a fading trail of dust.

Minutes later, the lifeless piglet hits the earth with a thud, as the coyote huddles over it. He is out of breath and his diaphragm is so strained, it has started to spasm, but that does not stop the coyote from feasting. He rips into the corpse, savoring every bite. The texture of the flesh feels wonderful in his mouth and when he bites down on a wad of meat, the pressure of the tissue against his gums makes him want to gobble down even more. He is both eating the meat and drinking the blood, savoring the warmth of the flesh, along with its salty, coppery taste of a fresh kill. He is so happy that he mutters soft yelps, while swallowing gobs of meat. This vocal expression of satisfaction causes him to choke, and he pukes up a soppy lump of tissue. No matter—he just gobbles it down again.

Soon, his belly is full, but he will not stop until hardly anything remains. He eats all the organs, every bit of meat and tendons. He gnaws on rib and long bones, and even scoffs down much of the fur. He does a fair job on the skull as well. Whether tissue be soft or hard, the coyote consumes it with greed, but for some reason he doesn't eat the hooves. In the end little is wasted, and although it was a bad day for the young javelina, it turned out to be a great one for the coyote. Tomorrow will come for the coyote, for he is the survivor of today. He has now earned his place as one of the great hunters of the Sonoran Desert.

As for the sow, she has indeed suffered a tremendous loss, but she does still have a remaining offspring. Now she will be able to invest twice the amount of energy into her one piglet, thus dramatically increasing the likelihood of its survival. If by chance she should lose that one too, then perhaps it would be a statement about her abilities as a mother. She will learn from this experience, so when the opportunity arises for her to become a parent once again, she will be an even better one.

Back at the lopsided barrel cactus, where the hognose snake lies, a miracle has begun to unfold. Now that the threat from the javelinas has passed, it seems that there is still some life left in this stubborn reptile. The resurrection commences with a twitching tongue, which slowly folds up from outside the jaw, until soon it is flickering with ease. The mouth that appeared to be broken slides from one side to the other and then slips back in place. The entire length of his body starts to undulate, and enthusiastic breaths draw in and out repeatedly. Finally, the snake's brightly colored belly begins to fold into the dirt, as his back rotates upward until at last he has managed to right himself. The hognose flexes and twists until all the kinks are out. Then, with a few flicks of the tongue he slips back into the dark, crescent-shaped grotto of the cactus. The hognose is no Lazarus, for he didn't truly perish—he just did an excellent job pretending he did.

You see, the hognose is a very skilled actor: He is a master at feigning death. When he loses all hope of escape, or when he fails to convince a predator that he is a deadly serpent through his dramatic bluff, the hognose simply plays dead. His performance is complete with the stench of decay, thanks to the potent musk glands tucked within his cloaca. As a species, the hognose snake is truly a marvel of nature, for it is a reptile that embodies the wonders of evolution. Like the coyote, the hognose too is a survivor, and I imagine that this particular individual will be back in top shape in no time. Soon he'll be visiting his old haunts in search of plump, amphibious fodder to feed upon.

Meanwhile, let us return to the shifting dune, where the sweep of sand and gravel meet. The dark crevice leads to the subterranean tunnel that is home to the ancient tortoise. Following the dank corridor down into the cool of the substratum, we pass the desert tortoise, which contentedly slumbers off a full belly. Further down lurks another reptile. She is a great lizard, at least a decade older than her roommate, and the two have been occupying the same den for nearly eight years. The lizard moved in with the desert tortoise just a year or so after the latter had excavated the burrow. This creature is perhaps the most mysterious and elusive of all Southwestern reptiles. It also happens to be my favorite species of lizard, the infamous Gila monster (*Heloderma suspectum*).

Pushing twenty inches in length, its width nearly as wide as my forearm, the Gila monster is the largest of all North American lizards. Perhaps the most remarkable attribute of the Gila monster is that it exists as one of the only two species of lizards in the world that are genuinely venomous. The Gila monster, along with its Central American cousin, the Mexican beaded lizard (*H. horridum*), belongs to the helodermatidae family, an exclusive club of lizards armed with a neurotoxic venom that is potentially deadly to both prey and predator. Gila monster venom is manufactured in glands in the lower gums. When a determined lizard grabs a hold of a victim in its vice-like grip, the viscous toxin flows from the gums and along a grooved channel that runs up the lower teeth. The venom is not injected but massaged into the flesh.

Here is the scoop about getting nailed by a Gila monster. It won't charge or pursue the aggressor; instead, it will first try to ward off the attacker with a menacing display of hissing, thrashing, and mouth gaping. If the Gila monster is compelled to bite, it will only do so upon being physically provoked by the assailant. So, if a Gila monster gnaws on a person, chances are that the bite occurred while the individual was attempting to either handle or injure the venomous reptile. Although the venom of this lizard is considered to be quite potent, I am not aware of any case in recent times where a human being has succumbed to a Gila monster's bite.

In my life, only twice have I had the rare privilege and pleasure of witnessing a Gila monster in the wild. Unfortunately, I have also had the tragic experience of discovering six impressive Gila monsters that had been squished dead on the road, apparent victims of hit-and-run accidents. There is nothing more devastating for a herpetologist than to run up to a beautiful Gila monster that appears to be basking on the tarmac, only to discover that it is roadkill. But the saddest, most depressing experience of all is to witness a driver intentionally swerve out of his way to hit a Gila monster, or any other herp (trade term for amphibians and reptiles) for that matter.

I once heard a story about a guy from Florida who was so pissed off at people intentionally and maliciously running over

Despite its strong survival techniques, the Gila monster (pronounced with an *h*, rather than a *g*) faces extinction.

endangered gopher tortoises, that he decided to implant a plastic model of a gopher tortoise with an erected railroad spike inside of it. He then set it up in the breakdown lane. Consequently, more than a dozen people were changing tires on the shoulder as a result of either poor driving skills, inebriation, or an innate cruel streak for killing critters. Perhaps this tale is nothing more than an urban legend, or rather, a rural one. Still, it does make you wonder, and perhaps be a better driver. Enough of this tirade; let's return to the Gila monster, resting deep within the burrow. She has awakened and is ready to make her move.

It is now just an hour before sunset, and more than two weeks have passed since the Gila monster has ventured upward to the world of wind and light. A yearning for sustenance has once again driven the great lizard to trek out from the stale, still air of her burrow to the land above. She crawls past the tortoise, who takes little notice of her. They present no threat to each other, since the Gila looks upon the tortoise as nothing more than a rock. The smell of fresh air, along with all the intriguing molecules carried by a whispering wind, motivates the Gila monster to crawl faster until she soon reaches the entrance of the tunnel. As the plump lizard exits the den, the light hitting her face causes her to squint briefly, while her pupils constrict until they have adjusted to the dramatic increase in luminosity.

The tawny glimmer of sunset reveals an absolutely gorgeous lizard. The head of the Gila monster, about the size of a large plum, is rather blunt, but with a slightly triangular shape. Her tiny black eyes sit above the gaping mouth that extends broadly between each jaw hinge. The body is cylindrical in shape but with a hefty girth. All four legs branch out low from her body, keeping the lizard close to the ground, and when she crawls, her legs swing out in a gait similar to a salamander's. At six inches in length, the Gila monster's tail seems somewhat stubby when compared to her great body size, yet it is nicely plump. A rotund tail indicates that she is in excellent health. Because Gila monsters store fat in their tails as an energy reserve for harsh times, her chunky behind suggests that she hasn't had the necessity to burn off much of her body fat. What is most impressive, though, is her color pattern. Scattered across her epidermis are hundreds of bead-like scales. Each is a jewel of unique color, ranging from cinnamon red and pumpkin orange to Indian ink black.

The Gila monster's reticulated mosaic of brilliant scales is similar to the complex pattern of an intricately woven rug. The distinctive and splendid coloration of the Gila monsters serves two purposes. The first is camouflage; the interwoven pattern of reddish-orange and black breaks up the lizard's shape, allowing her to blend in with the autumnal tones of the desert floor. The second purpose of her color pattern is to caution all other lifeforms that she is a potentially dangerous opponent. This strategy is called aposematic coloration. The bright colors of orange, yellow, and red stand out as a universal warning sign, indicating that this lizard is armed with an excellent defense and should not be harassed. While hatchlings are frequently preyed upon by raptors, carnivorous mammals, and even snakes, few creatures will mess with an adult Gila monster. Despite their strong survival techniques, these uniquely North American lizards are now facing extinction as a result of habitat loss and getting nailed by vehicles, as well as being illegally captured for the pet trade.

The Gila monster sits still by the tunnel entrance, collecting herself. Then she moves on. She decisively laps the brittle ground with a fat, fork-shaped tongue, until she detects an intriguing trail of chemicals that drives her to waddle onward. She knows this taste well, and if her senses are correct, the trail of residual molecules will eventually lead the hungry Gila to her next meal. Twenty minutes pass until the treasure hunt is over. The hungry monster arrives at a loose entanglement of wispy twigs that have been twisted into an untidy wreath and positioned on a gritty knoll, beneath the splintered shadow of an old creosote bush. Huddled over the concave center of the nest is a petite, pear-shaped bird with striking plumage. The bird's breast is gray, while its face displays a bold pattern of black, white, and cinnamon. Perched on top of the bird's head is a topknot, a tiara-like cluster of six tightly overlapped, comma-shaped plumes. This regal bird is a Gambel's quail (*Callipepla gambelii*), and when it spots the approaching marauder, it remains absolutely still.

This attempt to blend in will not throw off the Gila monster. Alas, it is not movement that the lizard detects, but a trace of molecules leading up to the vulnerable nest. Soon, the Gila monster is within a few inches of the nest. In a last-ditch effort to distract the Gila monster, the quail darts a few feet away from the nest and commences a panicked jig of circles and bobs. However, it is not the plump quail that the invading lizard seeks, but the precious contents of the nest.

The Gila monster's formidable jaws are powerful enough to dent a steel-toed boot, yet she can easily extract a fragile egg without rupturing its paper-thin shell.

Upon leaving the nest, the quail has inadvertently revealed a clutch of three gumdrop-sized eggs, each with its own unique pattern of auburn and russet specks.

The quail stops in mid-prance only to witness the great invader, as she plows across the ridge of twigs and begins to pillage through the spoils of her conquest. One by one, the warm eggs are gingerly plucked from the nest and swallowed whole. The Gila monster's formidable jaws are powerful enough to dent a steel-toed boot, yet when a more delicate approach is required, she can easily extract a fragile egg without rupturing its paper-thin shell. Five minutes is all the time needed for the Gila monster to empty the nest of all three eggs, thus forcing the forlorn Gambel's quail to begin anew. Now that her belly is full, the Gila monster needs some hydration. She creeps off, leaving the disheveled nest behind. The sun has been beating down on her hard, but just up ahead there is a place where she can cool down and perhaps lap up a little moisture. She arrives at the remnant pool that was brimming with fresh rainwater just nine days ago, but today it is nothing more than a sludgy, stagnant mess.

Although not the freshest water hole on the planet, it is at least still somewhat damp. So here she will stay for a bit, wallowing in the thick muck, and maybe filtering a few mouthfuls of tainted liquid. She crosses a quagmire that is thick with the desiccated bodies of sun-dried tadpoles. A thin, organic crust comprises the surface of this wide ring of death, which entombs a core of rot and stink under-neath as dense as your grandmother's chocolate fudge. The dull black stratum crackles beneath each labored step, as the Gila monster dawdles toward a soppy morass located in the center of the putrid halo. The wallow of sludge is not much wider than a turkey platter and is about ankle deep. The mucky center reeks of death, but the Gila monster doesn't seem to be at all offended by the stench. Slowly, she slides into the mud bath, al-lowing most of her body to be immersed within the tar-thick slush.

Her head sticks out from the muck as if decapitated and floating, while the re-mainder of her body squirms delightfully within the dark stew. She cracks open her mouth just wide enough to draw in a thin film of water that has separated from the muck. She contentedly settles in, for the 'warm mush is soothing against her beaded hide, as sheets of dead skin soften and slough away. Her eyes close as the sky softens above a fading sun, and soon she is asleep. While the Gila monster snoozes, another life has begun to stir. Wriggling beneath the Gila monster's coarse belly is a creature not much bigger than a pea. It fidgets and twists, until eventually it man-ages to struggle free from underneath the hefty lizard. The Gila monster remains asleep, as the little beast squirms up through the thick slurry and onto the reptile's submerged tail. The creature continues to crawl forward, concealed be-neath the brown mush, climbing up the lizard's spine until it finally reaches her shoulders. Having collected layers of mud on its way up, the creature looks like a blueberry-sized glob, formed at the nape of the Gila's neck.

The brown mass wobbles slightly, then bursts, releasing the small animal trapped within. Finally free, the creature, glazed with a coat of pungent batter, squats boldly upon the lizard's beaded head. In an instant, the glimmering brown coat of muck breaks when two bright orbs blink and then open wide. A stream of tiny mud globules spackle out from a pair of pin-hole nostrils. The Gila monster is oblivious to the great triumph tran-spiring above her tightly fixed eyelids. With one effortless hop, the energetic creature makes its first leaps from the scaly platform and onto terra firma. The battle to endure beyond the brutal boundaries of the deteriorating pool resulted in thousands of casualties, but in the end there were nearly a hundred survivors. This brave and resilient individual is the last of the great exodus of spadefoots. No longer confined by the limits of an aquatic existence, this youngster departs the caking pool for a new life and a new beginning. The glistening spadefoot has many challenges ahead, and there will undoubtedly be great dangers awaiting it. Its future is uncertain at best. Still, perhaps with a bit of prudence, luck, and tenacious spirit, this frog will yet return to the place where its precious life began to bring the next generation of spadefoots into the world.

OUR NATURAL HERITAGE

The Sonoran Desert is a uniquely North American ecosystem, which we, as citizens of the United States, should be proud to have as a part of our natural heritage. Of course, many of the creatures inhabiting this rugged and spectacular landscape are uniquely North American as well. It is important to note that the vastness of the Sonoran can give the impression that it is a limitless ecosystem that is impervious to disturbance. The reality is that the complex ecology of this desert community is highly sensitive, and the slightest bit of unnatural disturbance can have a devastating impact on the habitat and the wildlife living here.

Despite great efforts to conserve the Sonoran Desert of Arizona at the private, state, and national levels, this fragile ecosystem is still not being adequately protected. Although the overall trend in the attitude of today is to be more ecologically conscious with our approach to using natural resources, the cold hard truth is that we often fail to harvest wildlife and manipulate the environment in a manner that is truly sustainable. Unfortunately, the Sonoran Desert is vulnerable and has been negatively impacted as a result of the careless meddling of man.

In the end, no one creature is truly

greater than any other, and the loss of just one simple life-form can have a devastating impact on countless other organisms. Take the cactus, for example. With the extinction of just one species—such as saguaro, cholla, or prickly pear—an endless list of wildlife, from the cactus wren and Gila woodpecker to the lesser long-nosed bat and desert tortoise, would suffer. Then, if the desert tortoise should suddenly disappear from the Sonoran landscape, the impact on other wildlife would be immeasurable. Creatures like tiger salamanders, kangaroo rats, sidewinders, king snakes, gopher snakes, Gila monsters, geckoes, and burrowing owls would all lose access to their vital habitats; and many species of grasses, shrubs, and cacti would lose an important agent for seed dispersal. Although you may think that the tortoise is a ridiculous example of ecological cause and effect, the truth is that this species has come dangerously close to extinction in the past and is presently not faring all that much better.

With regard to being permanently erased from the ecological roster, the desert tortoise is but one critter living in the Sonoran Desert that faces possible extinction. Just a short list of the many Sonoran creatures tittering on the edge include all of the following: the San Xavier Talus snail, Sonoran tiger salamander, Tarahumara frog (regionally extinct since 1981), desert massasauga rattler, twin-spotted rattler, ridge-nosed rattler, flat-tailed horned lizard, Gila monster, Mount Graham red squirrel, black-tailed prairie dog, Mexican vole, lesser long-nosed bat, Mexican wolf, big-horn sheep, Sonoran pronghorn, jaguar, masked bobwhite, thick-billed parrot, cactus ferruginous pigmy owl, Mexican spotted owl, and Southwestern Willow flycatcher. The major contributors that impact the well-being of Sonoran wildlife include habitat and water loss, road development, and the illegal collection of wildlife. A shocking ninety-five percent of the riparian habitat in the Sonoran has dried up as a result of unsustainable water extraction for developing subdivisions. Because of this alarming decline in aquatic habitat, seventy percent of the fish species native to the Sonoran Desert are now listed as critically endangered by the state of Arizona.

Let me guess: I've pretty much reduced you to a state of utter depression. Well, before you roll the car into the garage, close the door behind you, and hit the gas, take a breather (outside of the garage!). While habitat is rapidly deteriorating as cities like Tucson and Phoenix grow at a cancerous rate, which of course displaces wildlife, there is still a lot of pristine desert just waiting for you and your family to come and explore. Millions of acres of fantastic Sonoran Desert habitat have been permanently protected in places like Organ Pipe Cactus National Monument, Joshua Tree National Park (which is part of California's share of the Sonoran), Saguaro National Park, Tonto National Monument, Kofa National Wildlife Refuge and many other wildlife refuges, and dozens of state parks such as Alamo Lake State Park and Catalina State Park. I would highly encourage you to visit these natural treasures, and trust me, if you go at the right time of day and in the right season, these majestic places will provide you with a chance to witness awesome wildlife.

When you chart out your expedition, though, make sure to plan for the challenges of this rugged terrain, which, for the ill-prepared, can be downright deadly. Bring lots of water, shade, sunscreen, and good hiking gear. Don't hike alone and whatever you do, don't get lost, or you just might end up as a desiccated mummy. While you're enjoying and exploring the many wonderful state and federally protected parks that Arizona has to offer, take lots of photos—just don't mess with the wildlife. Illegally collecting wildlife, be it lizard, snake, tortoise, or cactus, is devastating to the ecology of the region and has drastically depleted the populations of many endemic creatures. Now, if herpetology is your bag, then leave your bag at home. Trust me: I know the temptation to snag a critter and bring it home as an acquisition for the private collection. It is a bad habit that is all too easy to justify, but excuses like, "Well, it was going to die anyway," or "I'm a conservationist so I'll just privately conserve one specimen for myself," or "It's only one and I'm sure it won't be missed . . ." just don't cut the mustard. Individuals caught in the act of illegally collecting wildlife can face some pretty stiff penalties. Although an individual may think he is the only one out there when he comes across a hatchling Gila monster, the truth is that there are federal and state rangers with one objective: to catch poachers—and the collection of wildlife without a legal permit is, in fact, poaching!

I know this seems like a rather lengthy diatribe, and perhaps you're about to kick the soap box from underneath my feet, but I only bring it up because the poaching of animals and plants from the Sonoran Desert is a huge problem in Arizona. There . . . enough said. In the end, you shouldn't let the desert scare you, because if you respect her and treat her gently, she will reward you with an endless reservoir of wonderful memories of exploring spectacular landscapes and discovering amazing, one-of-a-kind critters. I hope that when you decide to trek across her painted earth beneath the stark shadows cast by jagged rock and bulbous cacti, your journey will be as rewarding as the ones that I have taken, and that you will return to the Sonoran Desert again and again . . . and again.

THE SAVANNAH
OF SOUTHEASTERN
AFRICA

y wife, Natasha, and I had returned from safari in Kenya just prior to my writing this book. It was Natasha's first time exploring the vast African continent. As for myself, I usually travel to Africa three or four times a year for work. I know, that sounds pretty cool, doesn't it? While most people travel to big cities like New York, Chicago, or Cincinnati for employment, I usually find myself in a remote and wild terrain in order to pay the mortgage. When I am exhausted from two days of travel, beat by sixteen hours of uninterrupted filming, or sick from an exotic bug that has set up camp in my lower intestine, I remind myself that I've got one of the neatest jobs in the world, and that I could instead be schlepping it out in a windowless cubby someplace coldly urban, where stark skyscrapers outnumber trees twenty to one. I am very lucky to have the opportunity to do what I do, and although it isn't always easy or fun, my profession has always provided me with unforgettable moments that occur on a daily basis. My work has taken me around the globe at least four times, and I have had chances to explore many of the exotic regions that have been on my wish list since I was twelve. Although I am smitten with many distant lands, such as Ecuador, Panama, Tasmania, India, Thailand, and Borneo, no place seems to get my heart all aflutter like Africa.

When I am in Africa, I often feel small and irrelevant, not in a humiliating way, but rather, in a humbling sort of way. I acknowledge that quite a few of the great life-forms there are very capable of squishing, out-running, or eating me. In the eyes of many African creatures, I really am insignificant, and in an odd way, I find this reassuring. Africa remains a vast frontier, brimming with excitement, adventure, and jeopardy. It is an extraordinarily diverse land, which possesses a spectacular coastline, intimi-dating deserts, entangled jungles, raging rivers, and sweeping savannahs that flow endlessly toward the horizon. In Africa serenity intertwines with conflict; life here, at every level, can be as cheap as it is precious. The energy flow from one or-ganism to the next is often brutal; the death of one creature to sustain another is delivered without mercy. It is a place where life unfolds on a grand scale. While Nature in Africa may appear to be unrea-sonably cruel to her subjects, she also gen-erously supplies moments of stillness, when her beauty, whether in landscape or in beast, remains unmatched in this world.

So there we were, the two of us, lounging across a fluffy bed, peering through the triangular opening of our tent, enthralled by the vista beyond the canvas walls. We had just traveled for seven hours along a viciously bumpy road until finally arriving at our camp, which was situated along the border of the Tsavo West Na-tional Park in southern Kenya. There was my wife, four months pregnant with our daughter, Maya, and sandwiched between us was a very precocious mongoose named Churchill. The young, ferret-like mon-goose arrived at the camp as an orphan, and after reaching adulthood had decided that life there was pretty posh, so he stayed. He would visit us each day to just check things out. He would begin by rum-maging through our suitcase before hop-ping up onto our bed. It had become very clear to Natasha and me that Churchill was a sexually frustrated creature, as he would frequently attempt to gratify him-self on our wrists or ankles. Churchill seemed more interested in trying to hump my wrist than observing the breathtaking landscape, and he was none too pleased that Natasha and I were paying more at-tention to the sunset than to him.

We were exhausted from the trek, but the extraordinary view from our tent had

My wife, Natasha, and I taking data from a sleeping hyena in Masai Mara.

clouds drifted by. Beneath the sky was a vast plain of tall, golden grass that stretched out to the horizon as far as the eye could see. The grass moved back and forth beneath a gentle breeze, like a sea of liquid amber. The air smelled of wet rye, yet it was dry and warm as it wafted into our tent, softly lifting the mosquito netting around us. We were in heaven, Natasha, Churchill, and I, lying back contentedly, the gleaming sunset washing over our limp bodies. Lost in the moment, my wife turned to me and said simply, "Now I know why you love Africa." Keep in mind, though, that the only creature we'd encountered so far was a horny mongoose looking for a cheap date.

In truth, I find the savannah and the bush country of eastern and southern Africa to be utterly breathtaking. When I am out there, in that endless stretch of grass, watching a herd of elephants pass or a pair of patriarchal lions wincing in the wind, I am both inspired and awestruck. When I sit on the hood of my Land Rover with a hot cup of coffee, while a never-ending river of migrating wildebeest flows on either side of the truck, just as an omi-

infused us with a second wind. We propped ourselves up on the straw-tick mattress, drew back the drape of mosquito netting hanging over the footboard, and just stared outside. It was a magical hour, as the colossal sun sank past distant Mount Kilimanjaro. The cerulean sky began to mellow to a rusty glow as a cluster of cotton-white nous storm begins to blacken the sky over-head—well, that is an experience that humbles the soul and ignites the spirit. I want to take you to *this* Africa, to the place where you can find yourself while getting lost in the wilderness, where the everlasting conflict between predator and prey has reached its zenith. It is here in the southeastern African savannah where competition is at its fiercest, as victors claim all the spoils at the expense of the young, the aged, and the weak.

Finding a specific location to set this story is a challenge because I can't think of any one place that outweighs the rest. We could go to the Masai Mara, Ngorongoro Crater, Tsavo East and West, or the Serengeti of Kenya and Tanzania. There are the magnificent plains of tall, verdant grass in Uganda, the dry acacia forests along the Chobe River in Botswana, or the bushvelt and salt pans of Namibia. And of course there is always Kruger National Park in South Africa. These places are just a few of the many extraordinary locations in Africa where splendid Nature is regularly displayed in all her glory. The

choice is certainly a difficult one, but I think I have come up with an alternative that will allow you to achieve a truly wild East African experience. But first, I want to remove the unnatural boundaries set by human beings, which abruptly divide one country from the next. Imagine that the dotted lines on a map do not exist—in fact, for many large species of migrating wildlife, they don't. We are on an expedition without borders, as we set up camp on a grassy bluff between a river and a water hole, beneath the splintered shade of a baobab tree. We could be in Tanzania or Kenya, but in truth, a specific location is of little importance.

THE LAST TERRESTRIAL BASTION

Now that the rains of the wet season have returned to the savannah, the parched earth, which had been dry for many months, is rejuvenated once again. The arrival of the sweet rain has replenished the crackling earth and withered grass, transforming the barren landscape into a luxuriant sweep of green fodder. A shifting wind rolls across the savannah, prompting the knee-high grass to ebb and flow with each pass. As we look out over the savannah, there seems to be no end in sight, as the fertile grassland spreads out to the distant horizon. Looking yonder from the great mound of black rock and tufts of bushy grass, it seems as though the savannah and the sky eventually collide, when the cobalt curtain above intersects with the breadth of green grass below. The sparse assemblage of trees scattered across the savannah are, for the most part, bent and twisted from decades of manipulation by wind, water, and wildlife. There is, though, one ancient tree that towers high and mighty over the grassland.

Like an enduring minaret, the corpulent baobab (*Adansonia digitata*) stands boldly atop the wind-scoured bluff. Its enormous bole, or trunk, is wider than a pair of elephant bulls standing side by side, and it seems to taper only slightly as it soars skyward, to well over eighty feet. The baobab's waxy trunk is practically naked of foliage, while the crown consists of crooked branches, radiating outward like the wire frame of an umbrella blown inside out. For nearly a millennium, the tree has stood upon this hill in semi-arid sub-Saharan Africa bearing witness to the eternal struggle for survival endured by all creatures of the savannah, whether great or small. Sitting at the base of the great baobab we can observe myriad dramas unfolding around us. Peering down at the water hole on the right, the river on the left, and the grasslands all around, we will follow the trials of life and death that all creatures inhabiting this land must face. We are here for a brief moment to observe the few hours separating sunset from sunrise and the many living things attempting to survive and prosper here.

Despite the expansive territory and abundant game, there is a limit to the quantity of large predators that the savannah ecosystem can sustainably support. As the level of competition among these supreme predators heightens, the consequences for all parties involved can be extreme, if not downright deadly. Here, like nowhere else, all life-forms are bound tightly and inescapably. Every creature occupying this terrain has earned a place at the great table of life, and each species is unique, with its own story to tell. What I find most exciting about the grassland ecosystem of southeastern Africa is its status as the last terrestrial bastion of our planet where a diverse array of colossally built creatures still exists. Of course, not all the wildlife inhabiting the African savannah is enormous, yet it is here, upon the never-ending stretch of grass, where we can find a twelve-thousand-pound elephant, a three-hundred-pound ostrich, a four-hundred-and-fifty-pound lion, a three-thousand-pound black rhinoceros, and a ten-thousand-pound hippopotamus.

In order for North America to emulate the Africa of today, we would have to travel at least twenty thousand years back in time. It was during the Pleistocene period when mega mammals, like mammoths, ground sloths, giant bison, and saber-toothed cats roamed the savannahs of North America. But these marvelous monsters have long since passed; thus we must look to the grasslands of Africa to get a feel for what life might have been like on the North American continent way back when. While there are still a few shrinking regions in North America where large land mammals, like grizzly bears and moose, still thrive, the concentration and composition of similarly sized and even larger creatures exists unmatched in Africa.

It's not only the wildlife whose size impresses here. In Africa, everything seems larger and utterly unconfined: the sky, the land, the sun. It is just before dusk, and the immense sphere that had been blazing intensely across the savannah has begun to sink behind the grassy plateau. The recent rains have reconstituted the river, which is now swollen to the brim of its muddy banks. The coursing waters are as murky as the dregs in the bottom of a coffee cup. The turbulent water rushes and rips over jagged rocks, causing the formation of small, floating islands of brown foam. Basking on the bank of the winding tributary is a gigantic Nile crocodile (*Crocodylus niloticus*) that stretches nearly

Nile crocodiles live in large communities and rarely venture very far from water. Though hunting them is illegal, poachers still seek their hides.

sixteen feet. The olive-colored reptile is spread out like a massive solar panel, as it fuels its 1600-pound mass in the sunset's warm and energizing rays. The great crocodile is wider than a dragon boat, its massive head is three and a half feet long from snout to nape, and its powerful jaw spans two and a half feet! The conical teeth along its snout are as large as my thumbs, and together, jaws and teeth are powerful enough to punch through a quarter-inch sheet of steel.

The crocodile is equipped with powerful limbs, and at the base of each rear leg is a webbed foot that's as wide as a pie plate. The creature's leathery back resembles the rubber strip of a tire that has been ripped off a tractor-trailer after a nasty blowout on the interstate. Running along each side of the croc's enormous tail are two corresponding rows of leathery, fin-shaped scales jetting up from its dark hide. The reptile is a massive monster designed to overpower prey ruthlessly and

(continued on page 91)

THE CROC THAT GOT AWAY

Not so long ago, I was working with a group in Uganda that was attempting to relocate a large Nile crocodile that had the nasty reputation of being a man-eater. Along with an expert croc capturing crew from Kenya, I arrived at the location with the mission of capturing the cantankerous reptile that had eaten four people in the last two years. I will never forget the first night I saw the beast. We were steering down the Nile River near Murchison Falls in a thirty-foot, motorized long boat. It was around nine o'clock at night when we came to the area where the croc had regularly been spotted. As we drifted by the bank, serving as the notorious croc's hangout, my gaze fell on what I thought was a slumbering hippo. When I focused a narrow beam of light onto the creature's face, instead of a hippo, I discovered the largest crocodile my eyes had ever seen. It was a huge eighteen footer, and although I knew that they could get this big, this size potential had never really registered. But at last, I was staring directly at one of the big boys. When he slipped off the bank and into the water, it was like watching a killer whale slide through the foamy surf. Slowly, he meandered past our boat and then just disappeared. Speechless, we all fell back into the boat, wondering how the hell were we ever going to capture it.

We had interviewed families who had lost their loved ones to the hungry reptile. We even met a survivor who had miraculously escaped the jaws of the beast, but lost a leg. He took us to the site where he had been attacked. By interviewing the victims of the ravenous crocodile, we were hoping to come up with a pattern of the attacks. We had two very important revelations: all of the attacks occurred at night, and each victim had been bathing alone. Frankly, I wouldn't jump in a croc- and hippo-infested river alone and at night for a million bucks, not even for a thirty-second dip. I'd rather take my chances entering, covered in honey, a cage with a dozen pissed off and hungry bears, than swimming blindly in a black soup of giant crocs and hippos. Anyway, we spent two weeks, working sixteen hours a day trying to capture the elusive giant. On four occasions we had actually managed to snag the monster croc, albeit temporarily.

During our first attempt to capture the reptile, we had attached a shank of rotten goat meat to the end of a sturdy thread of inch-thick hemp. We tied the line to a sizeable tree and then tossed the bait in the water, after which we moved off to give the croc a chance to come and grab the bait. We returned a few hours later to find the bait line taut and pulling on the tree so powerfully that it bowed toward the river with its foliage touching the water. Carefully, we exited the boat. I along with six other strapping men, gingerly clasped the line with trembling fingers, and then, ever so slowly, we began to pull. The line seemed to come out rather easily, as if we were heaving a water-soaked log. Now, after having time to reflect, I've come to believe that this was all part of the croc's plan. As the heavy mass began to levitate, our confidence grew with each pull, and then, without warning, the thick rope spun out from our grasp, stretching more tautly than a cable holding up a suspension bridge. A couple of the guys had fallen back, and as for myself, the skin on my palms was burnt bloody and smelled of melted plastic and singed hair. Instantly, we collected ourselves then grabbed a hold of the line again and attempted to pull once more. But this time, the line wouldn't budge at all, and a second later we all fell back onto each other. Quickly, I reached down and snatched the line, only to find it was as loose as unraveled yarn. As I pulled it in with ease, I found that the only thing I got a hold of was a dripping wad of rotten goat meat.

For our second attempt to capture the Nile croc, we set up a snare-trap on the riverbank where he would bask frequently. The line making up the trap had been tied to half a dozen solid saplings, so if he became trapped within, there was no way in hell he could escape. Dangling in front of the snare was a snack to lure him out, which was the same piece of goat shank that he had defiantly puked back at us earlier. After the trap had been set, we once again made for a speedy exit. We returned only to find that the bait was gone, all the ropes had been shredded, and at least three of the pole trees had been pulled out from the earth at their roots! Of course, there was no sign of the croc; he had managed to free himself from the kind of snare that even a raging cape buffalo could not escape. Our so finely and sturdily crafted trap was no match for him. The third attempt was a debacle not that much different from the first, but it was our fourth try that almost had me crying and biting my pillow, like the biggest wussy there ever was.

To ensure a successful capture, we again set out a bait line, but this time we looped a noose around the submerged rope. When the croc bit, instead of trying to pull him out, we would slide the noose along the line and across his muzzle until finally reaching the nape of his neck. Once we felt that the noose was around his neck, we would tighten the line and simply haul him out. Our plan was to use a fifteen-foot-long pole to slide the noose down over the croc's head. Finally, after the bait line and noose had been set, we returned a few hours later to discover once again a taut line with the submerged creature at the other end. Everything had gone according to plan, and after an hour of carefully synching the bait line forward, the croc, submerged just a few feet in the turbid water, was but moments away from capture. Slowly, I slid the pole down the bait line, and felt the knot of the noose hit a rock. "Oh my god," I thought, "that's no boulder, that the monster's massive

(continued on page 90)

THE CROC THAT GOT AWAY—CONT'D

skull!" I stayed focused, as the noose slid over the snout and past his jaws, until finally settling around his fat neck.

The air was thick with tension, and no one uttered so much as a peep, as I gently pulled on the slip of rope, which tightened the noose. Within a second of drawing the noose taut, the water exploded. All six men were quickly pulled to their knees and dragged to the water's edge. "Pull!" I shouted. "Pull with all the strength you've got!" Suddenly, an appallingly gigantic head, longer and wider than half my body, torpedoed out of the roiling water toward us. The monster croc kept his body parallel to the riverbank, and with one great swoosh of his tail, a waist-deep curl of water came smashing onto us. Down again he went, pulling us back and forth like a waterlogged rag doll. But then, as it had done twice before, the bait line went limp. In anticipation of the loss I yelled, "No, no, no, no . . . not again!" I dropped the bait line and anxiously pulled on the noose, but alas it came up from the depths easier than a thread through a button. Alas, the noose and the bait line had been snapped, and the monster croc was gone.

He had played us hard, and despite snagging him four times during the course of two weeks, in the end, the giant croc had eluded capture. I came to Uganda very cocky, and ready to kick some serious croc-ass, but in the end, the ancient creature had humbled me, providing a sobering reminder of the awesome power of these spectacular reptiles. Although we never caught the monster croc, our mission was not a complete failure. Watching the croc slip away, we came to the conclusion that the capture and relocation of these mighty creatures was only a temporary solution to the conflict between man and crocodile. In the end, the solution to this complex dilemma was rather simple. The crocodiles that had been attacking humans at Murchison Falls were opportunists, hunting people only when they were most vulnerable. By simply modifying human behavior a little, the human fatalities from crocodile attacks were dramatically reduced. The crocodiles stopped attacking when the villagers stopped bathing alone or at night, and when they constructed a rudimentary perimeter around their water hole at the river's edge. It is nearly impossible to alter the behavior of a wild group of ancient reptiles with more than sixty million years of instinctual hardwiring, but human beings are adaptive and are capable of adjusting their behavior when necessary. By not vilifying the crocodiles, while simultaneously recognizing their role within the ecology of Murchison Falls, the villagers now have an opportunity to share the river with these powerful predators without the fear of attack.

rapidly; while it will regularly consume fish, turtles, and birds, given an opportunity, this efficient predator will take down large mammals as well. I have worked with Nile crocs on many occasions, and while I greatly respect them and their ecological importance, I still can't help but feel a bit on edge when I am in their presence. Nile crocs are powerful and cunning predators, and to be captive in their grasp is a terrible fate that I would wish on no one. Despite their predatory nature, these aquatic reptiles are vital to the health and well-being of wetland habitats throughout the African continent, and without them, the ecology of this region would be incomplete. With that said, don't ever turn your back on one of them.

This particular croc has been laying out for most of the day, energizing his metabolism in preparation for the cooler temperatures of the evening to come. He avoids overheating by frequently drawing open his gigantic muzzle to allow excess heat to escape through evaporation off the moist tissue in his mouth. As he lies there, with a gaping maw upon the crackled mound of dried mud, his eyes detect a curious flurry of movement taking place a hundred yards downriver along the opposite bank. Like a descending drawbridge, the crocodile slowly closes his jagged chops before sliding silently into the muddy water. Except for the two rounds of bony flesh encasing his nostrils and orbits, the crocodile's body is completely submerged as he meanders downriver. Just as he is about to reach the muddy bank, he hovers for a moment and then sinks. As his head disappears in the water, two slightly opaque lenses, called nictitating membranes, sweep across his eyeballs. The membranes allow the croc to keep his eyes open underwater as he peers up from the murky depths, watching and waiting for just the right moment to make his move.

Gathered at the river's opposite edge is a small herd of eight plains zebras (*Equus burchelli*). Structured as a true harem, the herd consists of the dominant stallion, six closely related mares, and one colt. The largest member of the family unit is the gorgeous stallion, who stands nearly five feet to the shoulder and weighs

As you can see, zebras are very social. They exist only in Africa, but one species, the quagga zebra, became extinct at the end of the nineteenth century.

in at a very solid six hundred pounds. As with the rest of his clan, he sports a fantastic pattern of black and white stripes across his hide, which, like a human fingerprint, is uniquely configured to each individual zebra. The zebra's dramatic striping makes it difficult for predators to visually separate a single individual from the remaining herd. The pattern also functions as a visual bonding device among herd members, especially between mare and colt. In fact, when the foal was born, its mother separated it from the rest of the herd for a day or two in order to imprint the babe with her unique striped pattern. Because the colt is a male, he will be driven from the herd upon reaching maturity, but for now, he is just two months old and will have the pleasure of nursing for at least ten more months before he needs to worry about his independence. For the present, the colt is enjoying life. He is mischievous and curious; he is also very much loved by the other zebras. His existence up till now has allowed him to be the focus of attention among the other zebras, and as he spryly bucks and kicks with glee, he is completely unaware of the many dangers lurking beyond the security of the herd.

Close to the river's edge, a dense thicket of acacia trees is writhing up from the brittle earth. These thorny trees are just now beginning to regenerate the small, waxy leaves lost during the dry season. The lance-like thorns of the acacia are long and sharp enough to pass though a man's hand, while the branches and trunk are almost skeletal in shape. Although they appear hostile to visitors, and a man would surely skewer himself if he dared to climb one, many species of hardy wildlife depend and thrive upon these trees. Scampering through the branches is a troop of vervet monkeys (*Cercopithecus aethiops*). There are around twenty of these comical primates, which bang and jump through the thorny branches with great agility. Vervets are a relatively large species of African monkey with males weighing up to twenty pounds, while females are slightly smaller. Both males and females have a lustrous coat that is silvery gray, a smoky black face, and a long, wiry tail. Despite their similarities, there is one very distinct difference between the sexes: The males proudly sport a bright, cobalt-blue scrotum and a penis that is fire-engine red! How's that for sticking out in a crowd? Foraging among the

A foal weighs about seventy pounds at birth, can stand almost immediately, and runs within a day.

crooked branches, the vervets feast on tender shoots, leaves, insects, bird eggs, and small lizards. Much of the moisture they need is acquired from succulent fruits and from morning dew that collects on leaves. Rarely do they venture down to the river or to the water hole for a drink; it's just too dangerous. The troop is scattered throughout the acacia crown, and while some members are eating, others are grooming. Mothers with young babies gather beneath the crowns, while young males take sentry positions around the perimeter of the trees, diligently keeping watch for any signs of approaching predators such as leopards, rock pythons, and Marshall eagles.

A year-and-a-half-old sub-adult male, squatting on an arched limb, has taken an interest in the herd of zebras that has now wandered over to the river to quench its thirst. The first to drink is the stoic stallion, who cautiously spreads out his front legs a couple of feet, and then lowers his neck to the water. His ears rotate from front to back, as he listens intently for the slightest sign of danger. The remaining

Vervet monkeys walk and climb using all four limbs. They have an arsenal of more than forty calls.

herd watches for a few moments, and then approaches. Just as the other zebras begin to line up alongside the stallion, the giant crocodile bursts from the murky river and lunges toward the stallion. The water beneath the croc boils, while a foamy wake curls along his massive torso, which is now halfway out of the river, as if the leviathan is about to take flight. The immense jaws are jacked open at a seventy-degree angle, as the bolt-like teeth begin to graze the zebra's tensing neck. Pulling back, with hooves reeling in midair, the zebra is desperately attempting to retreat from the croc's deadly grasp, and as the arsenal of white fangs begins to scrape against his neck, the stallion manages to avoid a deadly blow to the carotid by rotating his neck around the croc's reaching muzzle. But as the top of his mane and ear slip past the predator's flailing jaws, the giant croc clamps down.

Like a sinking anchor, the croc plunges backward into the water, allowing his hefty body to pull the zebra down with him. The croc has viciously latched onto the stallion's right ear along with a substantial wad of mane and a chunk of nape flesh. As the croc sinks downward, the stallion is pulled violently forward until his front hooves are teetering at the edge of the crumbling bank. The remaining zebras are bellowing out from the rear in unified terror, as they witness the butchering of their patriarch. The mother and two other mares have formed a protective circle around the colt, whose father is now battling for his life. Meanwhile, one of the mares gallops to the stallion's aid. Once the mare is alongside him, she whirls instantly, until her rump is facing the river. Then, with all her might, she jackass-kicks the croc directly in the chops with both of her back hooves. The nictitating membranes roll reflexively across the croc's eyes, as the hooves smash against the side of his left jaw, but the determined reptile has latched onto the stallion, and he will hold on till the bitter end. Again, the mare plows her hooves into his snout with all her might, but the jaws are locked and he refuses to give in.

The terrified stallion whinnies pathetically, "Kwa, ha, ha, ha!" as the throbbing pain radiates throughout his face and neck. His head and neck are now awkwardly stretched out to the side, as the croc weighs him down, but the stallion will not surrender yet. With front legs locked and hooves wedged rigidly into the hard earth, the stallion stands rock solid as he battles for his life.

From the crown of their acacia tree, the vervets have been glued to the drama playing out below, and upon seeing the croc dive out and grab onto the zebra, many of the monkeys leaped back into the center of the acacia crown, terrified by what they had just witnessed. They continue to look down with horror, as the croc locks onto the zebra, while the latter pulls back from the reptile; the two stubborn creatures are trapped in a deadly game of tug-of-war. As everyone in the vervet troop watches, transfixed by the calamitous battle underneath, a pair of bright, piercing eyes is now gazing upon the monkeys. The vervets are so engrossed by the zebra's plight, that none of them notices the arrival of a snake eagle (*Circaetus pectoralis*) in a neighboring acacia, just twenty feet away.

The magnificent raptor stands upon the knotted branch. The folded wings and the raven-black plumage of his proud face shimmer in the warm light. The soft white feathers of his chest and legs stand out strikingly against the dark plumage. Eight merciless talons, capable of puncturing deep through the flesh of a variety of prey, from lizards and snakes to small mammals, are tightly coiled around the knotted branch. His face is broad and somewhat flat, giving him an almost owl-like countenance. His wide, glassy eyes shine with an intensely golden hue above a sharply curled beak. The eagle stares at the distracted monkeys with a menacing glare, but he has no interest in preying upon a vervet, for this mighty raptor prefers the flavor of reptilian flesh. Now that the

The snake eagle, or serpent eagle, enjoys a diet of lizards and, yes, snakes—even poisonous ones.

eagle has determined that the monkeys, whose attention was engaged elsewhere, will not disturb him with their petrified clamoring, he focuses on the edge of the water hole. There, between a large rock and a tuft of dried grass, two other enemies are about to engage in battle.

Stretched out on a slab of rock is another weighty reptile, dwarfed in size though it might seem when compared to a giant crocodile. The creature is a four-foot-long black-throat monitor (*Varanus albigularis*). If you're looking for an extant example of Dino from the *Flintstones*, this lizard would be it. Beaded and gray, its hide bears a lifetime of battle scars, received either as a predator on the prowl or the hunted on the run. With a body the size of a big loaf of bread, front limbs twice as long as my thumbs, and long strong hind legs, this rotund lizard can even climb trees. His corpulent torso is a testament to his hunting skills, but his ability to scrape up a meal will be tested once again. As he spreads out across the rock, the long prongs of his pinkish-white tongue tickle continuously the rough sur-face of stone, detecting the presence of something to kill and eat. As the fat monitor slithers off the rock and begins to crawl toward the grassy lump, the serpent eagle continues to stare down upon him with great interest, although not as a potential victim. The crafty eagle watches the black-throat monitor crawl off, gambling on the possibility that the lumbering lizard will lead him to his next meal.

Meanwhile, within the warm and wet darkness of an oval egg, a legless creature has been squirming about, waiting for the right moment to creep out into the golden light. The creature is just one of twelve newly hatched Egyptian cobras (*Naja haje*), all of which are preparing to leave the dark slimy comfort of their egg sacks for the hazardous world beyond the confines of their leathery shells. Over the last two days, the tiny cobras have begun to gain consciousness after nearly two months of development. They began as gelatinous embryos, until finally becoming perfectly formed serpents nearly two months later. Each cobra is complete with a rapidly pattering heart, novel lungs

The largest lizard in the Varanidae family is the Komodo dragon, which can grow up to ten feet long. Still, at four feet, this black-throat monitor would need a leash to be taken for a walk.

awaiting an infusion of fresh air, and a pair of tiny fangs ready to deliver deadly neurotoxic venom. At the tip of each snake's pinkie-sized muzzle is an egg tooth, used to slice through the eggshell encasing it. While some of the cobras have sliced a half-inch slit with their egg teeth just moments ago, other serpents in the clutch split their egg cases open twenty-four hours before. As a sliver of light penetrates each egg, causing the web of mucus around the coiled bodies to glisten, each little cobra must marshal every bit of energy and courage it possesses to whittle and push its way out from the darkness and into the light.

Encircling the clutch of a dozen eggs is a five-foot-long, wrist-thick mother cobra. She is innately driven to stand watch by her nest as the hatchlings prepare to emerge. Nothing, not even a predator, has deterred her from this obligation to her brood. Even though all cobras come into the world armed with potent venom, they are defenseless from predation while developing in their eggs and are an easy meal for many creatures, from mongooses to monitors.

Then, in a matter of minutes, it happens! One by one, tiny cobras slide out through the slits of their eggs and onto a patch of brittle grass and dried leaves. It's not much of a nest really, just a bed of plant material that has collected naturally over time. Each baby cobra comes into the world enveloped in a clear, slimy web of mucus, with slight streaks of bloody fluid smeared about their bodies. After a few moments of writhing within the sappy liquid, the cobras gain their bearings, as instinct pushes them to take cover. As they skirt and slither through the grass, one cobra inadvertently rubs against another. The sensation instantly rouses both cobras up to a defensive posture, their perfect miniature hoods defiantly spread. As the two snakes stare each other down, the remaining droplets of rapidly evaporating mucus, spackled across their stretched hoods, glistens in the yellow light like diamond dust. Soon after recognizing that neither snake poses a threat to the other, they begin to crawl off after their siblings.

The little cobras, decorated with shiny bands of yellow and black, emerge from their eggs with all the behavioral instincts and physiology needed for survival. As the pencil-sized cobras disperse, their mother prepares to depart as well. Now that her offspring are slithering away independently, her obligation to protect them has come to an end. The cobra does not give a parting glance to her progeny as they squirm off. She has no emotional response to the departing creatures that are her own flesh and blood. The bond between mother and offspring was severed when the little cobras slithered their way free from the leathery clutch of eggs, and if she were to encounter any of her children in the future, whether ten minutes or ten years from now, she would not know them. Just as she glides into the dense thicket of bristly grass concealing her abandoned nest, a black shadow has begun to stretch over the remaining fifteen inches of her body.

The cobra is the popular choice of snake charmers, who tease it into forming this defense posture.

tirely obscured by the woven turf. When she is seconds away from disappearing, she is violently jerked backwards. Again and again, the cobra is hit by an excruciating clamping sensation striking at her tender spine, just above the cloacal vent. She desperately tries to slither forward, but her determination to escape is overwhelmed by the fierce creature latching onto her back end. After a few more brutal tugs, the snake is wrenched from her safe hideaway. Now that she is vulnerable to attack, with no possible escape, the cobra has no alternative but to rise up and defend herself from the unrelenting aggressor. With hood defiantly spread, the serpent's menacing head is now hovering face-to-face with her attacker. Two pairs of eyes are now fixed upon each other. Both are reptilian: one, a snake armed with potent venom, the other, a lizard fortified with brute force. It is a face-off between the Egyptian cobra and the black-throat monitor. The two will commence a battle, but only one will survive.

The cobra's probing head has already entered the wall of grass; her tail is quickly following on through. She is completely unaware of the dark silhouette growing over the exposed section of her tail. The cobra continues to crawl forward, until she is just an inch or two from being en-

Behind the brave hood is a terrified serpent, who now must strike swiftly and accurately if she is to leave the confrontation alive and in one piece. Her only chance is to go for the neck and land a bite just behind the jaw, where the enemy's skin is more delicate. If her strike is successful, her fixed fangs will have a good chance of injecting a mortal dose of neurotoxic venom into the network of vascular tissue lying just under the dermis. Delivering a bite into the fast-flowing artery would allow the venom to make a rapid ascent into the lizard's brain, causing an almost instantaneous death. But if the cobra misses and hits, say, a forearm, or a shoulder, where the skin has an armor-like thickness, it is highly unlikely that her fangs will be able to puncture the monitor's hide, never mind penetrate into deep muscle.

The cobra has to surmount another challenge beyond the difficulties of a perfectly aimed strike. Although the serpent is determined, she is also weakened after standing guard over her nest, having been unable to rest. She will have just one chance, or two at best, to land a strike, and if she misses, the snake will not have

the energy for additional defense. Her spade-shaped hood waves slightly from left to right as she concentrates, waiting for the exact moment to attack.

Loping in a radial formation, with head hovering close to the ground and eyes facing the cobra's lower neck, just beneath her menacing hood, the monitor focuses on the snake. The lizard keeps his prey rotating around and around, as he circles the snake in an attempt to disorient her. If he can get her to panic and strike prematurely, the stalking lizard will have an opportunity to lunge forward. The cobra huffs and hisses in short bursts as the lizard swings around her body. Then, she initiates a strike, but doesn't follow through. She hesitates, then starts to strike only to pull back again. Finally, the cobra springs out at the monitor with mouth stretching wide and fangs reared to deliver a deadly bite, but the lizard anticipates her move. As she whips forward with all her might, the monitor flings his head and torso out of her reach, sending her head and hood plummeting to the hard earth. Her face smashes to the ground, and as the dust wafts up around her head, the monitor lunges down onto her. With ferocious speed, he pins her down, her head trapped inside his wet and stinking mouth, which clenches quickly around the nape of her neck. As the lizard's upper and lower jaws rapidly unite, a gnarly crunch of vertebrae and cranial bones within his muzzle resonates from his drooling mouth. Even though the cobra is mortally wounded she refuses to give up. Her tail is spastically flailing and whipping about, as she attempts to roll her neck out of the lizard's vice-like grip. Her futile struggle comes to an end instantly, when the monitor violently thrashes her back and forth like a cracking whip. Now that the cobra's neck has been broken and her braincase crushed, her body writhes and twitches from a surge of autonomic reflexes.

The victorious monitor whips the pathetic corpse around a few more times. Feeling confident that she is indeed dead, he opens his mouth and lets her limp head and deflated hood slide out onto the ground. Now that the monitor has killed the cobra, he will swallow the body whole, but first he begins to taste her gingerly. The prongs of his glistening tongue brush against her head, then down the length of her body, until finally arriving at her tail, which continues to twitch and curl. He decides that the most efficient strategy for swallowing the snake is to begin with the head, so, with an air of confidence, the monitor turns around and ambles back to her grisly head. Just as the monitor approaches the head, the snake miraculously springs off the ground and into the air, which sends the lizard scuttling backwards. The snake continues to rise; the monitor quickly gains his composure and scampers back to the kill site. Flabbergasted, he looks up at his ascending trophy, only to see her dangling from the talons of the serpent eagle. Within seconds, the eagle lands on the crown of the mighty baobab tree and begins to devour the cobra, ripping the juicy chunks of flesh from the limp corpse pinned beneath her talons.

As for the black-throat monitor, he continues to lap the earth where the cobra was lying just minutes before. He is confused and frustrated, because he can still taste the presence of his vanquished prey. Yet, no matter how much he licks the earth, the lizard is unable to locate his hard-earned meal. Soon he abandons his search, departing the scene hungry and deflated. Although he would search the whole night if he could, he needs to take cover in a tree or within a narrow crevice of piled rock. As his energy begins to fade due to the dropping temperatures of the approaching nightfall, other predators will be moving in, many of which would be eager to make an easy meal of the monitor.

THEY COME IN DROVES

The sky is red now, as the last trace of the fiery brim is smothered slowly by the blackness of an impending nightfall. Off in the distance, where the grass and the sky converge, an endless river of creatures flows across the expanse of fertile grassland. Although it appears to move as one, the great cluster of life is in fact made up of different species of game, each gathered into specific herds. These herds are then loosely connected to the greater gathering of different species of wildlife,

---

With ferocious speed, he pins her down, her head trapped inside his wet and stinking mouth, which clenches quickly around the nape of her neck.

---

most of which are various types of antelope. The borders of each herd contained within this immense drove of creatures are often quite fluid, with individual animals mingling and shifting from one group to the next. Some of these groups are residents, some are migrational, but together, they serve a greater good.

There are a number of different reasons that have brought this great horde of diverse wildlife together. One major contributing factor uniting many of these creatures is their need to migrate to the regions where fodder is plentiful and nutritious. Everybody moves together because essentially, they have a common goal: to eat. Another reason for the gathering of same-species herds within the collective is mate selection. Perhaps the most intriguing aspect of this great union is that many of these animals are vulnerable to predators, so gathering in large numbers dramatically decreases the odds that any one individual will be taken by a predator. Look at it this way: If a hungry lion encounters a herd of five wildebeest, each wildebeest theoretically has a twenty percent chance of being eaten. Those aren't great odds for survival. Now let's say there is a heard consisting of two hundred thousand wildebeest; then the prospect of one specific wildebeest being targeted by the lion is one out of two hundred thousand! Obviously, this extrapolation is far from exact, because there are many other factors to consider, namely, these wildebeest have to worry about more than a single predator. There are many carnivorous beasts, from the solitary leopard to communal hunters—like lions, hyenas, and painted dogs—who will capitalize on the great concentration of game

to gain access to prey. My point is that there is survival in numbers.

Blue wildebeest (*Connochaetes taurinus*) make up the majority of herbivores gathered in the great migration. There are many thousands of them grunting and snorting as they tread across the grassland. Few sites would take your breath away like the view of the Tanzanian Serengeti plains during the momentous migration of wildebeest. More than one and a quarter million of them move across the savannah to gorge on the succulent grass and to give birth to hundreds of thousands of calves. Amazingly, ninety percent of all calves are born within a three-week period during the early part of the rainy season. The wildebeest's great and perilous journey encompasses a three thousand mile trek through Kenya and Tanzania, as they abandon parched plains in search of the grasses that move with the passing rains. The herds of wildebeest can be so dense that more than one hundred thousand individuals can gather within a hundred-square-mile area. Wildebeest are much more hearty than their rather ungainly build suggests. The

Blue wildebeest, also known as brindled gnus, are actually part of the antelope family. Wildebeest are the most abundant wild grazing animals in eastern Africa.

front end of a wildebeest is more muscular and heavy than its spindly hindquarters. The coat is silvery tan with dark, vertical stripes. The large, anvil-like head sports a pair of outward curving horns at the top, while a luxuriant beard, grayish white in color, grows from chin to chest. The wildebeest's wide flat muzzle allows it to feed on very short grass.

Thousands of zebras travel alongside the herd of wildebeest. While wildebeest are grazing on the shorter blades of grass, zebras are mowing down the longer ones. The presence of zebras actually benefits herding wildebeest. Because the zebras have a heightened sense of hearing and sight, they can warn their herd-mates when predators, such as lions and hyenas, are approaching.

Additional herds of antelope include the sprite and delicate Thomson's gazelle (*Gazella thomsoni*). At around sixty-five pounds, Thompson's gazelle is a much smaller antelope, especially when compared to a five hundred pound wildebeest. Thompson's gazelles are high-strung animals that tend to keep to themselves in smaller herds within or along the perimeter of the greater gathering. Their guarded nature is due in large part to that fact that they present easy targets for many predators, despite their ability to sprint at sixty miles per hour. Creatures such as lions, painted dogs, cheetahs, leopards, hyenas, jackals, eagles, pythons, and even baboons will regularly prey on this diminutive species of antelope.

As the sea of roaming creatures washes over the grass in every direction, their presence has not been lost on a few beasts who would eagerly make a meal of them. In fact, the predators have been there all the time, hovering close by as they blend with the grass, while patiently biding time until the ideal moment to strike occurs. As the day fades into evening, the predators are preparing to spill the blood of the misfortunate. They will harvest the energy that has passed from the sun to the grass and finally been absorbed into the flesh of the grazers and browsers. One predator in particular has taken an interest in a small gathering of nervous Thompson's gazelles. She is huddled behind a wind-formed blind of tall grass with her adolescent cubs at her side, watching and waiting for the opportunity to kill. After scanning the herd back and forth, her eyes settle on a young Tommy, which has wandered a hundred yards away from the herd toward the hunter's hideout. Although the antelope is no longer a fawn, the Tommy is clearly lacking life experience as it continues to migrate toward danger.

The predator's heart begins to beat vigorously, as the thrill of the hunt with its potential for a triumphant kill motivates her to slip out through the grassy blind and initiate her pursuit of the naive Tommy. The stalker of the gazelle is none other than the fastest terrestrial mammal on Earth, the cheetah (*Acinonyx jubatus*). This is a creature perfectly built for speed. Because oxygen is needed to fuel her body in order to reach the remarkable speed of up to seventy-one miles per hour, she has expansive nasal passages that allow a generous and rapid influx of air to reach her lungs. To support the physiology needed for such acceleration, her lungs, liver, and heart are exceptionally large. Her body shape is fluid and streamlined, providing the cat with the ultimate in aerodynamic efficiency. The cheetah's delicate skeleton consists of lightweight bones, including a flexible spine, ideal for smoothly springing her limbs forward while she sprints toward prey. The wide eye sockets in her skull offer the cheetah a wide-angle view of the landscape, as the black tear-like streaks running from the corner of each eye down the snout reduce the glare from the sun. The cheetah's long tail promotes balance and stability, while the non-retractable claws of her paws provide traction when sprinting forward.

As the cheetah, hidden behind a veil of tall grass, slinks toward the gazelle, her two sons, both of whom are nine months in age, shadow her closely from behind. They bleat out to her softly and begin to purr in anticipation of a successful hunt. There is a very real chance, however, that she will fail, if she sprints forward too prematurely, or if the Tommy detects her approach and takes off. She must be successful, for three days have passed since her last kill. Although she managed to bring down a sizeable Tommy, the time to devour the antelope allotted to her and the cubs was all too brief. Minutes after she had made the kill, a spotted hyena drove the cheetah off her quarry. Not only was the lithe hunter denied her spoils, but the precious calories that she burned during the sprint and the kill had not been replaced. Ironically, the greatest obstacle impeding the cheetah's ability to survive is the very characteristic that enhances its chances for survival. A cheetah pays a steep price indeed for being the fastest terrestrial mammal. Its petite form renders it too fragile and weak to ward off the scavenging predators who attempt to capitalize on the delicate feline's hard work. When a cheetah makes a kill, the prey must be consumed rapidly, before other carnivores, like lions and hyenas,

move in and steal it. After a successful kill, cheetahs are often too exhausted to immediately eat their prey, never mind defend it from marauders. While the cheetah struggles to catch its breath, other creatures just stroll right in and appropriate the kill. So, if she is to be successful today, the cheetah, along with her hungry cubs, not only needs to take down the Tommy, but also has to consume it as quickly as possible. Otherwise, her competitors, waiting in the wings, will usurp the fruits of her labors once more.

The grass that conceals the cheetah from the Tommy has begun to thin, leaving her with a difficult decision. Should she creep up a few more yards and then dash forward into the exhausting hunt, or turn back and wait for a better opportunity to make a more reliable kill? The reality, however, is that she has only one choice: to make the kill. If she doesn't, and her cubs are unable to fill their empty bellies with life-sustaining

The cheetah paid for its speed with small teeth and weak jaws, rendering it rather defenseless against large predators, which has led to its endangerment.

meat, their health will be greatly compromised. Her brood knows enough to get down low in the grass and remain absolutely silent until she calls them in. Not only could they sabotage the hunt by failing to stay close to the ground, they could also be in very real danger of being preyed upon by ever-watchful hyenas, lions, and leopards. Tragically, as many as ninety percent of all cub fatalities occur when large carnivores attack while the mother is off stalking prey. Such a situation is brutal, but, alas, nature does not allow for the human concept of fairness. Moreover, in the wild, this system makes perfect sense. By executing and devouring cheetah cubs, a predator not only acquires a nutritious meal but also cuts down on the competition.

Both cubs are watching their mother intently, as she hunkers down in the grass and begins her carefully calculated pursuit. All three hearts beat in rapid unison; two hungry cubs anticipate a successful hunt, while their mother moves off nervously, fully aware of her sons' vulnerability. Nibbling on the succulent grass, the Tommy fails to see the cheetah, which is now but a few hundred feet away. Then, as the antelope pulls on a clump of lush grass, his eyes detect a strange mound. When observed from the periphery, it comes across as nothing more than a blurry lump of vegetation, yet instinct tells the Tommy that he is in danger. His jaw stops in mid-chew, as his head snaps up from the grass. All his senses alert, the young antelope is desperately trying to identify what has struck his instinctual core with such an overwhelming sense of anxiety. His ears rotate nervously from front to back, but they detect nothing. Apprehensively, he looks over his shoulder, only to discover that he has drifted dangerously far from the herd, and although he is still unable to detect anything particularly menacing, he just can't shake the uneasy sensation of being watched. He turns around again and suddenly discovers the source of his trepidation. When he finally recognizes the cheetah, the Tommy instantly transforms from a nervous antelope into a terrified quarry. At the exact moment when the eyes of predator and prey lock onto each other, a surge of adrenaline floods through both their bodies. For the cheetah, the hormonal rush rises up from the addictive thrill of the hunt, while for the Tommy, the adrenaline spike originates from absolute terror.

The gazelle has only one chance at surviving this encounter—to race back to the herd as fast as his nimble legs can carry him. He doesn't sprint just yet, however, not until he has determined in what direction the cheetah will run. Now that the cheetah has been discovered, she rises up confidently and then wanders off to the left of the antelope and away from her cubs. She continues to stride along the grass, as if she has all but given up and is just walking off into the sunset. With the exception of a nervously fanning tail, the Tommy remains absolutely still, as he waits to see if the predator is indeed moving off. The cheetah keeps strolling nonchalantly, until she ends up between the isolated Tommy and the remaining herd. Upon seeing the stalker moving across the grassland, the herd anxiously maneuvers back toward the sunset, a

move that further expands the distance between it and the solitary Tommy. Then, without warning, the cheetah makes a hard cut to the right and quickly increases her pace from a saunter to a trot in the direction of the gazelle. Seconds later, the Tommy darts to the side and begins sprinting parallel to the heard but in the opposite direction, while running adjacent to the wall of tall grass. The cheetah is now cutting across the plains as she races toward the Tommy. Two trails of dust are now heading for impact, as both creatures are sprinting at nearly sixty miles an hour. The hearts of both the gazelle and the cheetah are pounding at such a furious rate, that the valves are nearly fixed at full dilation. A continuous stream of blood gushes throughout their bodies, delivering freshly inhaled oxygen to myriad overworked muscles, desperate for the life-sustaining gas.

While the gazelle is now running at maximum speed, the cheetah pushes to full throttle, increasing her velocity to sixty-five miles per hour. Seconds later, she is gaining on the Tommy, but just when it appears that she is about to tackle the antelope, the cheetah zooms past him, until she is a hundred yards in front. Could it be that she has overcompensated in her attempt to reach the Tommy? Instantly, the cat fishtails at a ninety-degree angle, until she faces the gazelle. Without losing speed, the hunter continues racing toward the Tommy, who promptly skids to an about-face and is now attempting to flee the sprinting cheetah. Both prey and predator are running parallel to the high grass, one in hot pursuit directly behind the other. Unfortunately for the cheetah, the energy required to turn caused her to loose precious seconds. Now she is beginning to trail behind, until eventually, she slows down to a rapid trot. The gazelle, thinking he has outrun the cheetah, slows down as well, and veers off toward the distant herd. As if celebrating the cheetah's defeat, the Tommy begins pronking up to the red sky in a series of ten-foot-high leaps. Both his spine and head arch downward as all four legs simultaneously spring off the earth. As he leaps triumphantly away from the tall grass, the gazelle fails to detect the two quickly approaching shapes, closing in from behind.

Suddenly, he becomes aware of the rapid patter of approaching paws and glances back to the tall grass. He catches a glimpse of two young cheetahs, which are within seconds of pouncing upon him. He snaps his head forward and kicks into sprint mode. It is too late, and his back legs slide out from under him at the sweeping swish of a feline paw. The gazelle is now tumbling to the ground, and just before he hits the grass, the weight of seventy pounds of cheetah muscle pummels into him. The Tommy collides with the unyielding earth. Both cheetahs are now pinning the struggling antelope to the ground, as their mother, who has maintained her steady trot, reaches them. All three felines are purring with delight at their conquest, while their victim, who is still conscious, blurts out a series of breathy moans.

Now that the cheetah's offspring are nine months old and are nearly two-thirds her size, they are starting to take on the features of adults. The bushy mane of

Though this Thomson's gazelle could sprint at sixty miles per hour, it was no match for the greyhound of cats.

tawny fur enveloping their napes has begun to thin. The blurry spots, scattered across their coats, grow more distinctive with each passing day and indicate that they are well on their way to maturity. More important, though, the youngsters are finally starting to get a grasp of good hunting technique. Their mother is an excellent and devoted teacher. She has taught them well, and the chance to practice hunting on a live gazelle provides excellent preparation for the time when the cubs will be self-sufficient. But for now, and for many months ahead, the young cheetahs are still very much dependent upon their mother for survival.

Now that the family has captured a meal, they must devour it quickly, for spies have discovered the conquest and are now moving in. Vultures have begun to circle high overhead, volplaning atop warm streams of air. They serve as inadvertent signals to distant predators, informing them that there is meat on the ground below. Although the vultures will not move in until the cheetahs have finished, the rapidly approaching terrestrial predators will not be so polite. The cheetahs are quick to dig in to the hindquarters of the Tommy, who, despite his mortal wounds, is still conscious. As he feebly struggles to right himself, the cats are literally eating him alive. Five minutes into the cats' meal, the gazelle has bled to death; moreover, he is beginning to disappear rapidly. After ten more minutes, the vultures arrive in hopes of snatching up the scraps left behind. But today they will not be so fortunate, for the cheetahs have no intention of leaving anything to waste. They continue to feast on the vanishing gazelle, which has been rapidly reduced to a naked frame of blood-smeared bones. The cats have gobbled up much of the skin, every sinew of muscle and tendon, and all the organs. During their consumption of the many yards of intestine and stomach tissue, they manage not only to avoid swallowing the herbaceous contents but also to keep the material in the exact same formation as it was within the digestive tract. The neat, tubular stream of material is laid out in perfect sequence, depending upon the various stages of digestion. The arrangement begins with the

Nothing says satisfaction like the purr from a big cat.

recently swallowed soggy clumps of warm grass puree and terminates with the densely packed pellets of feces that were just minutes away from expulsion.

The cheetahs finish off the gazelle by crunching up the delicious, iron-rich ribs, and will spend a few minutes resting contentedly, before wandering off. Throughout the whole feasting process, the only sound louder than the chewing, tearing, and crunching was the cheetahs' continuous purring. Now that the cats are lapping the red smears of blood from each other's muzzles, this universally feline sound of satisfaction has grown even more intense. Today was a very good day for this family,

Cape vultures can soar so high that they become difficult to see from the ground.

naked necks, along with their bulbous heads, allow them to extract the slimy contents tucked deep inside a rancid corpse, while keeping the rank, putrid material from being smeared across their plumage. When it comes to unsavory meals, vultures are at the bottom of the food chain, but their role within the grassland ecosystem of sub-Saharan eastern Africa is no less important than any other life-form's. They are the sanitation workers of the savannah, cleaning up the dirty messes that carnivores and other predators leave behind.

for not only did they get to eat, they did so undisturbed by competing predators.

Unfortunately for the eagle-sized cape vultures (*Gyps coprotheres*), there isn't much left for them to pick at. Nevertheless, when the cheetahs rise up to their feet and slowly saunter off, the birds swoop down onto the paltry carcass. The vultures covetously squabble over the scraps and bones. They hop about in search of significant morsels of flesh, but to no avail. The vultures' acute vision and keen sense of smell directed these scavengers across the vast grasslands, as they sought out the dying, the dead, and the decaying. The birds' long

BACK AT THE WATERING HOLE

Reflecting on the surface of the water hole is the trailing brim of the vanishing sun. Slithering along the edge of the pool is a grotesquely fat serpent, which moves almost slug-style across the crumbling crust of sun-baked mud. Although the snake is no longer than my arm, it is stout, and its triangular head is more massive than my fist. In terms of stoutness-to-body-length ratio, he is the fattest species of snake on the planet; he also has the notorious reputation of having the longest fangs of any species of snake. The scales running down the serpent's back are roughly keeled, while the pattern spreading across his thick form is absolutely stunning. Vivid, leaf-shaped saddles of tan, cream, and chocolate straddle his spine. The bulky serpent is the Gaboon viper (*Bitis gabonica*), and he has recently slithered out from a patch of trees growing along the lower end of the eastern slope where the great baobab tree grows. Much of the snake's life is spent in this scanty scrap of dry dense thicket, where he passes the time coiled up on top of a soft pile of dried leaves. If you were to walk among the tightly clustered trees and look down at the snake, as he lies there all coiled up, you would not detect him, unless you actually knew he was there in the first place. His camouflage is absolutely flawless! Although most of his days are spent hidden

The Gaboon viper, the largest in Africa, can weigh more than forty-four pounds. Its fangs can reach two and a quarter inches long, and its bite can be deadly.

beneath the shadows of the scrubby patch of pole trees, acacia, and low-lying shrubs, today is an exception. A hearty appetite has driven him to leave the comforts of his grove, as he heads out in search of food.

Crawling along the water's edge, the Gaboon viper detects the presence of potential prey. The rhythmic flickering of his tongue increases as he gets closer to the source of the molecular discharge. Wallowing in three inches of water and mud is a blubbery frog of monstrous proportions. It is an African bullfrog (*Pyxicephalus adsperus*), who just happens to be the largest frog inhabiting sub-Saharan eastern Africa. About the size and shape of a honeydew melon, this amphibian is as wide as it is long. Her slimy skin is a lovely pea-soup green, with rows of ridged skin running from the back of her swollen head to the lower end of her body. This creature is practically all mouth, which is a good thing, since she spends much of her life devouring whatever forms of life she can get her jowls around. Do you remember the video game *Pac-Man*, where the yellow gobbler

would eat through an endless maze of dots? Well, the African bullfrog is the original Pac-Man frog, in both appearance and eating habits. It will eat rodents, birds, lizards, fish, small turtles, snakes, and even other bullfrogs! Cannibalism comes pretty easily to these guys; in fact, after copulating with an unusually svelte male a few years back, this hungry lass gobbled him up. Now, that's gratitude.

While her bloated body is enormous, her legs are ridiculously tiny. From snout to vent she is nearly ten inches long, which is about the same as her width, but her chubby rear legs measure only two inches long, while her front limbs are just over an inch! The African bullfrog is not designed for jumping, or for swimming, per se, but more for lying around, Jabba the Hutt-style. Although she is reduced to plowing through the mud in a most slovenly fashion while other, more slender frogs leap deftly from place to place, there is one physical activity that she excels at: digging. When the water holes evaporate and the muddy pools dry up, she doesn't abandon her habitat but digs out a shelter beneath it. Upon excavating her way down into a comfortably cool substratum, the frog becomes dormant for up to two years, or even longer. She survives by sloughing off her outer membrane of skin, which serves as a protective sack where she will rest. To keep nice and moist, she fills the skin sack with water that she has stored in her bladder. This year she spent nearly seven months buried three feet under the cemented earth, until the newly arrived rains drew her out to fill her belly, find a mate, and, if all goes well, maybe even eat him, too.

Although much of her life is spent filling her crop, it appears that today might be her turn to nourish another life-form, as the Gaboon viper is slithering dangerously close. He lies motionless behind her, and after one more flicker of the tongue he is ready to strike. Within a second of him lunging at her, however, she has hobbled off toward the deeper mud. He follows closely behind, but the sludgy muck causes him to get mired down. The bullfrog escapes, and the Gaboon viper is forced to retreat to the rim of the water hole. The African bullfrog continues to scramble clumsily onward, without ever seeing the corpulent serpent that nearly made a meal of her. As for the Gaboon viper, he continues to hunt along the perimeter of the water hole before returning to the comforts of his overgrown thicket.

Meanwhile, a herd of elephants (*Loxodonta africana*) arrives at the opposite side of the water hole. Our planet's largest ter-

The African bullfrog is also called the pixie frog, but it only earned its nickname from its genus, Pyxicephalus, not because it resembles Tinker Bell.

restrial mammals have come to wallow in the cool and soothing water. There are fifteen elephants belonging to the clan, which is made up of four generations of sisters, cousins, aunts, and daughters. The females will stay within the clan their entire lives. The males, who are doted on during their childhood and early adolescence, are often forced out as they begin to mature to adulthood. The clan is under the leadership of a wise matriarch, who, like her mother before her, guides the family through the best and the worst of times.

The matriarch is a large, six-thousand-pound cow, who at thirty-eight years of age is still well in her prime; her mother stayed healthy up to the ripe old age of sixty-five. Elephants are born with six sets of erupting molars, and after the ancient queen had worn her last set down to the jaw, she lost her appetite, grew weak, and then passed on a few weeks later. Even though the late matriarch has been gone a while, her kin still think about her often, as well as other family members that have come and gone over the years. Elephants are known to mourn their dead; they rec-

ognize and react to the remains of their own kind. What is even more startling, they actually visit the bone yard, where old elephants go to melt into the landscape. Whenever the herd passes through the patch of willowy grass, where the old matriarch's bones lie to this very day, they are reminded of her.

Today, however, they are not here to grieve, but to drink and play in the comforting mud. The matriarch and a few other cows begin to dig their tusks into the dense mud, which causes the water trapped in the earth to bubble up. Many creatures depend on the elephants to excavate a water hole, especially during the dry season, thus replenishing the surrounding wildlife and habitat. Despite the hearty nature of elephants, these intelligent giants require plenty of fluids—from thirty to fifty gallons of water every day.

Hovering close to the herd is a massive, fifty-year-old bull, who stands thirteen feet tall to the shoulders and weighs thirteen thousand pounds. He sports a spectacular pair of ivory tusks that are seven feet long and weigh two hundred

A herd of elephants dances in the dust at sunset.

pounds each! His need to breed is what draws him to the herd. The magnificent animal has entered the period of heightened sexual aggressiveness called musth. The oily liquid copiously weeping from the glands along each temple is a sure sign that he has entered musth. It is during this time that he is most dangerous. When he encounters a competing bull, the powerful hormones rushing through his body drive him to combat. In the presence of cows, on the other hand, his state of musth fuels up his sex drive. As he meanders through the herd in search of a mating partner, he delicately sniffs the puddles of urine left by the females and their genitals with his trunk. His sense of smell is so finely tuned that he can detect which females are in estrus and are ready to breed. So far he has not found a female whose reproductive cycle is in line with his, so he lumbers off to the other end of the water hole and proceeds to drink. He lowers his trunk into the water and draws up four gallons,

Leopard tortoises can grow to be two feet long and eighty pounds. Like other tortoises, they don't swim or draw their heads inside their shells, so when they're threatened, they use their scaly front legs as a face shield. Strictly vegetarians, they have no teeth, but their jaws are sharp and strong like a bird's beak.

which he then squirts into his mouth. As he continues to drink, the bull watches the cows and calves, who gleefully kick up clouds of dust in the amber light. He stands there for a few more minutes and then heads off in search of fresh fodder.

After arriving at a patch of tall grass, still green and fresh, he reaches down with his massive trunk, rips out a hefty wad and shoves it into his mouth. Each day, this mighty elephant spends sixteen hours foraging for sustenance, consuming nearly three hundred pounds of material, from grasses and herbs to fruits, foliage, bark, and branches. After inhaling every straw of green grass from the now disheveled area, the hungry elephant moves to a lush tree with a fourteen-inch-wide bole. With his trunk fully extended, the elephant stretches up and attempts to grasp the foliage, but the most succulent leaves are out of his reach. No problem; he just positions himself trunk-to-trunk, and, with a little twist of the tusks and a solid push, the tree comes crashing down. As he leans up against the tree, pressing his reinforced skull against the cracking timber, his left foot grazes the top of a steeply domed carapace. It belongs to the leopard tortoise (*Geochelone pardalis*), who had been resting quietly at the base of the tree. Despite the integrity of the tortoise's shell, it cannot support the weight of a newly born, two-hundred-pound calf, never mind a thirteen-thousand-pound bull. If the elephant applies just the slightest amount of pressure, the shell will explode and kill the leopard tortoise. Now, talk about multitasking! Not only can the elephant simultaneously knock down a tree and shove food into his mouth, but his mighty, column-like feet are sensitive enough to detect the tortoise underneath! He may be aggressive due to

musth, but he's not interested in assaulting this terrestrial turtle. He gently slides the tortoise backward, until the lucky reptile is well out of harm's way.

Soon he has filled his great belly with the entire foliage of the collapsed tree, and the great bull wanders off in search of a receptive cow that is fit to mother his offspring. As the massive elephant departs, he passes a group of three giraffes

The brown splotches on these giraffes are as unique as a fingerprint. Though they look about as stable as a newborn foal, they can gallop up to thirty-five miles per hour, and they prefer to sleep standing up.

(*Giraffa camelopardalis*), the tallest terrestrial mammals on Earth, gathered beneath the crown of a twenty-foot acacia tree. The tallest of the giraffes is a bull that stands eighteen feet tall and weighs thirty-seven hundred pounds. Despite its dramatic seven-foot length, the giraffe's neck is supported by only seven individual vertebrae, each measuring up to twelve inches long. The fuzzy-horned animals reach up to the acacia, plucking off its leaves with their pink-and-black prehensile tongues, which can grow to more than a foot and a half long. The long thorns of the acacia seem to be of little concern to the giraffes, who feed on the tree with great ease.

A few hundred feet behind the water hole, past the giraffes, are two black rhinoceroses (*Diceros bicornis*), who are facing off, horn to horn. The larger bull weighs around three thousand pounds; the other, five hundred pounds less. The smaller rhino has been challenged by his opponent for merely entering the larger's territory; so the two will now battle to determine who is more dominant. Each rhino is equipped with two sharp horns,

the largest of which is nearly sixteen inches long and more than four inches wide at its base. The massive horn erupts just above the rhino's nostrils, while the second, at half the size, comes out above it. Unlike bony antlers, a rhino horn is made of tightly fused material called keratin, a substance similar to human hair and fingernails. Although the brawny bulls are staring each other down, the residential rhino is not perturbed by the actual sight of the intruder. In fact, it was the visitor's foreign, somewhat unsettling odor that ticked him off. The trespasser, fully aware that the residential male is more powerful, has no desire to fight, but there is little alternative now. The resident bull charges, as his opponent quickly skirts to the side, unharmed. Again, they line up their horns and weave them together, until both rhinos are twisting each other's heads back and forth in an attempt to throw one another off balance. Then, the resident bull withdraws his head and lunges forward once more. As the intruder avoids the attack again by hobbling to the side, he receives a powerful blow alongside his torso. Lucky for him, his armor-like hide softens the impact.

The intruder has had enough and makes the wise decision to retreat. As he quickly scampers off, the resident rhino is charging closely behind and delivers one last poke, hitting the intruder in the groin and buttock. The latter's rump and rear legs are lifted up by the heaving head beneath. This sends the trespasser galloping as fast as he can (up to thirty-five miles per hour) out from the foreign territory. As he exits in haste, the intruder passes the stinking, five-foot-tall heap of rhino dung marking the resident bull's territorial perimeter. How the smaller bull had wandered into the foreign territory without smelling the dung heap is unclear, but it represents a significant oversight on his behalf. He has learned his lesson, and it is unlikely he'll return. He might have a fighting chance . . . if he packs on another five hundred pounds in mass.

Now that he has escaped the painful blows of competition, the bull settles down during these cooler sunset hours and begins to pluck up tufts of fresh grass with

Black rhinos are the third largest land mammal on the planet, after elephants and white rhinos.

the finger-like overhang of his top lip, which is prehensile enough to pick up the most tender shoots. His ability to selectively harvest plant material with his dexterous lip identifies him as a browser, as opposed to animals such as white rhinos or zebras that possess flat upper lips, allowing for proficient lawn mower-like grazing. His giant gray mass hovers over the green grass like a mound of dried mud, while his armored hide appears jointed where the sections of dermis fold near the shoulders and hips. The combination of a tough hide, sword-like horns, and size provides the

(continued on page 126)

RESPECT THE BEASTS . . . OR RUN!

I find elephants to be the most impressive of all of Africa's terrestrial mammals, and some of the happiest, scariest, saddest, and most exciting moments of my life have been spent with elephants. I will never forget the hot rush of blood that pulsed through my body upon witnessing a wild African elephant for the very first time. The encounter took place in 1997 during my first trip to South Africa, while my crew and I were filming in a private game reserve outside Kruger National Park. The crew and I, along with a park ranger, had been hiking through a spectacular meadow in search of a residential troop of baboons. All was going fine, until out of a small thicket of acacia came the most powerful bellow that I had ever heard. Hearing the booming call, I knew instantly that the trumpeting creature could be none other than an elephant. Due to the tremendous echo of cracking timber coming from the patch of scrub forest, I was also aware that the elephant was moving fast. But what really took me by surprise was that the massive beast was not running deeper into the forest but running right towards us! Very soon, the angry elephant came crashing through the wall of timber, charging us at full speed. I am not aware of anything that we had done to provoke him, but he was clearly in a rotten mood.

As his powerful legs thundered across the terrain, accompanied by the unending stream of glass-shattering trumpeting, I mustered every bit of courage I possessed to just stand there, absolutely still, while fighting the overwhelming instinct to flee. If an elephant ever charges you, the last thing you want to do is run. Chances are, he is just testing your resolve with a very dramatic bluff, but if you run off, he will consider that a challenge and will likely follow through. Usually, if the elephant charges with ears extended outward, he is just bluffing. If, on the other hand, those ears are flat against his neck, you'd best get out of the way. Now, if you are positive that the elephant is intent on stomping you and plans on filling your shorts with your guts, then, by all means, run—run as fast as you can! Just keep in mind that it's hard to outrun a twelve-thousand-pound beast that can sprint thirty miles an hour. I have seen charging elephants catch up to a Land Cruiser zipping off at full speed, pedal to the metal and all. Also, whatever you do, don't climb a tree, because if you do, and you've got a ticked-off elephant hankering to teach you a lesson, he'll just push the tree down to the ground with you in it. Your last memory may very well be that of an elephant beating you to death with a seven-hundred-pound tree limb.

Now, I love elephants, and the last thing I want to do is vilify them. Moreover, they are absolutely crucial to sustaining the health of the savannah ecosystem. Elephants are landscape architects that carve out habitat for many creatures. By merely consuming vegetation, they serve as important agents for seed dispersal. Simply put, elephants are a keystone species, and without their presence in the southeast African savannah, many other life-forms would perish. I have also met many kind and noble elephants, but with that said, elephants are powerful creatures that warrant a great deal of respect and space. When you lose respect for an elephant in the wild savannah, you put your life at risk. I personally met two men who had the misfortune of being killed by an elephant while working in the field. Could they have evaded the fatal encounter? I honestly don't know, but there are a number of steps you can take to prevent a confrontation with an elephant.

You should always avoid approaching a wild elephant on foot, especially if it is a cow with a calf or a male in musth. Elephant cows are devoted mothers, and like human mothers, they will stop at nothing to protect their offspring. To approach a bull in musth, while hiking, is an invitation for serious trouble. If you do come across a wild herd of elephants while bushwalking, try to keep as much distance as possible between you and them. Never head out alone or without a knowledgeable, licensed, and experienced guide at your side. And never feed a wild elephant, or any other wild creature, for that matter. Now, there are no guarantees, but if you follow these few rules, everything should turn out fine. Oh yes, one last bit of advice: Although it is hard to outrun an elephant, chances are, you're traveling with someone who runs a bit slower than you do. So wear a pair of good tennis shoes, because you don't have to outrun the elephant, just the slowest person you're traveling with.

So there I was, standing perfectly still, except for my dilating sphincter that was seconds from crowning a big one in my shorts. Yes, I was that terrified. Despite my fright I did not move, and neither did the elephant towering fifteen feet to my front. I remember trying to send a psychic message to the elephant, hoping that we, as sentient beings, could come to a mutual understanding of respect and tolerance. Even if he could read my mind, he didn't seem remotely interested in making a friend. He stood there for all of two minutes, but at the time it felt like eternity. Eventually, we were able to slowly back off and make it back to the road. I remember how, upon reaching the camp, the crew and I had laughed uncontrollably at the terror of it all out of pure nerves. Yes it was a scary moment, but it serves as a great memory and I regularly reflect upon it. Since then, I have had my fair share of bluff encounters with elephants, as well as a few genuine ones. The truth is, I am never completely at ease near a wild elephant, nor do I think I should be. I try never to forget that elephants are powerful, emotional, and intelligent creatures, demanding much respect.

black rhino with the luxury of having very few natural enemies. As for the unnatural ones, well, that is an entirely different matter.

As he contentedly browses in the grass and low-lying shrubs, his sensitive hearing detects a movement behind him, just before his nostrils pick up a foreign scent emitted not by a competitive rhino, but something much worse. Instantly, he spins around into the wind, with nose and horn held high. His giant head jerks nervously from left to right as his olfactory system attempts to hone in on the deadly odor. Then, the eerie silence is shattered by a rapid succession of thunderous cracks, as if an elephant had snapped down a row of trees. Immediately after hearing the deafening snaps reverberate through the air, an excruciating web of pain, worse than any blow from a combative rhino, rips through the entire side of his torso and neck. The mossy smell of wet grass transforms into the sharp odor that usually occurs after a bolt of lightning hits a tree. The agonizing pain has now spread deep into his chest and stomach. A warm stream of salty fluid pulses into his mouth and sinuses, until it begins to ooze out of his nostrils and mouth. The throbbing pain has taken over his body, and when he tries to rotate one of his legs outward, it will not move, for the ball and socket joint in his hip has been shattered.

Then he falls over, hitting the ground with a terrible thud. Although the air is still thick with the smell of smoke, it was not lightning that has struck the great creature down. As he labors to draw air into his punctured lungs, his eyes look up to see the deadliest of all creatures, a thin beast that walks upon two stilt-like limbs. Then, the two other limbs, which dangle awkwardly, like two elephant trunks from the sides of the frightful animal, extend outward. They are clasping a perfectly straight and shiny branch that smells of the same smoky odor floating through the air. The creature dangles the black and shiny stick directly over the young bull's head. As the helpless rhino stares up into the hollow end, it emits a blinding burst of light and another thundering crack. Excruciating pain hits the rhino above his left eye. The world dims around the wounded animal, until there is nothing. Standing over the dead black rhino are four men, each armed with AK-47 assault rifles. They have not murdered him in order to eat his flesh or to avenge someone who had been injured by the giant beast; they have taken his life for one purpose only, to steal his mighty horn. The irony is as bitter as hemlock: the rhino's sharp and powerful horn, a tool used by the creature to survive in the natural world, is now driving him towards the brink of extinction.

With hatchets and machetes, the poachers crudely whack and chop at the rhino's proud face, until the horns are extracted from the skull like bloody giant teeth. The men will take nothing else from the twenty-five-hundred pound corpse, only the horns, which weigh a few pounds. The rhino's carcass will be left to the vultures to complete the dirty work. The horns will pass through many hands, as they are smuggled from Africa to the Middle East or Asia, where they may fetch a handsome sum of many thousands of dollars. The horns may be retrofitted into an ornamental dagger sheath in Yemen, or perhaps, they will reach the black market in Hong Kong. There, they will be ground down into a powder and reduced to capsule form as a pseudo-medicinal product believed to cure erectile dysfunction. I find this bit especially moronic, since the keratin fibers making up a black rhino's horn possess about as much medicinal potency as fingernail clippings. My advice to those out there who are willing to pay hundreds of dollars for a small dose of ground-up rhino horn is to just gnaw on your fingernails, because it's a lot cheaper and equally effective. Or better yet, try Viagra!

When Teddy Roosevelt visited Africa in 1909–1910, there were approximately one million rhinos roaming across the vast expanse of the savannah. By 1972 poaching had reduced the black rhino population to sixty-five thousand, and then from 1992 to 1993 the total population of black rhinos had dropped down to just 2,700 individuals! Thus, because of human ignorance and greed, there exists a very real possibility that these magnificent beasts will be wiped off our planet during our lifetime.

ELSEWHERE ON THE PLAINS

A mob of a few hundred wildebeest is plodding back to the great herd as the darkness of night creeps across the ocher sky. An uneasy feeling has washed over the entire herd as a pack of twenty scruffy canines have begun ambling towards them from the shadow of lone trees at the edge of the horizon. The wildebeest are starting to pick up speed as the pack steadily approaches, and although they are still relatively far away, it will be only a matter of five or ten more minutes before the canines are dangerously close. The time for these creatures to hunt is quickly drawing to a close, for they prefer to kill from dawn to dusk, and as the black of night is fast approaching, it is unlikely that they will pursue their prey deep into the evening hours. But there is still time to make a kill and nourish the clan with the savory flesh of the unlucky beast that they may slay. This pack of prowling carnivores is none other than the very elusive and rare painted dog, or African hunting dog (*Lycaon pictus*). Tragically, in all of Africa, there only three thousand of these intelligent and cunning predators still alive, thus they are the most endangered predator inhabiting the savannahs of southeastern Africa. But this pack has no comprehension of just how close they are to becoming extinct, since life for them is not perceived in such a futuristic manner. For the painted dog, the joy of life comes from living each day, celebrating every second from sunrise to sunset surrounded by trusted and loyal kin.

Hovering beneath the shadow of a tall and lonesome tree, the pack begins to ritualistically gather around each other as they display a complex bonding behavior known simply as the meet. They are electric with excitement as they enthusiastically prepare for the hunt, and each dog greets the other with intense delight. They lick each other's faces, exuberantly piddle streams of urine, and emit an eerie, high-pitched twittering call as the entire

The only other African carnivore that is more endangered than the painted dog is the Ethiopian wolf. They suffer from habitat loss and disease spread by domestic animals.

pack rallies together as one, in preparation for the hunt. As the painted dogs feverishly mill around each other beneath the murmur of constant twittering, a dozen four-week-old pups scamper from a den on the opposite side of the tree. Quickly, the pups scurry to join the rally, where they are warmly greeted by the pack with gentle delight. Painted dogs are devoted to their pups, and while only one monoga-mous pair of dogs within the clan is allowed to breed, every member of the pack will help raise the offspring. Now that the meet is coming to an end, the dogs have decided who will stay at camp while the others head off to hunt. In addition to the pups, a few of the older dogs that are not fit enough to hunt will stay behind.

Now that they are united, the pack moves out. They are indeed a strange-looking horde of beasts, with each sticking out boldly and proudly against the other, as there is no attempt to conceal themselves while they approach their targeted

---

Now, I am not making a value judgment, it's just that when Mother Nature was passing out the good looks, the painted dogs got the short end of the stick.

---

prey. Painted dogs are quite odd in appearance, and if I may say, a wee bit homely. Now, I am not making a value judgment, it's just that when Mother Nature was passing out the good looks, the painted dogs got the short end of the stick. They have a gaudy coat, which garishly flaunts a blotched pattern of red, white, yellow, brown, orange, and black. Each painted dog has its own unique pattern of blotches, often looking as though it came across a painter's palette and then rolled around on top of it. By displaying an individualized color pattern, each dog can be visually identified by fellow members of the pack. They are however, often cursed with balding patches across their coat, while their tails, on the other hand, are covered by an excessive amount of wispy fur. The large, lobe-shaped ears have a somewhat comical appearance as they spring up from the top the dog's head, yet their unique design affords the painted dog with exceptional hearing. Ultimately, though, whatever the painted dog lacks in comeliness is overly compensated for by its character, loyalty, intelligence, and excessive goodwill. The generosity and tolerance expressed between pack members is unmatched by any other large-bodied carnivore inhabiting the savannah.

The pack is now within a few hundred yards of the wildebeest, which have begun to spook as the painted dogs approach. While the wildebeest are skittishly clustering together, forming one tightly bound mass as they attempt to flee, the pack of painted dogs moves in on them, calm and collected. The pack makes no attempt to hide or sneak, and while they are not necessarily moseying toward the wildebeest, they are not mad-dashing at them either. Their plan is to just stick with the herd and wait for signs of weakness, which they will detect visually. Painted dogs rely less on sniffing out prey, and more on spotting it, which is why they often prefer to hunt before the light of day has passed. Again, they approach as a collective, being that an individual painted dog, weighing between forty and eighty pounds, would have little chance in taking down an adult wildebeest by itself. The pack decisively spreads out and then loops around the herd, testing the wildebeest with quick approaches and retreats, as they attempt to flush out the one animal ideally suited for slaughter. Just when a formation of painted dogs nimbly slides past a perimeter of scampering hooves, the herd suddenly splits apart with individual wildebeest veering from each other, as chaos splinters the horde of fleeing beasts. That's when the candidate, an older bull, is revealed to the pack. When married with the herd, this bull looks to be of good health, yet when alone and flushed out into the open, his subtle weakness becomes more apparent.

Through the eyes of novices like ourselves, we keenly glare at the wildebeest and see a solid, rather healthy beast; on the other hand, the painted dogs detect signs of frailty that are as obvious to them as the blotches on their coats. As the painted dogs wander closer to the elder wildebeest, they observe that he has labored breath although he hasn't had to run all that much. When he does attempt to trot toward the distant herd, the dogs discover that he has a subtle limp, which you and I would not have noticed, but the hunters plainly observe that the wildebeest's rear left hoof is slightly lame. Now that they have selected their prey, the moment for taking it down has come. The canines loosely converge into a U-shaped formation, and as they move in, the wildebeest makes a desperate attempt to flee. Although he is moving off fast and begins to distance himself from the pack, the dogs do not rush after him but maintain a steady lope while always keeping an eye on him. In the end, it will be the wildebeest who decides when it is the best time to die, for when he is tired and can no longer resist or flee, the hunters will move in for the kill. The old beast begins to slow just as his pursuers slightly speed up, until they are running alongside him. Despite his exhaustion, he picks up speed, but he is not fast enough to escape. As he slows down once again, one of the dogs running parallel to the left of his hindquarters moves in.

The dog focuses on the cantering hoof, and just when it hits the spattering sod, she lunges forward until her jagged teeth rake against the rotating ankle. Painted dogs have a mouth full of phenomenally sharp teeth that can easily shear through tough flesh, hide, and even bone. Her strike is devastatingly quick, and when she pulls back her mouth from the flailing hoof, she can see the tendons that had manipulated and held it in place have been severed. Her nearly instantaneous snap has ripped open the wildebeest's ankle, exposing twitching and glistening muscle above a pathetically wobbling hoof. Like piranhas, the dogs running alongside their victim move in one by one, each targeting a specific zone,

which when struck, causes the wildebeest to slow. The final blow comes when one dog slides beneath the hobbling wildebeest and then tears out a mouthful of flesh containing a wad of bundled intestine. As the wildebeest continues his futile attempt to escape impending death, he unknowingly hobbles off as his guts are pulled out from behind like tissue ribbons streaming out of a popping party favor. He stops for a moment, wobbles a bit, then crumbles to his knees. But before the wildebeest has a chance to flop down onto his side, the pack is upon him, instantly splitting him open as they shred through his outer flesh until he is quickly dismembered into hundreds of unrecognizable gobs of flesh.

Although the mutilation of the bull may come across as cruel, the reality is that painted dogs are highly efficient predators who will deliver a merciful death more rapidly than other predators, like cheetahs or lions. I have seen lions eat a wildebeest that struggled for nearly half an hour as it was being eaten alive. As for their table manners, painted dogs do not exhibit the selfish hoarding of other carnivores, and there is very little squabbling over the kill, never mind true aggression.

Now that their bellies are full with fresh wildebeest flesh, they head back to the tree where the pack members eagerly await their return. Upon arriving at camp, the victorious hunters are met by both pups and older dogs that were too weak to attend the hunt. Even though they did not participate in the kill, they are still provided with an opportunity to nourish themselves, as a number of the returning dogs regurgitate piles of warm meat, which will be eaten by the adults and pups that were left behind.

So you're probably wondering why the painted dog is on the brink of extinction. After all, they are efficient hunters, devoted parents, and live in highly complex cooperatives. Well, the answer to this query is simple: the endangered status of the painted dog has less to do with their behavior and more to do with ours. Although attitudes have begun to change, the painted dog is still being aggressively persecuted throughout its range. Why? Unfortunately they are often looked upon as being vicious and savage, even though their hunting technique is often less brutal than other predators inhabiting the savannah. Unlike nocturnal predators such as the lion, leopard, and hyena, painted dogs are diurnal hunters; thus, humans have had more opportunities to witness these canines as they stalk and kill game. While lions are no less brutal to their prey than painted dogs, they often hunt at night, which means that they are less likely to be observed and ultimately scrutinized by *Homo sapiens*. The other challenge painted dogs face is from diseases that have been introduced by domesticated dogs; both rabies and canine distemper have devastated wild populations of painted dogs. Despite rigorous efforts to conserve the painted dog, this incredible species is still teetering on the edge of extinction. In the end, the future of the painted dog rests in the hands of the people of Africa, who are burdened with the responsibility for the management and conservation of this very special creature and the priceless habitat that serves as its home.

NIGHT FALLS ON THE PLAINS

At last the sun has passed, and while trailing fingers of lavender dance above a distant horizon, the fiery ball has now left the plains of Africa to slowly levitate above the landscape of a very different land. As the twilight of dusk fades to black, two great brothers, perched on the grassy bluff beneath the baobab, are intently gazing down at the riverbank below. As rulers of the pride, both patriarchal partners are burdened with the responsibility of defending their territory against wandering marauders seeking to appropriate all that they covet. They occupy a seventy-mile territory, which is plentiful with game, but even more intriguing to the competition eager to overthrow them are the four females that are at their reproductive prime. Weighing in at around four hundred pounds each, they are the largest species of terrestrial

Weighing in at up to 550 pounds each, these brothers discuss dining in or carrying out.

carnivore inhabiting the continent, the African lion (*Panthera leo*). Exhausted after a day spent unsuccessfully hunting for game, they have returned to their lookout hungry and beat. Despite their great predatory skills, they have only a thirty percent success rate when it comes to taking prey. In order to sustain their great bulk, adult male lions need to eat approximately fifteen pounds of flesh each day. While they have not yet eaten this day and are famished for a good meal, the night has just begun for the two brothers, and things are already looking promising from what they have just observed below.

As the warm air flutters through their luxuriant manes, the handsome brothers rise up on the windy mound and begin descending toward the river where a most peculiar situation is unraveling before their eyes. The lionesses are moving in as well, but not from the hill; from the savannah, where they had continued to hunt long after their pride masters' return. All six powerful beasts maintain contact with each other through a series of roars, which at an astonishing one hundred and fourteen decibels, can be heard from as far as five miles away. Muffled by the resounding resonance of the lions is the call of another animal whose eerie whooping howls, which sound like the cackling laugh of a madman, begin to grow louder as the creatures approach. It appears that the lions are not the only predators sleuthing for prey in the blackening night, for a large pack of spotted hyenas (*Crocuta crocuta*) have been drawn to the riverbank as well. Soon, the two formidable predators shall meet at the river

with the intention of capitalizing on an easy meal. Both species are alike with regard to predatory supremacy, but beyond their talents for delivering death to the victims they hunt, hyenas and lions are diametrically at odds with each other. Their mutual talents as pinnacle predators of the African savannah have pitted one against the other in an everlasting battle of intense rivalry. The competition existing between hyenas and lions has resulted in an antagonistic relationship where brutality and slaughter are an all too common occurrence whenever these two conflicting species converge upon the savannah.

Ambulating through the waving grass with their front limbs bizarrely longer than the rear ones, the hyenas are now but five hundred feet from the river and approximately seven hundred feet away from the four lionesses who are approaching from the opposite side. The pride masters are moving at a steady pace down the slope of grassy bluff and are now nine hundred feet away from the river, which places the two lions approximately at the halfway point between the hyenas and lionesses. There are at least twenty-six spotted hyenas belonging to the clan, but not all of them are on the hunt. A few of the hyenas are back at the den, but even still, this group outnumbers the lions nearly four to one.

Hyenas are dramatically different from lions with regard to behavior, social structure, and biology. First of all, they are not canines, as many people believe them to be. These very successful carnivores belong to their own unique family called Hyaenidae, and the African mammal which shares a very distant ancestry with hyenas is in fact the mongoose. Hyenas are powerful and rugged creatures with a number of physical characteristics that are rather peculiar, if not downright creepy, but when observed from the perspective of evolution, these unique traits are absolutely astonishing.

Before I begin delving into the mysterious and weird world of hyenas, I need to come clean. Personally, I think that hyenas are the coolest things since sliced bread. While many people regard hyenas as being dirty and stupid scavengers, in reality, this viewpoint could not be further from the truth. First of all, hyenas are in fact highly intelligent creatures, which, according to a number of scientists, exhibit an intelligence registering at a higher-primate level.

Unlike lion prides, which are patriarchal, the hierarchy within the socially complex clans of hyenas is matriarchal. Another difference between these two competing predator species is that lion prides are much more chaotic and less structured than their hyena counterparts. In lion society it is the strongest male who reigns supreme, while among hyenas, it is the most intelligent and powerful female who leads. In a hyena pack, the highest-ranking male falls short of the lowest-ranking female, which is usually nothing more than an adolescent cub. The highest-ranking hyena, or alpha female, serves as the queen of her clan, and the opportunity to rule often comes through inheritance; thus, her daughter, the princess, will likely lead the clan upon her demise. Beyond social expressions of dominance,

Life for hyenas is all about being female, and if fate should cast you as a male, well, you're simply at the bottom of the totem pole in hyena society.

female hyenas exhibit profound characteristics of their physiology that directly correlate to their supreme stature among clan members. While male spotted hyenas will max out at around one hundred and thirty-five pounds, females can reach one hundred and sixty-five pounds. Perhaps the most remarkable characteristic of a female hyena is that she is equipped with a pseudo-penis, which has an uncanny resemblance to the male's genitals, yet is indeed a functioning vagina. While working hands-on with a hyena study in Kenya, I was struck by how difficult it was for me to identify the sex of these creatures by merely looking at their genitals. The physiology of their dominance is so advanced that females even have a scrotum, yet they do not have testicles. The female's possession of male-like genitals is so profound, that until very recently it was commonly believed that hyenas were hermaphrodites. Unfortunately for the hyena, many of its strange characteristics have contributed to the numerous fallacies that many African people have about this truly unique creature. Perhaps it is the hyena's ghostly laugh and loping gate, or possibly it is the creature's sinister form; whatever the reason may be, the truth is that many people just simply loathe the hyena. Throughout Africa, the hyena is often regarded as an unnatural and malevolent beast that has its origins in witchcraft. Tragically, these creatures are persecuted in many of the regions they inhabit, and while the lion is looked upon as being the noble beast serving as the steward of the savannah, the hyena, on the other hand, is often regarded as nothing more than a moronically savage scavenger.

The simple truth is this: Hyenas are probably the most efficient predators living on the African savannah. When they hunt, they kill quickly, and when they eat, they waste nothing. It is not uncommon for a lion to consume only forty to sixty percent of its kill, while the hyena will eat just about every part of the animal, including bones, hooves, fur, and even teeth! They have even been known to devour mummified carcasses that a lion would just snub his snout at. The power of a hyena's jaws are unequaled by any other African carnivore, and I have seen them crunch up a rock-hard section of femur and hip bone from an expired cape buffalo as if it were nothing more than a chocolate-covered malt ball. Hyenas are capable of pounding down thirty-two pounds of meat at a single sitting, and when they are all gathered around the kill there is none of the squabbling and hoarding normally associated with lions. It is not impossible for a lion to be severely injured or killed by a fellow pride member while skirmishing over a piece of flesh. When hyenas join together to feast upon a kill, there is very little squabbling, and violence between clan members is extremely rare.

Back at the river's edge, long gone are the zebra mares and colt, and although they vigilantly stood by as their handsome stallion struggled against the mighty Nile croc, they had finally given up hope and made the difficult decision to move on. Although nearly three hours have passed since the croc latched on to the stallion, he is still standing there with hooves dug in and legs locked, refusing to submit to the monster reptile and fighting back with every bit of energy he can muster. The tattered body of the zebra trembles from the weight of the burdensome crocodile, which hangs off his face like an enormous pendulum. The crocodile's teeth are still tightly clenched onto the wad of hide and ear tissue, but the flesh is no longer being pulled from the top of the zebra's head and nape. He stares out into the black night with both eyes frightfully wide and unable to blink. His muzzle is slippery and wet from oozing blood, as the two rows of clenching teeth between the upper and lower jaws are completely exposed. The air passing through the wrinkled twist of skin where the nostrils once were gurgles as the zebra struggles to draw in desperate breaths. As the croc's great mass hung from the zebra, the skin around his brow had begun to tear. As time dragged on, gravity took its course until the zebra's entire face had torn away from the muscle and bone underneath. Like a grisly mask, the face has been pulled inside out and is now being stretched tight from the end of the upper lip, which is the only part of the zebra's head where the skin is still anchored.

As the crocodile relentlessly hangs from the zebra's face without mercy, a trail of fine bubbles is approaching him from behind. The painful silence is shattered by an upwelling of boiling water as an eight-thousand-pound bull hippopotamus (*Hippopotamus amphibious*) explodes from beneath the croc, torpedoing the reptile four feet out of the water. The croc hits the water with an sixteen-foot-long belly flop, and as he comes crashing down, the last bit of sinew attaching him to the zebra snaps. The faceless zebra tumbles backward just as

---

The hyena will eat just about every part of the animal, including bones, hooves, fur, and even teeth!

---

the raging hippo bombards the croc a second time. Terrified by the assault, the croc manages to shimmy up the bank and then scurries along the crusted earth for twenty feet before spearing back into the water. With a couple of labored kicks, he disappears downriver, wounded with a busted sternum and traumatized by the assault, but in the end, very lucky to be alive. The mighty hippo, which stands nearly five feet at the shoulder, widely snaps his colossal mouth open, with tusks flailing in the air. As he angrily bellows and grunts into the night, the hippo raises his massive rump above the water and then sprays out a six-foot-long torrent of

Male hippos can weigh as much as ten thousand pounds. Because their eyes and nostrils protrude, they can nearly submerge under water and still see and breathe. Though hippos can be very aggressive (including toward humans!), they are strictly vegetarian.

girth and hefty appearance, he's quite agile in the water, and if necessary, he can run along the bottom of the river.

The zebra stumbles back and forth; his face is oddly numb for such a devastating injury. The only real discomfort he is experiencing is coming from his throbbing eyes, which are painfully dry due to the lack of any eyelids to blink a soothing coat of moisture over them. While still facing the river with glazed eyes, the zebra wobbles a bit before making an attempt to walk. He is in shock, and even worse he is mortally wounded. His skin cannot regenerate and it is only a matter of time before the soft tissue of his eyes begins to crack before inevitably submitting to blindness. Already flies have begun to gather about his face and his eyes, but despite his dreadful state he longs for only one desire, which is to be reunited with his herd. Tragically, he may survive for days, slowly suffering until finally succumbing to infection. But as the stallion turns toward the savannah for his last journey to join up with cherished kin, it appears that his suffering is within sec-

feces. By rapidly fanning his stubby tail flush against his anus, the hippo spreads the streaming scat across the water. This is how he marks his aquatic territory; thus, his spraying scat is a blatant warning to trespassing wildlife, especially other bull hippos, that violators will not be tolerated. After a few more threatening yawns, the hippo submerges beneath the surging river until he finally vanishes. Despite his onds of coming to an end. Crouching in a half circle to his front are four lionesses, all of which are willing to provide the zebra with a swift and merciful death.

Only a single pounce is needed to bring him down to his final resting place upon a bed of dew-dappled grass. The lioness who pulls him flat to the earth is quick to clamps her jowls around the top of his neck, just beneath his lower jaw, and then she bites down with one effortless crunch, instantly crushing the zebra's windpipe. After just a few minutes he is dead, and as the remaining lionesses join, a deafening roar bursts out from the grass behind them. The pride masters arrive on the scene, which quickly sends their mates cowering away from the zebra carcass. Even though it was the females who brought the zebra down, it will be the brothers that will eat first, and only after their bellies are full will their lionesses creep forward to partake of the fresh meat. First, one of the lions slices a long gash down the zebra's belly, and then it disembowels the stallion by pulling out much of his digestive track. The two then eat the heart, kidneys, and liver before diving into the muscle. Throughout the feast, both brothers continue to growl at each other, and when one moves a little too close to the other, he gets a pawful of vicious claws raked across his muzzle. But as their bellies are stuffed with zebra, they begin to let down their guard, which is a signal to the lionesses that they may carefully slide in alongside the lions and partake of the rapidly dwindling kill. While the lions continue to gorge themselves on zebra, the shadows around them have begun to shift beneath the gray moon.

Then, the stillness is parted by a series of unnatural-sounding calls, which begin to bawl out from the black edge of night. The perverse cries of "whoop, whooop, whoooop!" begin sounding out from all directions as the creatures move in. All six lions snap up from the corpse just as the first spotted hyena ambles through grass and past the pride. This sends one of the lionesses pounding forward with heaving limbs as she commences to chase after the hyena. As the lioness begins to gain on the hyena, a sharp pain shoots through her

right buttock and sends her spinning about to discover that another hyena has latched onto the top of her thigh. She reaches out and smashes both of her paws against the attacking hyena's neck and then pulls the creature toward her mouth. As the lioness bites down on the hyena's shoulder, she is hit again, but this time along her left shoulder blade. She releases the first hyena, but as she turns away to have a go at the one nailing her from the side, the first one reels around from the lioness's haunch and then latches onto the great cat's neck. As the hyena's cavernous jaws begin to close around the lioness's nape, it immediately lets go while shrieking out. The lioness turns around to see that one of the pride masters has pulled back the hyena and is now ripping into its spine with his fangs, and then there is the hollow sound of crunching bone before the hyena's body falls limp to the ground.

Back at the zebra kill, a shifting wall of hyenas has encircled the remaining

If the pride master is present, the lioness must wait until he finishes with his meal before she can eat.

pride master and three lionesses. The lion charges out to the constricting perimeter, but the hyena he is targeting just lopes out from the chain and then slips back in as the lion is forced to retreat to the center of the circle. Finally, he lashes out once again, but this time he plows through the wall of hyenas and is followed by the three lionesses, who stay close to him as they escape. In a flash, they are racing up the bluff where the baobab awaits and are soon joined by the lion and lioness that had been attacked. The lioness has sustained significant injuries along her haunch and neck, but hopefully her strong constitution will help her to recover. In the meantime, though, the hyenas begin to rally around the zebra as they rip him apart. But as they devour the remains of the zebra, they discover that one of the hyenas is missing, and it turns out to be the matriarch.

A few of the hyenas wander through the tall grass only to discover that their queen is lying lifeless upon the ground, and as they sniff her body from head to tail, they determine that she is dead. After they finish devouring the zebra, a few of the hyenas amble over to the corpse of the matriarch and then begin to cannibalize her royal flesh as well. When you're a hyena, nothing is wasted, and in some cases that means devouring your own dead. The loss of the matriarch is a devastating blow to the hyenas, but walking amongst them is a spry and healthy hyena who just so happens to be the only surviving daughter of the dead queen. In the princess's body is the same genetic lineage that had contributed to her mother's success as queen. Now that she is of proper size, the princess takes on the role of matriarch and begins a new phase of her life as leader of the clan. As with many creatures of the African savannah, spotted hyenas are a resilient species, which despite the many adversities they face daily, continue to carve out a successful niche. Yes, Africa can be a forbidding land where death seems to come all too easily and where life is cheap, but beyond the rigors of its ecology, the southeastern Africa savannah is an exceptionally stunning land where one does not need to search long before discovering heaven here on Earth.

UNRIVALED BEAUTY AND DANGER

The trials of life that continuously play out across the rolling savannahs of southeastern Africa stand out as a great testament to the resiliency of the creatures attempting to survive here. I cannot recall any other ecosystem on Earth where the battle to survive is more spectacular and fierce than among the creatures of this expansive grassland. I have witnessed with my own eyes the suffering of prey as it is devoured by predators, struggling to survive to the bitter end, and all I can say is . . . I'm glad I'm not an antelope. Seriously, though, life for the unlucky and unfit often seems so unfair on the plains of Africa. Imagine you're a brand-new antelope, still wet from the amniotic fluid from your mother's womb. When you look up to latch onto a warm teat, you discovery that your mother has been driven off and a ravenous hyena is standing in her place.

On the other hand, this sprawling grassland is a place of unrivaled beauty, where an amber red sun sinking past the horizon can cast a radiance across the landscape powerful enough to soothe the most hardened of spirits. If life has you feeling a wee bit jaded, then set up a lawn chair along the rim of the Ngorongoro Crater in Tanzania with a nice glass of South African shiraz and a pair of binoculars at sunset. Trust me, the vista will have you feeling as right as rain in a matter of minutes.

The East African grassland is not only a breathtaking landscape where magnificent wildlife flourishes; it is also the cradle of humanity. This is the place where millions of years ago, our earliest ancestors stood upon two legs for the very first time and then ventured throughout the land as they colonized the entire continent of Africa and beyond. Today, there are very few places on Earth where we, the extant hominids begotten from our African ancestors, do not inhabit. The desire of modern humans to conquer the land and break the creatures that were here first has often devastated the ecology and wildlife

Distant rains fall upon the savannah against a fading sun.

native to these regions, which are now under the dominion of *Homo sapiens*. Unfortunately, Africa has not been spared the impact of modern man despite her role as the great mother of our species. We have a history of pillaging her natural resources for export abroad while ravaging her landscape in order to satisfy an appetite that seems never to be contented. Although Africa and her creatures have stood strong over the centuries while bearing the brunt of our insatiable avarice for more, she has now begun to wane. True, Africa is still a vast land where pockets of pristine habitat remain; the great question, though, is for how much longer. If it took only a century to deplete a population of black rhino from a million strong to just a few thousand individuals, then how long will it take before they are finally all gone—forever? Black rhinos aren't the only creatures facing extinction; many others are, as well, including the black rhino's burly cousin, the white rhino.

The types of African wildlife that are within a decade or so of slipping past the point of no return are tragically too many to list. If great action is not taken immediately, it is only a matter of a few years before there are no more painted dogs. My gosh, won't that be a somber day when the last of these marvelous canines slips through the very fingers that had failed to save them. Unfortunately, the issues of conserving African wildlife and habitats are daunting, but if we truly want to keep this great land pristine, we must immediately take aggressive action. Wildlife poaching is still a terrible problem throughout Africa. Each year millions of wild African animals are slaughtered for their body parts, which are then exported or consumed locally for medicinal use and for the manufacturing of prestige crafts. The gluttonous trading of illegally harvested bushmeat for the black market is yet another insidious contribution toward the potential extinction of many species. Everything from lizards to antelope, and even larger species like hippos and elephants, is still being illegally butchered for flesh. The great apes like chimpanzees and gorillas are regularly slaughtered for their meat as well, which, on the genetic level, is about as close to cannibalism as you can get before knocking your next-door neighbor over the head with an anvil and then throwing him on the hibachi.

Another challenge facing the conservation of African wildlife is a rapidly expanding human population. As humans expand beyond overcrowded villages and cities, their need to sustain themselves can lead to the exploitation of habitat for cattle grazing and other agricultural purposes. Of course, concerns involving an exponentially growing population of humans is truly a global issue. (If you're wondering just how fast we as a species are growing, in 1950, there were approximately 2.5 billion people inhabiting the planet. As of today, the population has increased to a whopping 6.3 billion people!) At current growth rates, there may be as many as 7.8 billion people living on the Earth in 2025. If the global population of human beings continues to grow at such an astronomic rate, it will only be a matter of a few more decades before our planet is no longer adequately fortified with the natural resources to sustain us. Other issues that have a negative impact on wildlife and habitat include mineral extraction (gold, petroleum, and diamonds), and the ever-growing conflict between neighboring countries within continental Africa where wildlife, along with human victims, is often caught in the crossfire.

So now you're wondering if it's too late to save Africa's wildlife. The answer is absolutely not! But if we are going to secure Africa's natural heritage for future generations, we need to begin working on the challenges today. Here are just a few of the many non-governmental organizations that are working hard to conserve Africa's wildlife and habitat: the African Conservation Foundation, the African Conservancy, the African Conservation Trust, and the African Wildlife Foundation. If you are interested in finding out what you can do to help, I'm quite sure that they would love to hear from you!

THE COSTA RICAN RAINFOREST

When I was thirteen years old, I asked my parents if I could go on an expedition to the jungles of Belize. Mom and Dad responded by telling me that if I really wanted to go, I would generate the funds to cover my expenses. By the time I was sixteen, I had spent the previous two years bussing tables at a local pub on weekends, trying to raise the funds for my trip during the summer months. For those two years we hardly discussed the subject, until I scrounged up enough money from the hundreds of hours of wiping down grease-glazed tabletops and polishing smoke-stained ashtrays. Finally, in the summer of 1984, I approached my parents, ready to take off for the wilds of the Mesoamerican frontier.

Again, my father reiterated our previous agreement that I would have to prove my readiness for the challenges of independent travel by securing the necessary funds. "Jeff, we had this conversation almost three years ago. We will entertain the idea of you going off to the jungle when you are responsible enough to pay for it." I nodded my head in accord, and then poured fourteen hundred dollars in tens and twenties out of a well-worn paper bag onto the kitchen table. "Let's talk passport, and oh yes, I'll be needing a signature from a legal guardian on this release form stating that I have parental consent to be an expedition participant." My parents sat there at the table, somewhat stupefied at my fiscal accomplishment. They looked at me in disbelief, thinking, is this the same kid who had managed to fall through the pool cover twice during the previous winter, who frequently showed up at the barbershop empty-handed after spending the money designated for a trim on candy, and who kept live salamanders in the toilet for weeks on end?

Let me explain: I rescued a couple of plump spotted salamanders from a storm drain and felt that the cold, highly oxygenated water in the toilet was the best place to keep them. The occasional shriek would flood in from the upstairs loo when visitors in need of relief would discover two very happy salamanders swimming in the toilet bowl in an almost synchronized fashion. Hearing this terrific commotion, I would scamper up the stairs to the rescue, screaming, "Don't flush! Oh God, whatever you do, just don't flush!" My dear mother has developed a slight facial tic, which she attributes to many such scenes that frequently played out in my youth. I truly believe that the statement, "I hope you have a child just like yourself someday!" was originally intended for me. As a kid, I was somewhere between Damien from *The Omen* and Bart Simpson.

So there I was, ready to venture off far from New England to the luxuriant and mysterious rainforests of Central America. I had a great desire to see and discover the extraordinary creatures unique to that habitat, armed with sixteen years of valuable life experience to get me through. I was definitely ready. I even had the confidence of my father, who, on my sixteenth birthday, was kind enough to leave me a note on the refrigerator: SON, MOVE OUT NOW, WHILE YOU STILL KNOW EVERYTHING! I had raised the cash, and my parents always kept their word, so a deal was a deal. I passed over the consent form and a pen to them, and two weeks later I was on a plane, destined for one of the most profound experiences of my life. The night before departure, I lay on my bed, unable to sleep. I had managed to count all the individual dots of plaster spackled against the ceiling (15,342, to be exact) before my dad took me to the airport.

I will never forget the first time I stepped past a wall of vibrant vegetation and into the humid understory of a tropical rainforest. The air was thick with moisture and smelled almost sweet from a cornucopia of trees hanging heavy with all manner of blossoms and fruit. The colors of the animals and plants were the most brilliant I had ever seen, making my memories of New England wildlife appear black and white. There were electric-blue butterflies, called blue Morphos, with wingspans wider than a man's hand. Giant vines twisted every which way, as bromeliads and ferns seemed to cling to every branch. There were powder-white bats sleeping beneath tents that they had ingeniously constructed from bowing palm fronds, and termite mounds twice the size of blue-ribbon pumpkins wherever I glanced. Lizards were chasing each other from twig to twig, as troops of howler monkeys crashed through the treetops. I was blown away by the density and richness of life inhabiting this chaotic forest, and I longed to better understand its many secrets. When it was time to depart, I did not want to leave, but I consoled myself by knowing that I would return the very first chance I got. It has been nearly twenty years since that first life-transforming trip, and I have had the good fortune of returning to the rain-forests of Central and South America nearly a hundred times since.

PRECIOUS JEWELS OF BIODIVERSITY

I have always been utterly thrilled by the display and the complexity of life in a tropical rainforest, and no matter how many times I visit this remarkable ecosystem, my sense of wonder and amazement for the weird and wonderful creatures living there remains strongly intact. For a biologist, there are few places on Earth that are as stimulating and exciting as tropical rainforests. They contain densely packed, thriving communities, where life has reached its zenith. The exploration of tropical rainforests led nineteenth-century naturalists, like Darwin and Wallace, to develop their evolutionary theories that still to this day serve as foundations for modern biology. Tropical rainforests are precious jewels of biodiversity; they exist as reservoirs for much of our planet's wildlife. Globally, tropical rainforests take up less than five percent of the surface of the planet, yet contain more than fifty percent of all life on Earth. Just a few acres of tropical rainforest can have more species of plants and animals than the continents of Europe and North America combined. A single tree in a tropical rainforest may have as many, if not more, species of ants living on it than all of the species of ants inhabiting the entire state of New Hampshire.

The uniqueness of a tropical rainforest lies in the fact that many of the great and exciting critters living there are often diminutive in stature and manage to blend in perfectly.

I like to think of a tropical rainforest as a hyperactive ecosystem where life travels at a frantic pace and most of the inhabitants are forever linked in a massive conglomeration of interconnected organisms. If you aren't focused in your approach to this ecosystem, it is easy to miss many of the strange and marvelous individuals united in this living maelstrom, organisms that are superbly designed to survive in this evolutionary wonderland, where survival often depends on an exceptional defense and where the beautiful are often as deadly as they are bold. If you don't explore this symphony of nature piece by piece, you risk overlooking all of its distinct performers, each unique in its contribution to the entire opus. Each one reveals secrets to survival in this very competitive arena, where winners pass on their genetic lineage, while losers become lunch. When I worked as a tour guide in Central America, I heard, on more than one occasion, people vent their disappointment at an inability to spot any creatures. That was when I would usually transform into that blind martial arts master with the Fu Manchu goatee and the fake-looking cataract contacts—you know, the wise old man from the television series *Kung Fu*. "Tell me, Grasshopper, how do you know what you have not seen, if you do not know what you are looking for?" After this pearl of wisdom, they'd get really pissed off and tell me, "Listen, you jerk, I paid you two grand to show me a wild jaguar and you want to talk about grasshoppers! If you don't start anteing up some animals real soon, I'm going to round-house kick your butt back to Massachusetts."

The uniqueness of a tropical rainforest lies in the fact that many of the great and exciting critters living there are often diminutive in stature and manage to blend in perfectly with the layered backdrop of vegetation. The tops of the tallest trees, fanning out over the forest like giant beach umbrellas, form the emergent layer. Just beneath this layer are trees that grow almost forty feet tall. Their dense blanket of leaves forms a canopy, and only a few of the tallest trees will push through this ceiling to join the ranks of the emergents. But they're not the only trees vying for a shot at the big league; smaller pole trees with thin trunks form the understory layer, growing until they reach the canopy and then waiting until a gap appears where they can punch through. Ferns and small shrubs fill in between the understory and the forest floor, where a mere two percent of sunshine ever reaches.

THE QUINTESSENTIAL KEYSTONE

Here, in an old forest in the Central American country of Costa Rica, at the bend of a creek, stands a great emergent tree called the strangler fig (*Ficus watkinsiana*). At around eighty degrees, the temperature beneath the canopy of leaves feels rather pleasant, while the humidity at nearly ninety percent is beyond balmy. Very little of the intense sunlight above manages to poke through the canopy, so the understory remains nicely shaded. This strangler fig began life thirty years ago, when it was nothing more than a vine, wandering through the branches of the canopy. Today this emergent towers more than one hundred feet tall. It would take four men in a circle, with arms stretched out and their fingertips barely touching, to encompass the tree's massive base.

The fig's colossal roots, twice as thick as a fire hose, radiate out and across the forest floor. Some of these roots extend more than twenty feet from the tree. Like the squirming tentacles of a monstrous octopus, the roots connect to the base of

The strangler fig can grow to be 150 feet tall.

interweave to form an almost cheese-cloth-like barrier just inches beneath the soil. Lying on top of this dense root mat is a two-inch thick, nutrient-rich stratum of decomposing organic matter, called the humus layer. Above the tier of brownie-moist humus rests a six-inch deep deposit of foliage in various stages of rot, called the leaf litter. As the leaves break down over time, they form the mulch-like humus, which then passes on the valuable nutrients to the root mat. The fibrous roots in the root mat have special ni-trogen-fixing bacteria called mycorrhizae, which aid the tree in the absorption of minerals, since the soil resting beneath the root mat is often nutrient poor. Many trees of a rainforest recycle more than ninety percent of their nutrients because they cannot depend on the soil in which they grow to supplement their desperate need for the additional minerals that sup-port healthy growth.

the tree along the buttress, forming a mantle of innervating channels and cavi-ties, some cavernous enough to conceal an adult human. The roots provide structural support for keeping the emergent stable and steady, as well as an expansive surface area for the absorption of both water and nutrients. Woven between the greater roots are millions of filament roots, which

The rainforest continually locks death and life in an eternal embrace. Think of it as a closed ecosystem, with most of its life contained between the canopy and the root mat. The life cycle in a rainforest begins when sunlight hits the leaves of the canopy and is then converted to energy through photosynthesis. All that energy gets locked up in the tissue of leaves, wood, fruits, stems, flowers, and roots. This energy then passes into the insects and animals eating the plants' material. The energy often goes a step further, when carnivorous or insectivorous critters devour herbivorous critters. When plant material falls to the forest floor either naturally or as animal waste, the warm, moist air will cause quick decay, thus releasing nutrients to the root mat. Dead animals on the ground further contribute to the richness of the leaf litter. The rainforest harbors very little waste, and the energy remains within the ecosystem. Various hosts, animals and plants alike, act as temporary keepers of energy fragments until they pass them on to the next guardian.

In the process of survival, the strangler fig has created layers of habitat that house many creatures. If an animal is not using the fig tree for housing, it may be thriving on the tree's fruit or leaves. Similarly,

some critters, instead of consuming parts of the strangler fig, prey on those who do. With such a great diversity of creatures dependent upon this great tree for survival, the strangler fig is the quintessential keystone species. It is the navel of life in this little clump of Costa Rican rainforest, towering like a rich old man, burdened with the many needs of a greedy, clinging family. But benevolent this fig tree is not; there is a reason why it is called "a strangler." Not long ago, there was another tree that once stood in this very spot. In order for the strangler fig to transform into the towering pinnacle of today, another tree was sacrificed, literally crushed within the strangler's deadly grasp.

Decades ago, a lithe vine slithered its way out of the canopy and onto a great ironwood tree. After making contact, the vine sent out hundreds of thread-like tendrils that began rapidly fusing together, until eventually, the liana spread across the entire surface of its doomed host. Once the vine reached out with its deadly touch, it was only a matter of a decade before the strangler fig completely enveloped the ironwood, like the gelatinous ooze that covered its hapless victims in *The Blob*. The strangler fig is a body snatcher, assuming the space and shape of the original tree. After fifteen years, the remnants of the ironwood were all but swallowed up by the parasitic predator plant, completely encased by a living coffin. The strangler fig replaced the roots of the ironwood with its own; it even sent aerial roots deep into the decomposing host to extract any remaining nutrients locked within. Eventually the ironwood rotted, until only a hollow cavity remained. Today, the strangler fig is an independent tree, complete with branches, leaves, and roots. Now this emergent, like its victim before it, serves as a host to many other organisms that capitalize on its newly acquired good nature.

THE NEOTROPICAL NETHERWORLD

The cumbersome air looms sweet and sultry, as droplets of gooey dew adhere to the surface of many of the surrounding leaves and shoots. Underneath an herbaceous layer of club moss, scattered tufts of fern, and clumps of nasty nettle are hovering shadows that repel the soft light of the understory. Cowering in the muted corridors of corresponding roots, dwells a tightly bound community of creatures. I like to think of this knee-high layer as the Neotropical netherworld, home to unassuming animals and often ignored by misguided biophiles who are enamored of the larger, and supposedly more charismatic, species. There are no jaguars or tapirs to be found at this lowly layer. As if reaching for celestial bliss, a regal orchid insists on opening its blossoms nearly six feet above the world of overlooked members of this rainforest community. A spider or howler monkey will rarely venture here; in fact, any animal designed to live high above would avoid this humble abode, far beyond the world of crisp light and a fluttering breeze. But there are creatures here, and as minute as they are, compared to the beings above, their presence is equally unique and vital to the overall integrity of the rainforest ecosystem.

Check out the mandible on this leaf cutter.

queens and hundreds of cohorts, flies through the jungle in search of a new empire of her own. Each of her royal companions will have to do the same. The queens split up, as instinct demands that each matriarch claims and conquers her own territory.

As the fleeing queens and their courts of fervently following suitors buzz across the forest floor, an assorted assemblage of ravenous predators craving an easy meal is ready to pounce. Flycatchers swoop in, snatching up Attas left and right. Spiders scamper down their nearly invisible cables of sticky silk that lead to trapped ants, who struggle pathetically against the coils of web. The Attas are crude navigators, with very rudimentary flying skills. One bumbling ant manages to survive a crash onto a philodendron leaf unharmed, only to be swiftly ensnared in the sickle-like grasp of a praying mantis. The few Attas fortunate enough not to have been gobbled up while in flight reach their designated landing spots only to be attacked by a second wave of predators.

One such miniature citizen finds herself banished from her subterranean kingdom. She has been flying for nearly an hour, and although instinct drives her to fly as long and as fast as she can, her wings have begun to fail, and soon they will collapse. She is a royal member of the clan of ants called Attas, also known as the leaf cutters (*Atta cephalotes*). The young queen, exiled with a couple dozen other

A large queen hits the ground running

with a convoy of lusty suitors filing behind her in quick pursuit. Her cumbersome wings, no longer useful for flight, are holding her back as the stalking procession begins to pick up speed.

Marching enthusiastically toward the queen, the males hone in on the pheromone-laced trail dappled across the leaf litter, which indicates that Her Royal Highness has a biological need to breed.

But not far away, another creature has more than ant fertility on his mind. He's thinking breakfast! Just as a dozen sex-crazed males begin to ambush the Atta queen, a giant Bufo marine toad (*Bufo marinus*) comes plowing out of a crevice in a hollow buttress at the base of the strangler fig. He barrels forward and begins to suck up most of the Attas. The queen, along with three males, quickly slips through a channel running under a bulky root of strangler fig and away from the rapacious toad. Discovering that there are no more delicious Attas to swallow, the great toad retreats into the hollow of the tree with his appetite far from satisfied.

About the size of a ripened cantaloupe, the giant Bufo marine toad is grotesquely gigantic. This rotund amphibian is so corpulent in girth, he makes Jabba the Hutt resemble the Lord of the Dance. You would almost need two hands to hold this blubbery toad. The alert eyes of the toad are nearly as big as my thumbnails, and his mouth is cavernous enough to engulf a small bird. Growing up, I kept an exceptionally large specimen that was capable of eating half a dozen adult mice in a single sitting. While the quaint toads of North America and Europe are filling their crops with delicate moths and dragonflies, this Neotropical monster is gobbling up mammals! Perhaps even more overwhelming than the marine toad's appetite is its defense.

Bubbling up from the tan skin across the toad's back are hundreds of warts, varying in size from a pubescent pimple to a black-plague boil. Two pit-riddled pads, called paratoid glands, straddle each eardrum-like tympanic disc on either side of the toad's face. These spongy cushions contain a milky, Elmer's Glue–like liquid

Bufo marine toads have been introduced as pest control in the Caribbean and parts of Australia and are now considered pests themselves.

that just happens to be a deadly neuro-toxin, strong enough to drop an adult man in minutes. Perhaps you've been in your backyard when dumb old Rover decided to chew on a North American species of toad. He probably gagged for a bit, then spit out the toad, whimpering from the burning residue in his mouth. You likely took the whining Rover into the house and poured some water down his maw. If you (and he) were lucky, he only splattered out some Bufo vomit all over your favorite chair in gratitude. The Bufo toxin secreted by the marine toads of the Neotropics has, on the other hand, a far more devastating effect than the eye-itching, mouth-burning defense of their North American cousins. If good old Rover should happen to get his mouth around a *Bufo marinus*, you can pretty much bypass the rinsing stage and just head straight for the shovel in the tool shed.

Having escaped to the other side of

DON'T LICK THAT TOAD

Now, I am sure you have heard of the dirty little addiction secretly taking place in the dingy back alleyways of morally questionable neighborhoods throughout Eastern Europe. Of course, I am talking about none other than the shameful habit of toad licking. Well, I hate to be the one to break it to you, but the slobbering practice of sucking on marine toads for psychedelic exploits is nothing more than an urban legend. This myth, I believe, although am not absolutely certain, was started by the Reagan Administration. I can assure you that, what one may actually experience from the excessive licking of a marine toad can go far beyond a mere high; it just might bring about death. It is impossible to achieve any mental euphoria from licking a toad. Trust me, I know. And don't look so shocked! We are talking about the same kid who at eight years of age spent four hours in the emergency room undergoing a pussy willow extraction from his sinus cavity. But enough about me.

the fig tree, the male Attas immediately resume the task of mating with the queen. They are quick to satisfy themselves and after all three males have finished their task, they crawl off. The male Attas have accomplished what nature had intended for them. Now that the three have sired a future kingdom that may well reach five million ants strong, they are obsolete and will scamper off into the forest, where a quick death awaits them. While the males are useful only for sex and die soon after copulation, females have a much longer lifespan, and a queen may rule for a decade or more before she perishes. The queen and her mates part ways, and she scampers off in search of a bit of underground lot to claim as her new kingdom. The queen will never need to submit to the desires of male Attas again because this blue-blooded hymenopteran carries within her all the sperm she will ever need to secure a future metropolis. Assuming she survives the perilous journey to the substratum, the queen will quickly undergo an astounding transformation from a svelte pioneer to an engorged egg-laying machine.

But first, she needs to rid herself of the burdensome wings clinging to her back. I imagine that for an ant, the sloughing off of a deteriorating pair of wings is similar to the sensation experienced by a child whose restless tongue probes the pulpy root of a stubborn milk tooth dangling from a sliver of gum. The queen begins to bite and tear at the tattered membrane structuring her wings. Like a throbbing hangnail, the translucent wings fraying from her thorax irritate her to no end and she longs to amputate them. Finally, she rips them away and scampers toward the wet earth, soon to be out of the glow of daylight forever. No time is wasted in her fight to reach the humus. The impregnated queen fumbles from leaf to leaf, as she climbs down through the stacked layer of desiccated foliage making up the leaf litter. Spiraling down through the leaves, she lands upon a slender branch. Suddenly, the twig she

is rushing across stirs. Her steps quicken, as the long cylindrical mass beneath her twists out from a veil of leaves and into view. In her hasty journey through the foliage heap, the anxious Atta has accidentally stumbled upon Costa Rica's most venomous serpent, the infamous coral snake!

This is a serpent I know all too well; it can be as deadly as it is mesmerizing to the eye. The colors displayed across the coral snake's back are a vivid reminder of its defense. Bands of bright red, yellow, and black loop their way down the snake's shimmering body. At around eighteen inches in length, and not much wider in diameter than my pinkie finger, the coral snake (*Micrurus diastema*) is a rather diminutive serpent. Its head is small and rounded, disproving the theory that all venomous snakes have triangular-shaped heads. The tiny, black eyes are perfectly round and iridescent. Coral snakes are shy and mild-tempered, and they spend much of their lives hidden beneath logs and stones. When they slither about, it is usually done under the concealment of leaves and scattered debris. Although coral snakes are not a rare species of reptile, they are not commonly encountered due to their secretive nature. When a coral snake is flushed out from the cover of leaves and into the light, it is capable of transforming from a placid reptile into a deadly adversary, equipped with a formidable defense.

Coral snakes are the only snakes living in the New World that belong to the Elapidae family. Other members of this notorious club include cobras, kraits, taipans, tiger snakes, and mambas—lethal serpents that inhabit places like Africa, Asia, and Australasia. What most elapids share in common is that their fangs are moderate in length and fixed, meaning they don't retract. The snakes also tend to produce some of the most potent venoms known to man. The venom that flows from an elapid's fangs is neurotoxic, which means it is capable of permanently shutting down the nervous system of prey or predator at an alarmingly rapid rate. Like other elapids, coral snakes have been blessed with this extraordinary defense,

which I experienced firsthand one fine summer day.

The vivid color pattern of a coral snake serves as a visual warning for predators to keep back, thus reserving the potent venom for killing prey: small lizards, frogs, and even other snakes. This type of color configuration is called aposematic coloration, and while camouflage is the survival strategy of many other life forms, the coral snake is a creature that is designed to be noticed. Aposematic coloration is not unique to coral snakes; think yellow jacket wasps or monarch butterflies (nice on the eyes but terrifically nasty on the palate). The universal warning colors of yellow, orange, and red, often made even more distinct against a backdrop of black, can be found among many potentially dangerous creatures in the natural world. This aposematic strategy has given rise to a great plethora of mimics, animals that probably taste pretty good but are often left alone by predators because of their uncanny resemblance to the genuine article. The monarch has the viceroy, a butterfly that

In theory, one bite from a coral snake is lethal enough to take out fifteen full-grown men.

from their deadly counterparts. I know of few creatures, with the exception of a slightly soft-headed herpetologist, who fail to take heed of the obvious aposematic display that marks the coral snake as a reptile not to be trifled with.

As for this particular coral snake, in truth, it has no interest in the bumbling Atta; instead the serpent slithers into the compact leaf litter until it soon disappears. As the snake slides through the crunchy layer of leaves, the Atta queen is scraped off the back of the serpent and onto the moist earth. Immediately upon flopping down onto the soil she is compelled to dig, and the determined ant does just that, until she has excavated a narrow tunnel running a foot into the earth. She is quick to carve out a tidy chamber before regurgitating a most precious blob of goop that had been stored in a small cavity at the back of her mouth, called the buccal pouch.

The mushy lump is warm and sappy with a slight musty odor. While it looks to be nothing more than an insignificant fleck of ant puke, it is in fact the foundation on

is nearly identical in appearance to the real McCoy but without having to undergo the costly process of manufacturing and storing toxins in its flesh. Counterfeit corals, like tricolor kings and scarlet snakes, are harmless imposters that, if it were not for a slight switch of the red and yellow bands, would be indistinguishable

(continued on page 167)

A LIFE LESSON LEARNED

It was 1996. At the time, I was knee-deep in my graduate research on bats, as well as running a field station in Central America. Beyond bats, I was also conducting an inventory on the amphibians and reptiles native to the region. Out of the numerous amphibians and reptiles I had observed that summer, coral snakes became one of the most commonly encountered species. By the last day of a four-month investigation, I had probably found twenty individual coral snakes, so why I felt so compelled that fateful day to capture one more still remains a mystery to me. All the students were back at their respective homes, and I had just finished closing up the field station for the rest of the season. I was going to be heading home soon and I thought it would be nice to embark on one last hike in the surrounding jungle-covered hills. I headed out alone, with plans on being back by lunch. I frequently went on long hikes in the rainforest by myself. After all, I had been exploring this particular tract of forest off and on since my teenage years, and I knew the terrain like the back of my hand. I loved being out there, beneath the soaring minarets of ironwood, ceiba, and mahogany, alone in the misty understory of the forest, where I could meld with the surrounding environment. I found that without the annoying distractions generated by a bumbling gang of spectators, I was more adept at focusing on the secretive creatures hidden behind the endless layers of foliage. After about an hour of spotting the usual—a few iguanas, the blur of a sprinting agouti, and a couple of keel-billed toucans—a lustrous and colorful serpent slithered across my path.

Whenever I come across a snake, whether a common garter or a king cobra, my body undergoes the same autonomic reaction, an affliction that has haunted me since I was six years old. My heart races so hard, it hurts. Blood flushes across my face, and my limbs begin to shake. So there I was, with joints trembling and sweat beading down my spine, trying to stay as still as possible until just the right moment to strike. Then the snake bolted prematurely, causing my left foot to instinctively shoot out and pin it down. When I normally do this, I never press down hard, just firmly enough to immobilize the snake. Moreover, I hardly ever attempt this maneuver with venomous snakes (unless I am feeling unusually lucky), especially if I am wearing Tevas. Yup, you've guessed it: I was trying to foot-pin a highly venomous coral snake with sandals on—certainly not a high point in my all-too-few moments of brilliance. (But then again, we are talking about the same kid who, at sixteen, while taking his father's brand-new Caprice Classic for a test drive, confused the gas pedal with the break pedal, thus causing the car to plow through a stockade fence until finally teetering over the rim of the family swimming pool. Anyhow, back to the most dim-witted day of my [post-pubescent] life. . .)

Immediately, my brain signaled my body to pull up from full-throttle to back-pedal mode, but it was too late. Seconds after pinning the coral snake with my nearly naked foot, the alarmed serpent reached back to deliver the bite of my life. As my lips muttered out a "What the hell are you doing, Jeff . . . " an explosion of pain, a thousand times more intense than a paper cut plunged into a beaker of boiling vinegar, shot out from the knuckle of my big toe and up my leg. Alone in the jungle, I had been nailed by the coral snake. There was no one to help me at the field station, I was at least an hour hike and a two-hour drive to the nearest phone, and to make matters worse, I was hundreds of miles from the nearest vial of antivenin. It takes approximately four hours to succumb to an envenomed bite of a coral snake. The clock leading up to my potential demise had started to tick, and time was not on my side. As the victorious serpent slinked off, I gave one last stare, while mumbling the old poem that had been burned in my memory since childhood: "Red touches black—friend of Jack. Red touches yellow . . . kill a fellow." Unless I had suddenly become dyslexic, the escaping snake was no coral mimic, but the real deal.

I tried to convince myself that I had probably just received a dry bite, but the sharp, nerve-twisting pain that grew more intense with the passing seconds was a rude reminder that I was in serious trouble. I tried to keep my wits about me as I made the two-mile trek back to camp. The more anxious I became, the quicker my heart raced, which meant that the neurologically corrosive venom traveled that much faster through my body. The pain quickly spread up my leg and into my chest, causing my heart to beat at an erratic rate. The salivary glands in my mouth began to exude copious amounts of drool, as my eyes liberally watered up with a continuous stream of uninvited tears. By the time I departed the shady forest and hit the dusty road leading to a nearby Mayan village, my leg had lost much of its mobility. I pathetically swung it out to my front only to have it wobble backwards and then drag from behind. I decided that my best chance for survival was to hobble down to a Raleigh International Mission that was building a new schoolhouse in the area. I knew that Raleigh had a resident British physician on standby, just in case one of the volunteers got injured. More important, they also had radio contact with the British Embassy.

About an hour had passed when I finally reached the Raleigh mission, and although they did not have any antivenin on hand, they were more than eager to crank up the radio on my behalf.

(continued on page 166)

A LIFE LESSON LEARNED—CONT'D

After going through the appropriate diplomatic channels of both the British and American Embassies, a British Defense Force helicopter was dispatched to airlift me out of the jungle and off to Belize City for medical treatment. Time was running out; it took a little over an hour for me to drag myself to the Raleigh International Mission and half an hour of radio talk to get permission for the airlift. It was going to take a good forty-five minutes for the helicopter to arrive from the Cayo District to the north, then there would be time needed for medical treatment on the ground before finally taking off for the hospital in Belize City. Remember, in as little as four hours one can succumb to the venom of a coral snake bite, and at least three and a half hours would pass before I received my first round of antivenin.

My symptoms of swelling, pain, cardiac arrhythmia, and excessive mucus production had become more severe. The medical officer had decided that because of the possibility of my developing an allergic reaction to the antivenin, he would limit the field treatment to intravenous fluid replacement, a very pleasurable dose of morphine to cut the pain and take the edge off, and steroids to decrease tissue damage. By the time they strapped me to the litter and slid me into the helicopter, I was feeling no pain. Soon, I would be injected with antivenin and be well on my way to making a solid recovery.

In all honesty, I never felt that I would not survive the bite of the coral snake. What hit me more than the venom was the realization of my own stupidity and a very sobering reminder of my mortality. It was a very important life lesson for me, and my regard for the exceptional power and extraordinary defensive abilities of venomous reptiles has yet to wane since that fateful day. Although I still work with venomous snakes, I do so only in what I feel are legitimate circumstances, while engaging an appropriate and responsible handling technique. I reflect upon my experience with the coral snake's defensive bite as a constant reminder of the respect and admiration that all venomous reptiles deserve. The serpent's intent is not to be malicious or wicked; its venom represents a remarkable adaptation of evolution that has but one purpose: to secure the snake's survival in an extremely treacherous world of "eat or be eaten."

My point is that we all have regrets, and being nailed by the coral snake certainly has earned top billing in the category of why I should probably be weeded out from the gene pool.

which the Atta species has thrived. This ostensibly ordinary little wad is called inoculum, a miraculous fungus that grows nowhere else on Earth but in the bowels of an Atta city. The task of nurturing this strange life-form falls to the diligent cast of gardener ants, and without their loyal care, this rare basidiomycete fungus could not exist. In turn, the fungus is the only food that one hundred percent of all Attas will eat. It is the fuel that drives the great hymenopteran metropolis, and should it fail to thrive in the colony, millions of inhabitants would surely perish.

The queen carefully kneads the fungal pulp for a few minutes and then waits, huddled over this ambrosia, until the time comes for her to lay a few precious ova in order to nurture the fungus. The first round of eggs, along with squirts of fecal fluid, is infused into the fragile bundle of fungus as a fertilizer to promote rapid growth. She will guard and cultivate her tender patch of fungus, for the future of her entire kingdom depends upon it.

As the queen waits patiently for the mycelia of the fungal pack to multiply until it is stable enough to support the first ravenous wave of consumers, a battle is underway at the base of the great strangler just a foot or so above her chamber. Face-to-face, two warriors are sizing each other up, coldly glaring upon one another, waiting for his opponent to make the first move. At no more than an inch in length, they are tiny but formidable with regard to territorial defense and keeping predators at bay. Adorned with ruby-red bodies and purplish blue legs, they are some of the prettiest little frogs inhabiting the rainforests of Costa Rica. Commonly called strawberry poison dart or blue jeans poison dart frogs (*Dendrobates pumilio*), these jewel-like amphibians, although diminutive in build, pack a mighty wallop when it comes to defense. They are precocious and fearless, petite frogs hailing from a notorious clan of amphibians—the dendrobatids, or poison arrow frogs. As with the coral snake, the dendrobatids engage a brilliant display of vibrant colors to remind the potential predator that to snack on a poison arrow frog is to taste death.

The destruction of the rainforest has had a detrimental effect on the pretty little "blue jeans" frog.

(the golden poison frog), is presumed to be the most poisonous terrestrial vertebrate on Earth. *Phyllobates terribilis* can be deadly to the *touch*, and it is said that the poison of just one of these weenie, fingernail-sized frogs is potent enough to instantly slay approximately one hundred brave, strong, and strapping adult men. The secret to their deadly success lies in a series of alkaloid-based poisons, called batrachotoxins, which are secreted from glands in the dendrobatid's skin. Batrachotoxins work by shutting down the nervous system, with death usually resulting from respiratory paralysis.

So, just how potent is the toxin manufactured in the skin of a poison arrow frog? This is a question that I get asked quite regularly; it's an inquiry that ranks right up there with "Why do zebras have stripes?" Well, toxicity among the dendrobatids varies from species to species. As for the strawberry poison dart frog, its toxin level registers at a bellyaching, vomit-wrenching, and diarrhea-squirting potential. While the strawberry poison dart frog may not be downright deadly to the taste, its Colombian cousin, *Phyllobates terribilis*

Despite their potential to deliver death so efficiently, batrachotoxins have great value to surgeon and hunter alike. In many operating theaters throughout the Western world, these dendrobatid-originated toxins have been synthesized to take the form of anesthetics, muscle relaxants, cardiac stimulants, and fibrillation controllers. For the Choco people, an indigenous community inhabiting the rainforests of western Colombia, the dendrobatid toxins are carefully extracted from the frog's skin, then applied to the tip of a blowgun dart. When blown out and penetrated into prey, the batrachotoxin-laced dart brings about instant paralysis, followed by death. So as the old joke goes, why did the monkey fall out of the tree? The answer is, of course, because it was dead—most likely knocked out of the canopy by the silent and practically painless delivery of a blowgun dart infused with lethal frog toxin.

At first glance, the opposing strawberry poison dart frogs appear to be fragile in form and disposition, but in reality they are quite resilient, and are prepared to battle to the death for territorial claims. The invading frog perches high on all fours as he rocks from side to side, while emitting a series of insect-like clicks and bleeps. The buzzing call coming from the intruder serves as a challenge to the resident male, an invitation to fight it out. It's a game of high stakes, with the victor securing access to prime real estate—along with lots of good frog sex with resident females—while the deposed combatant loses stature and terrain. The fearless frogs

stare at each other with their brilliant black orbs. The intruder taunts the resident by pressing forward until one slick muzzle rams against the other, and all the while the two rivals produce an incessant chirping clamor.

Finally, after growing weary of all the threats and posturing, the resident frog makes his move. The occupant of the entangled buttress roots leaps forward, and soon the challenger finds himself trapped within an angry embrace of grasping fingers and pressing limbs. The invader has been wrestled to the ground, and no matter how hard he resists, the frog on top will not let him free. All the wind in his tiny lungs has been wrenched out, as he is held flat against the moist earth, barely capable of catching a breath, never mind squirming free.

Nearly twenty minutes pass before the victor finally lets up, allowing the pathetic loser to regain his breath and sulk off. In celebration of his triumph against the competitor, the winner boastfully chirps until his call is met by an inquisitive female, who, after observing the valiant battle, creeps down from a flaring root in order to get a better glance at the charming champion. Though unable to return his call, she strokes his back with her front feet.

Love is in the air, and the bond between potential mates is further cemented through the twittering whir elatedly emitted from the vibrating throat of the spirited male. The receptive female likes what she hears, so she advances. Submitting to the droning bachelor, she allows him to lead her to a tidy patch of freshly fallen leaves. The female wants to bond but is still a bit apprehensive. Attempting to calm her, the male reaches out and strokes her jittering head with his forearm. Then to relax her further, he flutters his chin across her delicate head. Upon feeling that she will reciprocate, he presses his pelvis against the bed of leaves, and then, after a few quick jerks and thrusts, he withdraws, leaving behind a spattered glob of sperm. She hesitates, but after a few more comforting caresses from his gentle reach, she concedes. The ripe female moves in and lines up to him, back-to-back, cloaca-to-cloaca, with no true amplexus, or mounting, taking place. Carefully, she hovers her vent over the spot of sperm and then pinches out a gelatinous mass containing five precious eggs.

Amazingly, this is just the beginning of the parental journey of the two copulating strawberry-colored frogs. What comes next for these little gems is an astonishing and intricate process. The few fortunate humans who have had the privilege to witness this near-miraculous event often feel compelled to reconsider the argument that complex parental behavior is limited only to larger species of a more sophisticated design. But we'll have to wait another week to find out how their story ends.

Meanwhile, another, very different, egg laying is taking place. The Atta queen has been patiently waiting for a few days, cloistered within the darkness of her sultry chamber. She has been hovering close to the prospering mound of fungus when, finally, it happens. Her engorged abdomen begins to throb, until one by one, a series of rice-shaped eggs, tiny and moist, come spurting out from her dilated vent and onto the soft earth. Before long, they will hatch into ravenous larvae, hungry for grub. They are quick to grow and soon will separate into their predetermined castes, carved out by millions of years of evolutionary tweaking. Before the ants can serve, however, they need nurturing. The queen mother will raise the first round of offspring on a medium of the now-established fungus and unfertilized ova.

These firstborn, upon a dramatically rapid rise to maturity, will don the robes of nursemaids. Some will only service the queen, making sure that as she grows ever more grotesque and helpless; she will want for nothing in her endeavor to bring an endless stream of Attas into the world. The nursemaids will do everything in their power to keep her clean, comfortable, and safe, stopping at nothing to secure the success of her sovereignty. Not so much as a mite or other parasite, whether insect or rogue fungus, will be allowed to tap into her life source. All her energy must be honed in for one purpose only, and that is to lay egg after egg after egg,

for what will hopefully be a long and prosperous reign.

Workers from the first generation of ants that do not tend to the queen will take on the roles of nannies for fragile pupae, ensuring that the great oncoming horde of minions grows to fulfill its duty to the collective. Every single ant is forever bound to serve the great kingdom, be it as gardener, forager, sanitarian, architect, or warrior. While they all will have their places in the great metropolis, there will be no individuals. The ants must dedicate their entire existence to the super organismic structure of the Atta society. Those who perish will be quickly replaced by another generation, produced by the forever-fertile queen. Her transformation into a corpulent egg-laying machine is dizzyingly fast, and over the next few months thousands upon thousands of ova will stream from her body, as the population of the subterranean city of Attas multiplies at a rate faster than urban sprawl. As the novel Atta kingdom begins to flourish beneath the leaf litter, the world above the compact earth has once again grown dark.

THE STORY OF THE UNDERSTORY

While the moon slips high over the canopy and all grows ashen and dappled beneath her filtered gleam, a diverse assemblage of creatures is now awake, many of which are ravenous for sex and for flesh! It is in the black-and-gray world of night when many of the creatures upon and around the old strangler fig become most active. As the last light of sun fades, they creep out from shadowed crevices of wood and stone. They slither up from the twisted roots and down through the knotted vines. Some will scratch their way out, while others may hop, skip, as well as fly into the maelstrom of competitive chaos. Some will prosper, while many others will perish. But despite all the drama, tonight is just one more stream of moments that plays out each evening around the strangler fig tree, where Life unfolds in all her painful and miraculous glory.

Curled from snout to rump, resting upon a mat of bent twigs and crumbled foliage in the crooked elbow of the emergent, is a creature that sleeps more soundly than a fetus floating in its mother's womb. Alas, the glowing moon has once again interrupted his pleasant respite, just before his rumbling belly finally breaks the beast free from his daily slumber. He is a wonderfully weird creature with a strong, prehensile tail that any Neotropical monkey would be proud to swing from, but a primate he is not. Menacing talons, fit to shred the toughest of hides, hang like sharpened sickles from the quick of each toe. Yet he bears no relation either to the hunters of flesh, such as felines, or to any members of the weasel family. His curious snout is remarkably long and narrow, swinging out from the diminutive face like a boomerang clenched in a thrower's fist. So, just who is this mysterious dog-sized beast hanging sixty-plus feet off the forest floor? It is none other than a tamandua, of course.

As you might well know, the tamandua (*Tamandua mexicana*) is a moderately built anteater that has carved out a successful niche in the highly competitive rainforest arena by being a specialist. The tamandua is uniquely designed to sniff out, dig up, and then suck down huge quantities of tiny creatures, mainly ants and termites. He can chow down an entire generation of termites like no one can. To watch a tamandua feed is to witness a moment of destruction and greed. Observing this voracious predator pillaging a colony of hapless invertebrates provides a rare opportunity to experience nature at its best, in a near-perfect manifestation of evolution in action.

The tiny dark eyes of the tamandua are foggy and seem impassive against his bizarre, funnel-shaped head. His narrow muzzle is nearly eight inches long, yet the shimmering wet lips wrapping the mouth stretch no more than an inch or so in width. Although the pair of nostrils riding above the mouth may appear to be rather insignificant, they are, in fact, extraordinarily keen at detecting the faintest of odors, especially the aroma of potential prey. Except for the brown saddle strapping his back, the dense, bristly fur covering the tamandua is mostly blond.

His arms stretch out and shiver a bit. His slick lips perk up, and a long slippery tongue, sixteen inches in length, rolls out for a few seconds before sliding back in.

Any Neotropical monkey worth his salt would be proud to swing from this tamandua's tail.

He is quick to unravel from the tuft of branches, as he reaches up with extended claws, grasps onto a dangling vine, and then descends through the layers of dew-sopped foliage. With all claws clamping tightly to the wobbling liana, the nimble tamandua climbs down to the forest floor, face first. So as not to slip, the anteater wraps his limber tail tightly around the brittle bark of the vine. A palm-like wedge of hairless skin running along the underside of the tail allows the creature to hold on tight.

As the tamandua continues to amble downward, his sensitive nostrils identify the fragrance of prey. He stops to sniff out the source of the scent, and when he hones in on the location, the hungry beast reaches out to a neighboring branch and changes course. The anteater is so eager to get to his quarry that he nearly tumbles off a vine as he swings onto an overhanging branch. Now heaving upward at a forty-five-degree angle, he loops from branch to vine, and then to branch again, stopping only once at a jagged clump of bromeliad leaves, before reestablishing the scent and getting back on course. The odor of turpentine is growing stronger, which means the tamandua is getting close. A goiter-shaped sphere, as big as a beach ball, is growing out from the massive tree trunk almost sixty feet off the forest floor. Finally the tamandua arrives at the mound of crackled bark. The bulbous mass hangs off the tree as if it were a tumor, sucking the life out of the great emergent. Living within the morbid-looking orb are hundreds of thousands of termites, all of whom are completely oblivious to the great destructor that is closing in. It will be an attack so fierce, that on the human scale, it would make a furious hurricane seem no more treacherous that a gentle puff of wind.

At first glance, the nest of Nasutitermes termites appears to be a primitive, disorganized jumble. In fact, it is a complex structure, functioning as a microcosmos, where the inhabitants are completely in charge of their self-created environment. Life in the Nasutitermes colony is based on order and control. Similar to the Attas, the individual is of little importance; all work as one to ensure the prosperity and success of the collective. The universal pathway of communication shared by the termites is based not on auditory vibrations and visual cues, but is expressed through an intricate array of chemical messages, called pheromones. As with the Attas, specific commands to forage, defend, breed, and build are carried forth throughout the community by an invisible but tangible pathway, consisting of chemically diverse odors. The termites construct the nest by cementing together globs of spitball-thick wood pulp with a kind of fecal glue they secrete from their rectums. The outer layer of the nest is somewhat soft and papery, while the inner chambers leading to the core of the colony are more rigid.

Although termites chew and swallow wood, they in fact don't really digest the wood fibers in their raw form. Living in the gut of each termite is a microscopic creature called a microbe, and when a termite swallows a tough wad of plant fiber (cellulose), it is the microbe that breaks it down, separating valuable nutrients from waste. The termite benefits by being able to acquire previously unavailable energy that was locked in the wood, while the microbe enjoys a warm, cozy, and slimy gut it can call home. This obligatory symbiosis is a win-win situation for both termite and microbe. When it is time to forage for plant material, the termites travel through channels and runways, which are enclosed beneath a protected

It is only a matter of a few more seconds before this intricate and highly organized utopia of invertebrates receives the wrath of the great predator.

layer of cemented cellulose and run from the nest throughout the forest. Not all the termites, though, are designed to head out into the wilderness to harvest plant matter. There are many thousands of termites whose missions keep them locked within the chambers of the nest, and who never venture beyond its carton walls.

There are three different castes making up Nasutitermes society. There is the reproductive caste made up of kings, queens, and nymphs. Beyond the breeders, there are two sterile castes of termites that are incapable of reproducing yet are equally vital to the survival of the colony. Workers are members of this celibate caste that must carry a great burden of responsibilities ranging from foraging for plant material to constructing the nest. While workers have diverse missions, soldiers, on the other hand, have one primary directive—to defend the colony from attack. Also known as nasutes, they are the Green Berets of the termite world. The loyalty of these soldiers is absolute, and they will stop at nothing to defend the colony, gladly sacrificing themselves in battle to secure the future of the collective. The innate drive to defend and battle to the death is a noble trait indeed, especially considering that the soldiers' unwavering resolve is about to be tested. All hell is just a few seconds from breaking loose.

Except for the muffled burr coming from millions of rustling limbs, quivering in the commotion of everyday life within the Nasutitermes colony, everything is tranquil and undisturbed. Then, a second later, the peaceful silence is abruptly shattered, as a great claw rips deep into the nest like an atomic wrecking ball. With one single swish of the claw, hundreds of termites are instantly smashed to death. The massive talon lops off row upon row of termite heads, crushing dozens of bodies into unidentifiable bits. I have often wondered what goes through the minds of termites under attack. Chances are, it's all just autonomic hardwiring, with reactions based solely on instinct driven from millions of years of evolution. But what if they were fully cognizant of life unfolding around them, if they could assimilate the impact of a situation, completely aware of the profound consequences generated from action and reaction?

Whether sentient or automatic creatures, the Nasutitermes termites respond to the tamandua's assault, and despite their minute size, they are capable of dispensing a formidable defense. The claws slash deep into the nest again, slicing through hundreds of corridors and chambers, killing thousands of termites trapped within the collapsing path. The tamandua waves his nozzle-shaped snout over the gaping tear, draws in a few breaths, and then resumes his marauding of the nest. Panic has infested the damaged colony, as much of the population muddles about in an attempt to escape the invader. Hundreds of termites tumble out of the chasm in the nest to their death upon the forest floor below.

Finally the tamandua cuts his way through the fibrous core by jamming both of his front paws into the gash while simultaneously bending his elbows outward with claws brutally dug in. Then, with one quick pull, the nest is ripped in two. The cap of the nest, filled with a hundred thousand termites, hurdles down through the canopy until it smashes against a protruding stump and explodes into bits, while the remaining two-thirds of the nest is still attached to the tree. The termites that have been left behind are now completely exposed to the long-nosed monster, who now, after tearing into the utopian city without mercy, will begin to slobber and suck up as many of the remaining survivors as he can. Like a Shop-Vac set to high, the ravenous tamandua probes the surface of the damaged colony, extracting hundreds of squirming victims with each draw. His sixteen-inch-long tongue flickers in and out of his small mouth, penetrating many of the narrow corridors which run deep into the nest. The tongue is as tacky as flypaper, and once it touches the termites, they are helpless to free themselves from its sticky grasp. The tongue slides in and out swiftly, about a hundred times per minute. It pulls in a mouthful of termites and grinds them into protein-rich slurry against a firm palate of flesh in the oral cavity.

Although the loss of termite life is immeasurable, the battle is not over yet. The chemical signal to attack resonates throughout the tattered nest, calling all surviving nasutes to the trenches to defend the realm from the ruthless intruder. Charging up from the bowels of the nest, a battalion of nasute warriors rushes toward the assailant. The nasutes flank each other back-to-back, while raising their pin-shaped faces to the tamandua. Each nasute's elongated head forms into a conical, syringe-shaped snout, called a nasus, and although the nasutes have no teeth for biting the attacker, they are indeed armed. As the tamandua pillages through the

---

When rainforest trees are clear-cut for industrial purposes, there's a ten percent increase in the deforested region's temperature due to termites.

---

crumbling nest, the nasutes resort to chemical weaponry. They squirt out sticky, turpentine-like liquid from their nasuses toward the anteater's mouth. The tamandua is momentarily deterred by the volatile substance, but still continues to suck up streams of termites. The first flank of nasutes is instantly crushed beneath the tamandua's muzzle. No matter; the reinforcements are quick to file up to the front line. Again, they shoot out copious gobs of repellent liquid, which now nails the tamandua not only in the mouth once more, but in his left eye as well. The anteater's lid winces and his eyes begin to water, as his mouth clots with gooey webs of mucus. The predator has had enough. He will now withdraw into the shadow of the forest, where he'll nurse his irritated eye, while attempting to expel the caustic juice from his mouth.

The reaction to the liquid defense will soon pass, and now that he has filled his belly with termites, the tamandua will nest down for the night. He will rest contentedly, until the following evening. Then, once again, he will fulfill his role of a wrathful deity who will smite yet another unsuspecting colony of Nasutitermes. As for the surviving termites and their disheveled nest, they will rebuild. In fact, within seconds of the tamandua's departure, the workers arrive at the site of the massacre and begin to raise new and stronger walls from the rubble. It will only be a matter of a few months or so before the nest is as good as new and the population of the collective has been restored.

The tamandua is not the only creature that is partial to termites, for these small creatures contribute vast amounts of protein to a diverse array of consumers. One termite may appear to be insignificant, but a whole nest of them can sustain a creature of great mass. In fact, much of the health of the rainforest rests on their backs. Beyond being a source of food, termites serve the rainforest community by releasing energy locked in plant material back into the ecosystem. Because of the heat, moisture, bacteria, and termites, a tree that falls in a rainforest can be broken down in about a season or two. The termites eat that tree and convert the energy in their bodies, then build their nests or become food for others. As they munch, they create a significant amount of nitrogen, carbon dioxide, and heat energy that infuses the environment. In fact, this heat energy can be measured on a larger level. When rainforest trees are clear-cut for industrial purposes, there's a ten percent increase in the deforested region's temperature due to termite activity. This is just another example of little things having a big impact. Without termites, many species of mammals, reptiles, amphibians, birds, and insects would perish.

Elsewhere on the strangler fig, there is another anteater that has begun to feed, but this creature is not a tamandua. It is a tiny, delicate beast with velvety soft fur and an angelic face, called a silky anteater (*Cyclopes didactylus*). Its dense pelage is as soft as cashmere and has the color of golden honey. It even smells nice, like clean linen. I have only seen the highly elusive animal three times in my entire life. This mysterious, almost magical creature sends my heart aflutter each time I have the rare privilege to set my eyes upon it. The Mayas of Belize refer to the silky anteater as the Seraph or angel of the forest. The ghostly creature had even me perplexed on one occasion.

Like the tamandua, the silky anteater has made a career out of eating great quantities of tiny creatures. As a specialized consumer, the anteater possesses a unique design which allows it to procure specific prey. It has the characteristic elongated, toothless snout, Ginsu-sharp claws, north in the very recent past thousands of years. In the United States, we can actually see the migrational flow, as this armadillo has moved from Mexico through Texas and Louisiana to Florida.)

This particular silky Seraph is hidden behind a flowing tube of aerial root which hangs six or seven feet above the forest floor. Like its greater cousin, this little anteater is nocturnal, woken up by a desire to feed. It hangs there, hunkered tightly to the dangling root, as it tweezes open a pencil-thin vine with its sharp claws. Upon being split, the vine spurts out a stream of tiny black ants that come shooting out like blood from a severed vein. Silky anteaters prefer ants to termites, and the hordes of crunchy and sweet creatures flowing from the torn climber will be greatly savored. The little beast lowers its head close to the wounded vine and then laps up every ant it can capture. It may be tiny and cute, but the silky anteater is an efficient predator, and after only five minutes, the fuzzy critter has devoured nearly an entire colony of ants.

The silky anteater is not so helpless after all. If it were, it would have joined the endless list of really cute extinct creatures.

and prehensile tail. Anteaters are members of an extraordinary and weird group of mammals, called the Xenarthrans. This ancient order of mammals is unique to the New World tropics, with the exception of one species, the nine-banded armadillo. (In fact this creature demonstrates evolution in action. All Xenarthrans evolved in South America, but the nine-banded armadillo has been migrating

Not more than a yard away from the buttress of the strangler fig tree is a pool

A MAYAN MYSTERY

I was nineteen when I spotted my first silky anteater. I had discovered a pair tucked beneath a bowing palm frond during a late-night hike along a mountain trail. I was utterly smitten with them at first glance. Both anteaters weighed no more than half a pound each, and they were about the size of a small stuffed teddy bear. They were tiny and precious, but what I found most wonderful about them was their fur. I was unable to tear my eyes from their adorable form. I was also saddened by their vulnerable appearance, thinking melancholically, "How could anyone hurt such a precious creature, and who will protect these innocent, wee little beasts?"

I was so terrified that I would never have another chance to observe them again, that I thought I would borrow them for the evening to take some photos, with the intent of returning them to where I found them the following morning. I bundled up a couple of snake bags and then carefully scooped them up. Holding the two creatures gently swaddled in cloth and with my eyes closed, I lowered my face close to their velvety bodies, inhaling their herby, almost wholesome scent. "Don't worry, little guys, I won't hurt you, shshshsh, it's ok . . . "

That's when it happened. Just as I was contentedly savoring this harmonious encounter, a sharp, eye-watering pain throbbed in my right nostril. The peaceful silence was broken by a howl that started out "Owee, owee, owee" until it quickly progressed into an "Ahhh! Ayiyi! Yi!" I quickly opened my eyes to discover that, while I was getting lost in the tender moment, one of the innocent silky anteaters had shoved his little paw up my nostril and dug his razor-sharp claws deep into the super-sensitive skin beneath my sinuses. The pain was so intense, that it made a nasty ingrown hair zit in the nose seem about as traumatic as losing an eyelash. Tugging on the creature only caused my nose to bleed more, as his talons quickly shredded the thin nostril membrane. I froze and waited until the little monster pulled his paw out of my nose.

After arriving back at camp, a friend of mine from a local Mayan village seemed rather impressed by my discovery of the anteaters, as well as my bloody nose. He told me of the folklore surrounding the silky anteater, including the accounts of how they can magically disappear and reappear. I moved off to find a safe and secure place to keep them overnight and nurse my wounds. I lined a cardboard box with blankets and a couple of branches before placing the pigmy anteaters inside. After closing up the box nice and tight, I went to bed. The next morning, when I went to retrieve the anteaters, I discovered that they had vanished, yet the box was completely closed in the same manner as I had left it. I have no idea how they could've escaped.

of water that has formed within a perimeter of polished limestone rocks. The pool is a few yards wide and contains relatively clear rainwater about eight inches deep. Although the pool is shallow, the liberal amount of rainfall unleashed during the rainy season keeps it full for nearly half the year, which is the approximate length of the rainy season. In fact, the "dry season" should really be called the "less rainy season" since this forest receives nearly one hundred inches of rainfall annually. A severe dry spell, however, can still hit this lush community every few years, raising a lot of havoc. The creatures that live here like it wet, and when the environment experiences a long and pronounced dry season, the wildlife tends to suffer.

High above the glassy pool, a forceful call consisting of a series of "choc . . . choc, choc . . . choc" begins to echo through the branches of the understory. The creature behind this intense and hearty call is in fact a frog of a rather delicate frame. It is merely two inches in length, although its legs stretch out long and gangly. Its toes radiate out like toothpicks, and while each toe tip sports a nifty suction disc, the toes of the rear legs have elaborate webs of membrane stretched between them. The frog's dorsal surface shimmers bright green, while electric-blue bars spread out across the sides of his torso. Just when you think a frog couldn't be more spectacularly colored, he rotates from back to front, revealing two perfectly rounded orbs that are cherry-red and as large as gooseberries. The splendid beauty is a red eyed tree frog (*Agalychnis callidryas*), who has tiptoed onto a wobbly twig in hopes that his amorous call, along with his comely looks, will nab him a mate.

The ardent frog is not alone at all, however, but surrounded by numerous competitors each resonating wildy into the night. He is nevertheless determined to attract a mate, and finally, after two hours of bellowing out the "choc . . . choc" call, his persistence is rewarded. A lovely, three-inch-long female responds by sliding down a ribbon-like tendril of philodendron until she is left dangling but an inch away from him. Not even a second passes before the excited frog jumps off his twig and onto the female. He quickly slides onto her back, wraps his arms around her torso and then interlocks his thumbs close to her sternum. Together, the bonded frogs slither downward from branch to branch, tumbling through the leaves, as if free-falling, to the gleaming pool below. And yet, they maintain total control of their descent. Their arboreal lifestyle is made possible by a magnificent sense of balance, limber body structure, powerful leg muscles, and a remarkable talent for adhering to just about any surface, be it upside down or right side up. Eventually, the lovers reach the pool of water, but their courtship does not come to an end there; in fact, it is just beginning. For a minute they sway there, at the end of an overhanging leaf, intertwined like two tangled strands of Christmas lights, and then make the plunge into the iridescent liquid.

After a few laps, the female wades over to a slab of limestone at the pool's edge. Meanwhile, her mate is on her back, still latched on tight. She kicks her legs a

The red eyed tree frog can become so enraptured during sex that it can be oblivious to predators.

few times, spreading them wide for a second or two, before hauling out of the water and onto a stretch of the strangler fig root protruding at the edge of the pool. Her reason for going to the pool was not to lay her eggs, but to fill her bladder with water. The male's reason for tagging along was to ensure that he gets first dibs on breeding with her. Together, they follow the winding root back to the buttress and then ascend into the branches. They meander laterally from one twig to the next and across a bridge of entangled vines, until they are positioned directly over the pool.

With her mate clasping tight, the female slides beneath the underside of a large leaf. With only her front limbs grasped around a narrow stem, she hangs there, dangling beneath the leaf. The copulating frogs would lose their grip and fall to the ground if it weren't for the powerful vacuum created by the suction cups at the tips of their fingers. After a little bit of fidgeting she is no longer dangling, as she manages to position herself laterally on the underside of the leaf. Now that both frogs are safely in place, the female begins to lay eggs along the soft undersurface of the leaf. The exiting eggs are large and encased in a generous sheaf of gelatinous protein, made all the more thick and gooey by the water she has taken into her bladder. Not only does the clear layer of jelly allow the egg mass to adhere to the underside of the leaf, but it also serves as a protective layer that keeps the embryos moist during their development. As she squeezes out egg after egg, her mate does

his part by covering the fresh ova with his sperm, thus initiating the remarkable formation of new life. After they have finished amplexus, the pair of red eyed tree frogs will leave behind eighty precious embryos, each with the potential of developing into an independent frog.

After approximately eight days of development within the slimy pillow of jelly, the tadpoles will leave their protective glob and enter the aquatic world below. The invitation to be freed from the gelatinous mass will come from a raindrop that will spatter against the leaf. The impact will stimulate the tadpoles clustered underneath to wriggle and squirm, until finally they are able to slide out from the viscous blob. As the rainfall increases in intensity, the water dribbling across the leaf will carry the tadpoles from the shimmering lump to the vein running down its center, until they slither off the drip tip and drop into the pool.

Unfortunately for this cluster of eggs, however, there will be no development into beefy tadpoles, no frolicking in the clear water of the pool, and no metamor-

The parrot snake is remarkably thin for its length. Never mind how I got him to smile.

phosis into red-eyed, tree-climbing adults. Locked in their intimate embrace, the mating frogs were not alone. A stranger was hovering nearby, following them down through the branches and to the leaf where the female deposited her eggs. From the flickering shadows he watched, patiently waiting for the right moment. When both frogs were consumed by passion, the brilliant, emerald-tinted hunter moved in. The stealthy predator is a parrot snake (*Leptophis ahaetulla*), a six-foot-long serpent not much wider than a pencil. But the prowler's target is not the amorous pair. Instead, he craves the copious gobs of fatty, protein-rich eggs flowing from the female's cloaca.

Resembling a vine, the parrot snake hangs dangerously close to the frogs, but to them, he is no more than a floating shadow against the leaf they had perched beneath. Ever so slowly, the serpent creeps in closer and closer, until he manages to sneak in on the preoccupied frogs. Eventually, the parrot snake gets close enough to touch the female's vent with the tip of his snout. As she begins to lay, the snake just opens his mouth and literally drinks up the eggs. The copulating frogs never even look behind them, as every single egg goes directly from the cloaca and into the serpent's belly. Most of the eggs have been swallowed before the male even has a chance to fertilize them. After the frogs have finished mating, the male releases the female from his grasp, and they go their separate ways. Unaware of the tremendous loss of energy and investment, both frogs depart absolutely ignorant of the foul play that has taken place directly under their feet.

AMONG THE TREETOPS

Beyond being a sexual playground and haven, the great strangler tree also provides its tenants with sustenance. Thousands of plump, lush figs, heavy and ready for plucking, hang scattered throughout the branches. Ripe figs are just over an inch long with a "nipple" at one end and are dark purple with yellowish spots.

Many creatures, from toucans to raccoon-like coatis, feed on this nutritious fruit.

One mammal in particular favors these succulent figs. This inquisitive animal wanders through the branches of the strangler's crown, just below the weave of dense foliage of the canopy. During the day he is as sluggish as a stone, but at night he comes alive like an atomic particle. Each evening, well after the sun has been stifled by the boundless firmament of black atmosphere and twinkling stars, the mischievous kinkajou (*Potos flavus*) wakes up and ventures out through the treetops in search of food. Like a monkey, he has a prehensile tail, while his body shape is rather cat-like. His ears are short and bent above a face that resembles a fox, yet with a stubbier snout. The kinkajou's intense eyes appear especially dazzling in the moonlight, and his short coat of glossy fur glistens with a golden hue.

This nimble beast scampering along the narrow branches is in fact a member of the raccoon family (Procyonidae). While your neighborhood raccoon has been raiding garbage cans, his Neotropical and arboreal cousin has successfully carved out a livelihood by tracking down seasonal fruits, sweet nectar, tender shoots, insects, small animals, and eggs. An assorted diet consisting of animal and plant matter qualifies the kinkajou as an omnivore, yet he prefers fruit most of all, with figs placed high on his list of regional delicacies never to be passed up. He gorges on the figs with such greed that his cheeks transform into tightly stretched pouches that seem ready to burst. While to the kinkajou the fig represents just one more soft and squishy object that is both tasty and filling, there is much more to it than that.

Kinkajous prefer to go it alone as they move about the canopy.

Truth be told, the fig is a remarkable fruit that can only be produced through a very specific and complex process involving a most surprising symbiotic partner, a tiny hymenopteran called the agaonid wasp. Both wasp and fig are completely dependent upon each other for reproduction. These unlikely partners share one greater goal: survival.

Life for a fig begins when a near-microscopic female wasp, no more robust than an eyelash, lands on a small, mushroom-shaped, immature fig, called a synconium. She is attracted to the synconium by its scent, and once she has arrived, the minuscule wasp immediately aims to get inside the undeveloped cavern of the fruit. Sealed within the synconium are the male and female flowers, which can only be pollinated by the tiny wasp. The relationship between these two life-forms is so specific that each species of fig has its own unique species of corresponding wasp for pollination. The pregnant wasp enters the fig through a tiny hole the size of the eye of a needle, called an ostiole, covered by densely packed scales. As the wasp squeezes past them, the scales scrape her delicate wings right off, as well as any contaminants, like bacteria and fungus, that she might have transported on her body. In addition to the fertilized ova, the female wasp brings with her pollen that has been stored in sacks along her central body segment, called the thorax. Once inside the synconium, the female fumbles over many of the tightly clustered female flowers (stigma). Her passage causes the pollen to be released from her body, thus allowing the pollination to take place.

Pollen is pressed down into the stigma when the wasp begins probing the florets with her ovipositor, a thin tube at the end of her abdomen that deposits the eggs. Pollination takes place while the female is trying to reach a tiny, cyst-like gall at the base of the floret where she will lay her eggs. Each synconium may host multiple invading females in search of a gall to lay their eggs. Although many females will enter the synconium, none will leave it, for soon after laying their eggs, the females die within the undeveloped fig. Soon the eggs develop into larvae. Think about that the next time you bite into a big, juicy fig! To prevent fig-hungry creatures from eating the fruit, the larvae produce a chemical that prevents the fig from ripening, rendering it unfit for consumption. After about a month passes, the wingless male wasps hatch.

Newly hatched males will often battle each other to the death, leaving only the strongest competitors alive and ready to procreate. Surviving males then go in search of females, who are still developing deep within the florets. Upon discovering a dormant female, the male cuts a hole through the thin wall of the floret and then slips the tip of his abdomen inside. This is when copulation takes place, and after he has passed on his sperm, the male wasp retracts his abdomen and then retreats to the outer core of the fig. Here he begins an arduous excavation of a tunnel to the outer world, which is forever to remain a mystery to him, as males are not destined to reach the outside. The wasp is driven by pure instinct; his goal is to create a passage large enough to allow his impregnated partner to depart the fig unscathed. The ostiole, the opening in the fig through which the mother wasp had to initially squeeze in order to lay her eggs, was so miniscule that she was forced to sacrifice her wings to enter. Her daughter, on the other hand, will need her wings on the outside, if she is to find a home for her ova.

As the male bores his way through to the other side, the carbon dioxide that had built up in the synconium, delaying the emergence of the female, floods the newly dug tunnel and finally gets released from the fruit. Once he has completed the grueling task of cutting through the fibrous layer of fig skin, the industrious digger falls prey to exhaustion and dies soon after. The male leaves behind an impregnated female, who, in a final testament to his ephemeral existence, is oblivious to his presence. The fresh infusion of air from the outside provides a boost to the quiescent female, stimulating her to complete her development and emerge from the sarcophagus-like floret.

Like Juliet rising from her deathly sleep within the dank mausoleum, the gravid wasp awakes. She pulls herself out from the floret and then begins her momentous journey toward the newly excavated channel. As the wasp passes over a bulging field of male florets, fresh pollen is smeared over her slick torso, filling the sacks around her thorax until they are packed tight with the dense powder of pollen grains. As she exits, she may have to chew through the outer skin of the fig where the male left off. He may still be clinging to life, but they will not know each other. Soon she is free from the fig's catacomb and is ready to launch her maiden flight—ironically a first and final voyage for her, yet a new beginning for the next generation of agaonid wasps. Like the Atta ant and the basidiomycete fungus, the Nasutitermes termite and the gastric microbe, the fig and the tiny agaonid wasp are obligated to ensure each other's survival.

Utterly unaware of the complex life history of the mealy fruit, the kinkajou greedily grabs another ripe fig. The gluttonous creature is also oblivious to the fact that he serves as the final stage for the development of future figs. After the mushy balls of fruit are eaten and the nutritious pulp is digested, the kinkajou will defecate, spreading its scat across the landscape and thus serving as a disperser of seeds. In the end, this crude bodily function of the kinkajou, or any other frugivore (fruit-eater) for that matter, is vital to initiating the germination of new strangler fig trees. As the kinkajou continues to gorge on the endless bounty of figs, another hungry creature is slinking in from behind. The beast silently observes the feasting kinkajou, waiting for her turn to indulge. The mysterious creature looming behind a veil of leaves does not yearn for a bellyful of figs, but a bellyful of kinkajou flesh. As the kinkajou slobbers down fig after fig, a deadly feline is hovering close, watching and waiting for the precise moment to pounce.

The stealthy hunter is an ocelot (*Felis pardalis*), an absolutely stunning cat, sporting a pair of bright golden eyes that gleam brilliantly against a marbled coat of black and orange. Ranging in weight from fifteen to thirty-five pounds, the ocelot is a substantially built feline, the third largest cat species living in the Americas, after jaguar and puma. (Pushing up to three hundred and fifty pounds, the jaguar is indeed the largest feline of the New World. It is also the second largest Neotropical carnivore, the highly endangered spectacled bear of South America being the first. At two hundred and fifty pounds, the tawny-colored puma, or mountain lion, closely follows the jaguar in size.) Though smaller than their feline cousins, ocelots are adaptive hunters, inhabiting a variety of ecosystems throughout Central and South America. If there is prey to pursue, be it in the rainforest, flood forest, cloud forest, or open savannah, the ocelot would be one of the chief predators. This lissome cat is a proficient hunter, capable of seizing a variety of quarry, including fish, reptiles, birds, and moderately sized mammals, including deer. Although a

Despite being protected in most countries, the ocelot has been hunted to near-extinction for its pretty pelt.

skillful tree climber, the ocelot is more adept at hunting on the forest floor, where she pounces upon plump, ground-dwelling birds, like the pheasant-like tinamou or the colorful oscillated turkey. Still, the kinkajou feasting in the treetop presents a tempting meal indeed.

Ever so slowly, the ocelot slinks toward the unsuspecting kinkajou and then pauses, her prey within a paw's reach. She is so silent in her approach that the only noise to be heard, aside from the slurping sound of figs being mashed in the kinkajou's overstuffed maw, is the high-pitched shrills of surrounding insects and bats. The kinkajou is now teetering at the thinnest overhang of the branch, while the ocelot is poised just twelve inches behind. If the cat creeps forward any further, she will not have enough surface area to stand upon and will most likely lose her balance. Should she decide to pounce on her target, both hunter and prey will fall from the branches and to the forest floor, possibly to their deaths. So she decides to wait patiently, in hopes that the kinkajou's next move will be to a more stable stretch of branch closer to the trunk. The disciplined cat will not so much as flinch while waiting out the situation. Then, after a few minutes pass, the kinkajou begins to move off, but to a location that is even more precarious than the first. While the kinkajou reaches up and grasps a tangle of hanging foliage, the shadowing hunter instinctively bows down to the level of the narrow branch. Just as the kinkajou begins to pull himself up to the snarl of thorny twigs and leaves, the ocelot leaps forward.

An earsplitting shriek rips through the canopy as the ocelot, her claws hooked deeply into the flesh of the kinkajou's haunch, dangles beneath him. The ocelot is swinging about in an attempt to maintain her grip on the squealing kinkajou, who, with his paws latched onto the hanging bramble, is being stretched downward by the great cat's weight. The ocelot miscalculated her attack and now both creatures are in desperate peril. The kinkajou continues to screech wildly, while the predator sways beneath him, refusing to let go. The strength of the kinkajou begins to wane, as the two fistfuls of foliage start to slip out of his grasp. Soon, there is but a thread-thin tendril of vine suspending both prey and predator. And then it snaps. The pair is sent spiraling downward through the understory, and as both creatures plummet to their deaths, the ocelot releases the kinkajou from her grasping claws. They tumble violently through an onslaught of branches, plunging toward the hard earth below.

The jagged foliage whips against their thrashing bodies while they free-fall to the earth, when both creatures miraculously halt in mid-descent. An outstretched tree limb that had been concealed by many years of epiphytic growth has broken their disastrous fall. Multiple layers of soft moss, wispy lichen, and mounds of bird's nest fern have softened their landing, and although the dramatic drop has left these two quite tattered, they are still in rather good shape, considering the intensity of the ordeal. The kinkajou quickly leaps up from the bowing branch and soon disappears into the canopy, while the ocelot is left behind to gather her wits. As the swaying branch begins to settle, the ocelot regains her equilibrium, and, like the kinkajou before her, she too makes a hasty retreat. Unlike her targeted quarry, the ocelot chooses not to venture above, but to return to solid ground below.

While the ocelot has failed to make a kill in the canopy, there is yet another, more agile feline that wanders over the twisted and slippery branches of the canopy with deadly precision. A willowy predator of elegant design, weighing about eight pounds, she is similar in size to an ordinary house cat. The name of this dexterous feline is the margay (*Felis wiedii*), and she moves as soft as a shadow through a soaring wall of gnarly foliage and serrated snags of timber. All felines seem to possess a certain mystery, but the margay even more so. This cat is quite capable of living out much of her life high above the terra firma in the densely woven canopy, although she will venture down to earth from time to time. She is truly one of the most beautiful cats you will ever set your eyes upon; that is, of course, if you are given the rare privilege of witnessing her striking form.

Like the ocelot, the petite margay has

The margay is hands down the best tree climber of all cats. Its hind feet can rotate completely around!

a plush coat of marbled rosettes sur-rounded by black rings that stand out brightly against a background of tawny fur. While her spotted coat may appear striking to us, it is designed to break up her shape so as to be nearly invisible as she stalks her prey. Yes, the margay is truly exquisite to behold, but for the small-bodied creature lost in sleep, she is more deadly than beautiful. As long as the

---

The margay is truly exquisite to behold, but for the small-bodied creature lost in sleep, she is more deadly than beautiful.

---

prey is not much larger than she is, there is little in the world of arboreal life-forms that the margay will avoid attacking. The diet of this sprightly cat includes insects, frogs, lizards, snakes, mammals (like rats, opossums, squirrels, and small monkeys), and of course birds.

Tonight, the margay has targeted a plump bird nearby, and as she follows her nose through the entangled foliage, she comes upon a keel-billed toucan (*Ramphastos sulfuratus*) fast asleep. With its plumage all fluffed out beneath its colossal bill, the bird appears to be almost as big as the margay. The napping toucan has a lemon-yellow breast, while the rest of its plumage is jet black. The naked skin around its closed eyelids is green, as is much of the toucan's eight-inch-long bill. A chestnut-red streak runs along the upper edge of its bill all the way to the tip. The keel-billed toucan sleeps in the oddest position: He wraps his cumbersome bill around his shoulder until it lines up along the center of his spine. The tail feathers, which are fluffed up like a kitschy fan, fold straight back until they envelop the grand, back-turned bill. For a margay, the discovery of an accessible toucan in deep sleep is a rare treat indeed. The toucan spends much of its life confined to a nest hollowed in an old emergent, so the cat is lucky to find one of these spectacular birds resting out in the open.

The toucan's bill has many uses: It is a pincer for extracting fruit and prey from tight crevices; it is a comb for grooming plumage; it can toss food into the receptive bill of a nesting mate; and it is used as a foil for sparring with competitors. The canoe-shaped bill is surprisingly light for its size, and the toucan wields it with little effort. Unfortunately for this toucan, the bill doesn't do much good against a powerful predator like a margay, especially if the bird is fast asleep. The best defense for the toucan would be to fly from the margay's line of sight before the spry cat lunges forward. But the sneaky feline is just too silent as she swiftly makes her move. The toucan doesn't even have a chance to flutter out a breath before becoming entangled within the barbed paws of the margay. The bird never even knows what hit him. The spine and nerves of the unlucky creature's neck are severed just seconds before he gurgles out a deflated death rattle.

Enthused by her triumphant kill, the margay drags the toucan's corpse up onto a platform of compressed foliage and commences the feast. It takes the hungry cat just ten minutes to pluck away tufts of feathers and peel back the bird's thin, membranous skin before devouring much of its muscle and organs. Now that her belly is full, the margay coils up into a tight ball and quickly falls asleep. As the feline contentedly slumbers away, the black shadows of the night begin to soften in the glow of early morning light.

A NEW DAY

Nearly one hundred feet above the Attas, the forest floor, and the arboreal frogs, up in the canopy, a troop of mantled howler monkeys (*Alouatta palliata*) hangs out. Their territory spans approximately thirteen acres (about the size of seven midtown Manhattan city blocks) and includes the strangler fig, which functions as a home base for the troop, sprouting up directly in the center of their home range. These arboreal primates move through the branches like seasoned trapeze performers. The howler monkey's lanky and flexible forearms are ideally built for swinging, climbing, and suspension. Its back legs are shorter than the front ones but are equally powerful, with dexterous

Howler monkeys are among the largest primates in the Americas. The reddish hair on this guy's neck and hands distinguishes him as a mantled howler.

toes that provide additional grip. A powerful, limb-like prehensile tail aids the howler's talent for skillful maneuvering through the woven gauntlet of vegetation forming the canopy. There are eight members in this particular troop, which consists of one dominant male, four adult females, one adolescent male, and two babies. They are stretched out like sheets of tarpaper over the natural platform of foliage, vines, and intertwining branches. The dense, dark fur covering their bodies is wet from the billows of moist vapor flowing upward, and they are lying in the blazing sun in hopes of drying out a bit. As the sun grows more intense, the howlers escape the glare by sliding past the outer blanket of the canopy's leaves and into the comfortable shade of the understory.

At nearly twenty pounds in weight, the dominant male is the largest member of the troop; the next one in size is a six-year-old female who weighs about fourteen pounds. Tight bonds exist between each member, and the entire troop feeds, sleeps, and moves together. The only real tension lies between the dominant and adolescent males. In fact, they are father and son, but now that the younger of the two is reaching maturity, his father has begun to push him out of the troop. Ever since his mother gave birth to a new daughter three months earlier, the tension induced by his presence has grown even stronger. The adolescent male will often try to appease his father by grooming him or pretending to be much younger in age by behaving childishly or by emitting soft, submissive sounds, in the hopes that his father might not expel him from the only family the young monkey has ever known. Despite all his efforts, however, he eventually will have to abandon the comforts and security to which he has grown accustomed. He soon will head out alone and find a little piece of jungle to call his own.

The howlers lounge around in the branches of the strangler fig, trying to do as little as possible. The younger females are playing with one of the babies, while the other infant suckles away on a warm and comforting breast. For the moment the father and his elder offspring are getting along. To keep the peace, the son is intently picking out bits of dead skin along with the occasional tick from his father's back. The older howler is dozing off, as the adolescent obsesses over every tidbit of alien matter buried deep in his father's fur. Upon extracting a small tick, which is desperately clinging to a long strand of hair, the young male promptly pops the doomed parasite into his mouth and chews it up. Just to keep dear old dad content, the conciliatory son pretends to find another tick that does not exist. His elaborate performance is flawless, as he concentrates on the extraction, examines the tiny scrounger, and then eats the imaginary tick. The youngster is attempting to buy a little more time with the troop by demonstrating that he still plays a useful role within the family unit.

"I TOLD YOU I HEARD A JAGUAR!"

I will never forget the moment when I first heard such a frightful roar; it echoed throughout the forest like the sound of a great emergent crashing to the earth. I was seventeen at the time, and out on an early morning jaunt through the Belizean jungle. The serenity of the surrounding forest was shattered by the loudest growl that I had ever heard. It was an endless, deafening roar that drilled deep into my skull. I froze in my tracks as the terrible howl continued. My heart was racing along with my legs as I sprinted back to the local Mayan village as fast as I could. Huffing and puffing, I rolled into my friend Maurizio's thatched hut. Staring at my startled and tattered form, he observed, "Hey man, you look like you just saw a ghost."

"Worse!" I responded, "It was a jaguar, and if I hadn't high-tailed it out of there, he probably would have gotten me." Intrigued by the account of my near-death experience, Maurizio insisted that we go out and track down the great predator. Now, had I known what he knew, I probably would have refused the offer, called it a night under the belief that I had barely escaped the jaws of death, and been a better man for it. But like the numbskull that I was back then, I gullibly went along with the plan. After Maurizio mustered up a few more men for the trek, we headed out in search of the elusive beast that had nearly taken my life.

Grooming is not unique to howlers and is common among many primate species. For monkeys and apes, grooming is an essential behavior that builds trust, strengthens friendship, and diffuses tension in a close-knit community of highly intelligent, social creatures.

Although foraging for food is a priority for the troop, nearly seventy percent of the day is spent sleeping. This time of the day, when the temperature rises, is a fairly sedate period for the howlers. A few monkeys are eating freshly ripened figs, while others are chewing on the soft, newly developed leaves. Howlers prefer to eat younger leaves, which tend to be

It took us no more that fifteen minutes to bushwhack our way to the spot where I encountered the ferocious cat. Maurizio searched along the ground for tracks but saw none. "Where exactly did you see the jaguar?" he asked. "Well . . . um, I didn't actually witness the mighty cat with my own eyes, but I certainly heard it. It was big, it was close, and it definitely was a jaguar." In response to my defensive retort, Maurizio muttered, "A jaguar, you say? Hmm, interesting." Now I was beginning to believe that Maurizio and the few lads that had joined up were in doubt of my allegation. Then, the roaring happened again, but this time, thankfully, I was not alone. As the strident series of roars thundered loudly, I yelled out, "You see, you see, I told you I heard a jaguar!"

Every time I remember this story I wish that there indeed had been a jaguar to drag me off to my demise, so that I could avoid the extreme dose of humiliation I was about to endure. The awe-inspiring growls coming from the forest were soon drowned by a very different kind of roar that came not from a jaguar but from Maurizio and his mates. They were cut up in a fit of hysterical laughter. Maurizio managed to interrupt his rib-tickling tizzy to tell me to look up, and when I did, my eyes set upon a most horrifying site. Slung over the branches forty feet above our heads there was indeed a roaring beast, but not a jaguar. The creature hollering down at us with great fury was in fact nothing more than a howler monkey. In the end, my life had been spared the deadly clutch of the mighty jaguar, but my pride . . . well, that was another matter.

suppler, more nutritious, easier to digest, and lower in toxins (many trees manufacture poisons as they mature to prevent herbivory) than older leaves. Except for the rasping call of a passing keel-billed toucan and the constant buzz of the irritating flies, which incessantly swarm over the mostly slumbering troop, all is quiet.

Then, a great crash of ripping leaves and snapping twigs echoes within the perimeter of the troop's territory, just a few hundreds yards beyond the towering strangler. The clamor of crackling foliage is soon followed by a most menacing roar, so fierce in delivery that the alarming sound reverberates for a mile throughout the treetops. Instantly, all eight howlers snap up from their languid poses. Mothers quickly secure their babies, as the dominant male and his eldest son dart to the top of the strangler's crown to catch a glimpse of the intruder.

Swiftly and tenaciously, the troop races up to the pinnacle of bowing timber radiating from the strangler's crown. They look down to discover an invading clan of howlers consisting of five individuals that have swung and swooped their way to the ends of a few outstretched limbs of the strangler. With elbows locked and all four limbs defiantly erect, the dominant male of the resident troop straddles an arching branch and then angrily bounces up and down. A thunder of cracking leaves echoes as he thrashes about, then with chin held high, he bellows boldly up to the sky. His vociferous roar resonates from his lungs like an exploding bagpipe. He generates his tremendous howl by narrowing his windpipe, while simultaneously forcing air through it. The pressurized air flows into a chamber in his throat where the sound is generated. The flush of air expands his vocal chamber, which causes his hyoid bone at the base of his tongue to vibrate and his resonance muscles to contract until sound is created. In order to create the perfect sound, the roaring patriarch balloons his cheeks and purses his lips while pushing the air through. The adolescent male joins in and proudly hollers at his father's side. A few of the females howl as well, although due to a much smaller voice chamber, they emit a roar that is much softer and less daunting.

The invading troop takes heed of the boisterous howls coming from the locals. By vigorously sounding out, howler monkeys use their powerful call as a vocalized marker to establish and defend territory. In essence, the call of these primates diffuses conflict between neighboring howler monkey communities by reducing the need for physical combat. The raucous roar of howlers serves as both shield and sword. If you ever have the good fortune of being in the Neotropical rainforest and should hear the blistering call of this great primate, enjoy, because there is nothing more exciting for the ear than the menacing growl of a howler monkey.

OPPORTUNITY, OPPORTUNITY!

While much of the canopy surrounding the strangler fig tree is rather thick, allowing very little sunlight to penetrate through, there is an area of forest just outside the strangler where the canopy is broken. The gap formed when a lofty emergent fell to the earth and took other trees to the ground with it. Some had been smashed to the ground when the falling emergent collided with them; a few other neighboring trees, connected to the doomed giant by the intricate network of strong vines, were pulled down as the tremendous tower of timber collapsed. But the awesome formation of this gap was marred by the destruction of five ancient emergents, along with a multitude of creatures who went down with them. Although the gash in the canopy brought about the demise of residential wildlife, the formation of the substantial puncture ultimately served as an invitation for new life to colonize the territory. The rupture in the dense canopy foliage allows light to flood the forest floor. The introduction of sunlight into the previously dark area stimulates the germination of dormant seeds that have been waiting many years for this opportunity to sprout. It gives us the opportunity to witness evolution.

The organisms that first capitalize on the formation of this gap are true pioneers; they arrive by wind, on the backs of birds and insects, or as latent seeds trapped within the soil bank. While some of these plant species—high-quality trees like mahogany, ceiba, Santa Maria, tropical cedar, and ironwood—are slow growing, others develop remarkably fast; heliconia, palmetto palms, philodendrons, acacia, and passion flowers are all swift to mature. As new colonies of plants establish themselves in the gap, other lifeforms quickly follow. Butterflies, bees, and humming birds arrive in search of nectar. Bats, birds, and small mammals, hungry for fruits and seeds, find their way there as well. Of course, there are many predators, like the various raptors, pole-cats, frogs, spiders, praying mantis, lizards, and snakes, who find the newly formed opening to be an excellent hunting ground. Within just a few months, the gap transforms from a traumatized tract void of life into a thriving jungle, teeming with a cornucopia of life-forms. Soon, the chaotic amalgamation of life in the clearing has more species of plants and animals than the pristine expanse of old-growth forest that had stood there prior to the collapse and formation of the gap. Competition between life-forms in the gap is intense, and success for many of the first colonists is defined by how fast they can grow and how quickly they can re-produce. If a colonizing species is capable of quickly producing a high quantity of vi-able offspring, its chances of establishing itself as a residential species increase dra-matically.

One of the first colonizing plants to make its mark in the newly formed gap is a cecropia tree. The seed from which this cecropia has sprung laid buried in the soil bank for nearly two years. Through chaos and disturbance comes life, and soon after the gap formed, the influx of intense sun-light upon the humus caused the tiny ce-cropia seed trapped within to take root. The cecropia grows at a phenomenal rate, developing from seedling to skinny pole tree in just a few months. With the passing of each year, the thriving tree adds another eight feet to its height. Just three years after its germination, the cecropia stands nearly twenty-five feet tall! The long, leafless trunk of the tree towers above the entwined network of vegeta-tion. Despite its height, the diameter of the cecropia is approximately eight inches at its base, narrowing to about three inches at the crown. Aside from three, six-foot-long wobbly branches at the top, the cecropia's trunk is naked. The ce-cropia's large, palmate leaves have a radius of approximately two feet. The floppy leaves, which project in clusters off a thin stalk at the end of each branch, are spher-ical in shape, with eight to ten lobes radi-ating from the center of each leaf.

Because of the cecropia's success, many other species of wildlife prosper.

MIND THE GAP

Although life in the foliage clearing may appear serene, there is a battle underway within the verdant mesh of flora. A young forest of sun-hungry plants shoots up to the sky in a race to grow as fast and as tall as possible. The first trees to spring up and establish a crown of dense foliage end up shadowing the vegetation growing beneath them. Trapped under these expanding umbrellas of foliage, the sun-loving plants are inevitably choked out, leaving the triumphant competitors with more space to grow. For the moment, the cecropia towers victoriously above the surrounding vegetation, but hidden within the low-lying herb layer, hovering less than a foot above the ground, are sprigs of shade-tolerant flora that will continue to grow slowly and steadily over time. After a decade or two, these shoots will transform into trees themselves and will eventually tower over the cecropia, which grows more slowly as it ages, causing it to perish along with much of the remaining sun-greedy vegetation. After sixty years, the gap will have been long since filled in, the fast-growing pioneers extirpated by the giant emergents. Although the early colonists will no longer thrive there, the seeds that they have left behind are tucked away in the black earth and moist humus. The dormant seeds will linger patiently, until one day a tree falls to the earth once more, opening another gap in the canopy. Precious light will flood in, which will induce the seeds to rise up from the wet darkness and reach up to the light, as the cycle of life begins anew.

One creature in particular, the three-toed sloth (*Bradypus variegatus*), benefits greatly from the presence of the cecropia. Perched sedately on the bowing branches of the cecropia crown, he looks like some sort of outlandish aberration, a hybrid of a monkey, a koala, and a bear. In truth, the three-toed sloth shares no phylogenic ancestry with any of these creatures, but is in fact a member of the mammalian order of Xenarthra, the same group that includes armadillos and anteaters. The three-toed sloth has a most curious build. This animal possess many intriguing characteristics, but I think his most unique attribute lies in the fact that he is the least active

Just look at that face!

and is externally earless. The sloth's blunt muzzle is slightly canine-like with a long, upturned grin that stretches from cheek to cheek. His small brown eyes are set widely apart, and they also appear to be smiling. At the end of each of his long and powerful forearms are three, four-inch-long arched claws, shaped like meat hooks. His hind limbs, which are also equipped with sickle-shaped talons, are half as long as his forelimbs. A blunt tail a few inches in length is buried under a mane of coarse fur. For the most part, his rather shaggy pelage is tan in color, with the exception of a wide swath of mossy green dappled across his back. You can tell this one is a male because of the small, orangey yellow patch with a black stripe in the center of his back. At just under three feet in body length, and a total weight of around ten pounds, the three-toed sloth is not very large, but if you're looking for the cutest mammal living in the Neotropics, this guy comes in a close second to the silky anteater.

mammal on Earth! The sloth is a wonderfully odd-looking creature, ranking as one of my all time favorites. Now, if you've ever wondered where George Lucas or Jim Henson got their inspiration to create the fantastical creatures in many of their films—an Ewok, for example—then look no further than a three-toed sloth.

The small head of the three-toed sloth has a somewhat heart-shaped face

Ever so slowly, the sloth reaches up with his long claws, pulls down a fresh cecropia leaf, and folds it into his mouth. Nearly five minutes pass before he finishes chewing up the leaf and swallows it. All his movements appear to occur in slow motion, as he continues to feed upon the endless supply of cecropia leaves. His metabolism is so slow that it will take up to seven days to digest a bellyful of leaves. He in fact has the slowest metabolic rate of any mammal of this size. Internally, he runs at a snail's pace, and in order to keep himself properly energized, he basks lethargically in the sun's unremitting warmth to fire up his metabolism.

The body temperature of the sluggish Xenarthran functions at a near-reptilian rate, and when he sleeps at night, his body temperature drops twelve degrees in an effort to conserve energy. With regard to sleep, he spends twenty hours a day doing just that. He is truly arboreal, spending nearly ninety-eight percent of his life in the treetops. Only when it is absolutely necessary will he slowly descend to the forest floor and crawl to his next location. There are few sights more pathetic than that of a sloth crawling across the flat earth. His muzzle hovering humbly just an inch above ground, with his limbs splayed and thrashing about awkwardly, the sloth drags himself across the ground. If need be, he can also swim, but to see a sloth at his best is to witness him sling from branch to liana, as he slips through the woven greenery as adroitly as any nimble primate could, albeit much slower.

After he finishes his salad of cecropia leaves, the sloth contentedly naps away with his back exposed to the bright sun. While the morning rays gaze down onto his bristly coat, a few of the individual hairs begin to twitch, ever so slightly, beneath the greenish hue that is spread across the fur of his back. If we zoomed down through the thicket of fur, we'd discover that the greenish tinge is not hair pigment, but a rare species of algae, which grows nowhere else but within the sloth's dense pelage. In fact, this minute environment houses a plethora of tiny creatures, all of which are found nowhere else on Earth but here. Scampering along the shafts of hair is a variety of beetles, moths, and mites, which, like the algae, are unique to the sloth's densely woven fleece. So not only does the fur serve the sloth, but it also functions as a miniaturized ecosystem. The life-forms inhabiting the sloth's coat aren't mere freeloaders. The algae, for one, provides its sluggish host with camouflage. By crawling incredibly slowly, while simultaneously blending in with the neighboring foliage, the sloth improves his ability to evade capture from predators, like harpy eagles. When the sloth is grooming his fur, he ingests an enzyme that is produced by the mites and which enhances the digestion of fibrous plant material. This relationship between the sloth and the biota inhabiting his fur is just another instance of the bonding between unlikely partners that leads to a more prosperous life for all involved.

The sloth hunches against the pole of bowing cecropia contentedly, until a bubbling in his gut, along with the pressure sensation in his bowels, causes him to stir. Slowly, his head rotates, his eyes blink, and he begins to methodically unhook each claw from the crown of branches be-

fore beginning his descent. To give you an understanding of just how slow a sloth is, you have to realize that it takes the beast twenty seconds to simply rotate his head ninety degrees, nine seconds to blink his eyes, and just over a minute to readjust his posture for his descent down the tree. Gradually, he cautiously continues to move one limb past the other, like an unbelievably slow-motion fireman inching down a pole, until after twenty minutes of downward climbing, the sloth finally reaches the bottom of the tree. He hangs there for another five minutes, strapped to the bole of the cecropia, with his scruffy behind hovering a few inches above the leaf litter. Then, he moves further down, until his stumpy tail begins to compress the leaves and eventually penetrates the mulch-like layer of decaying matter. Then the sloth raises his rump off the ground an inch or two and begins to defecate into the impression left behind by his tail. His eyes wince as he concentrates, and after ten minutes have passed, he finishes pinching out his warm morsel of scat. Upon completing his movement, the sloth commences the slow journey back up to the cecropia's crown.

You're probably wondering, why all the effort to take a simple crap? Why doesn't he just aimlessly expel his bowels up in the canopy like all the birds, monkeys, and other arboreal creatures do? Well, you will be relieved, no pun intended, to know that the sloth does not need to defecate every day. In fact, because his metabolism runs at such a slow rate, he only needs to pinch one out once every seven to nine days! According to one theory, the sloth implants his scat near the root system of the cecropia in order to fertilize the very tree he feeds upon.

As the sloth slowly graduates up the cecropia trunk, a slender four-foot-long vine bends toward the interior of a neighboring shrub. The straw-thin vine waves as if bowing to a soft breeze, while continuing to slip into the twisted mesh of

tendrils and twigs. The front end of the supple vine resembles a lance with a needle-like twig projecting from the tip. Indeed, this is no gaunt liana, but a Mexican vine snake (*Oxybelis aeneus*), and the

The forelimbs of two-toed sloths end in two large curved claws, while their hind limbs have three claws, which come in handy in self-defense. They are quite different from their three-toed relatives: They're nocturnal, a little less flexible, and larger, being a bit longer than two feet and weighing up to twenty pounds. Like their relatives, however, they carry algae on their pelage.

This snake is so vine-like in appearance that both predator and prey often pass him by without notice.

serpent is an efficient hunter, with lizards and frogs making up much of his prey. Hanging along the top jaw at the back of his mouth is a set of rear fangs, capable of delivering venom potent enough to paralyze a gecko. At the moment, though, the vine snake is not on the hunt, but is attempting to avoid becoming prey. At least a third of his body is jetting out from a tangle of branches, as he tries his best to blend in. If the branch that he is dangling from sways just a little, so does he. Even an ant crawling over his face does not cause him to flinch. Despite the serpent's masterful attempts to meld with the tangled background of vegetation, his cryptic cover has been revealed to two other creatures. They have already grown curious about his presence and decide to test whether he indeed is just a branch . . . or a tasty treat!

thread-thin shoot jetting out from the pointed snout is his forked tongue.

The purplish gray scales running from the top of his head to the tip of his tail are stacked like shingles, while the flat scales running from his chin and along his lengthy belly are cream colored. The elegant serpent is equipped with large eyes, perfectly positioned upon his head for excellent depth of vision, an important trait for maneuvering through the obstacle course of branches, thorns, and foliage inundating his habitat. The vine-mimicking

To the vine snake, the creatures that are looming so dangerously close seem gigantic, yet they belong to the second smallest species of primate living in Costa Rica, squirrel monkeys (*Saimiri sciureus*). Whether scampering through the canopy, understory, or across the forest floor, be it in a gallery of ancient forest or in an overgrown patch of jungle, squirrel monkeys are generalists, capable of thriving in a variety of habitats. Balancing now upon the bow of a drooping vine that splices through the center of the vine snake's camouflaging shrub, the primates are poised to make a move. The two alert squirrel monkeys are indeed similar in size and color to their namesakes. Each squirrel monkey weighs no more than a pound and a half, while standing approximately fifteen inches tall, head to toe. The fluffy fur on their bellies has a whitish tone, while silver, tan, and gray tint the coarser pelage on their backs. Unlike the howlers, the long tail of the squirrel monkey is not prehensile but serves to enhance the primate's balance during climbing from branch to branch. Squirrel monkeys are a gregarious species, and the two prowling individuals that have slinked their way to the interior of the shrub belong to a substantial troop of twenty.

Squatting along the sulking liana, the curious monkeys glare intently at the pur-

The squirrel monkey is the second smallest species of primate in Costa Rica. The smallest is the chipmunk-sized rufous-naped tamarin (*Saguinus geoffroyi*).

plish vine as they try to get a fix on the situation. Usually, squirrel monkeys have an aversion to snakes and will screech in terror upon stumbling across one. If approached by a large snake, such as a Boa constrictor, the monkeys will rattle the branches loudly around the invading serpent in an attempt to either drive it away or to let the powerful snake know that they are well aware of his presence and will watch his every move—sometimes a vulnerable creature can avoid attack if the predator comes to think that the prey will outwit it. Although squirrel monkeys will occasionally hunt small lizards, it is extremely rare for them to prey on snakes, even small ones. Much of their diet consists of fruit, seeds, shoots, tender foliage, sap, insects, and bird eggs. For some reason, though, the monkeys are fascinated by this serpent, who is doing his very best to remain undetected.

The snake stays stock-still, while one of the monkeys slips off the vine and onto a branch running parallel to the petrified snake. He remains rigid, right up to the moment when the nimble fingers of the monkey's outstretched hand are within seconds of grasping his scaly tail. As with other primates, it is the nature of the squirrel monkey to explore. It learns to survive and prosper through the process of discovery. This inquisitive monkey plans to find out what the creature is, yet it is equally cautious, reaching out warily and slowly. Then, just when one of the primate's digits hesitantly touches the odd vine, the stiff serpent instantly breaks free from his rigid stance and whirls wildly around, until he is facing the monkey snout to snout. Startled by the snake's reaction, the probing monkey leaps backwards and blurts out a menacing shrill. Both primates retreat quickly to an extending branch, but the snake refuses to give up as he levitates toward the monkeys. The furious serpent has inflated his neck like a balloon—his jaw unlocks and his long muzzle snaps open. His gaping mouth is stretched open at a ninety-degree angle, revealing a glossy wet flesh so deeply lavender in color, it appears almost black. But it is all for show. In truth, the vine snake is absolutely harmless, but the startled squirrel monkeys don't know that. They have gotten more than they bargained for, and they scamper off into the forest to reunite with their troop. It doesn't take long for the vine snake to settle down. He slithers deeper toward the shrub's center, until he eventually dissolves into a tangle of twigs and leaves.

Aside from the vine snake, there is another serpent with exceptional camouflage. But unlike his thin, vine-mimicking cousin, this snake has no need to bluff. This beautiful serpent, which masterfully blends in with the surrounding mosses and lichens, is the eyelash viper (*Bothriechis schleglii*). It is a mild-mannered snake that would much rather merge with the verdant background than confront an adversary. If it needs to lash out, however, the eyelash viper is capable of delivering a deadly bite. When hunting birds and small mammals, this viper detects them with heat-sensing pits beneath its nostrils. The serpent comes in a wide variety of morphing colorations, including banana yellow, moss green, and copper red. This stunning snake is named for the tiara of raised scales cresting the top of each eye. The viper rarely descends to the forest floor; it is utterly arboreal in design, even sporting a prehensile tail. The squirrel monkeys, busied with the vine snake, don't even notice the eyelash viper that has been hidden nearby all the while, dangling from a branch above their heads.

The eyelash viper is one of the smallest and most dangerous poisonous snakes in Central America—but it's not aggressive.

Luckily for the monkeys, they did not detect him. Had they attempted to bother the eyelash viper, there would have been no bluffing, but instead a deadly strike!

BACK AT BASE CAMP

Sunlight sifts through the morning mist like laser beams cutting into smoke. At the base of the strangler fig we find that the male strawberry poison dart frog is still hovering close to his treasured clutch of eggs. Anxiously swirling inside each translucent sphere is a plump and healthy tadpole, eager to break free. Their dependable father has stood by them since fertilization, and now that seven days have passed, they are just moments away from hatching. Throughout the eggs' development both parents have been attending to the clutch. Whenever the father felt that the eggs were getting a bit dry, he would keep them moist by urinating on them. No, he's not a bad parent. Rather, this complex behavior is just one of the many examples of the quality of parental care that these fantastic little frogs provide for their offspring. Finally, the efforts of both parents are paying off as the first tadpole bursts from the elastic capsule that has surrounded it for a week. This moment marks the beginning of the deeper investment that these Lilliputian parents are prepared to make to ensure the welfare of their progeny.

The emerging tadpole quickly responds to the cues given by its father and squirms towards the parent. Meanwhile, the father hunkers down, until the tadpole slides onto his back. The frog produces a sticky mucous from his skin glands, which allows the tadpole to adhere to its parent's slimy back. Ever so gently, the father carries the vulnerable tadpole, piggyback-style, through the branches of the lower understory, until he finally arrives at an epiphytic plant, called a bromeliad. Resembling the bundled leaves of a pineapple top, the bromeliad possesses a funnel-shaped cavity within the dense spiral of its prickly foliage. The tightly bound leaves form a cone-shaped crater in the center of the bromeliad, where a five-ounce pool of rainwater has gathered over time. After transporting the tadpole to the bromeliad, the devoted father carefully slips his larva into the water. As the tadpoles continue to hatch one after the other, they are transported to different pools of water scattered throughout the frogs' home range. Not every tadpole will get its own bromeliad, but by dispersing their offspring, the parents decrease competition and stress amongst the tadpoles, thus also reducing the opportunities for cannibalism.

As the tadpoles develop within their protective nurseries over the course of a month and a half, their mother will make frequent visits to provide her offspring with nourishment. Most people never think of frogs as dedicated parents, considering them primitive and unremarkable. But these extraordinary little frogs actually feed their offspring in a way that is similar in concept to mammalian milk production. The female frog knows where each tadpole has been carefully concealed, whether singularly or in small groups, and upon each visit she brings with her a life-fortifying tribute, which she has generated from her own flesh and blood.

The female strawberry poison dart frog is making her first visit to the tadpoles that have been spread about in bromeliad nurseries around the massive tree. Her first trek takes her along a low-lying branch, where a tadpole eagerly awaits its mother's arrival. The petite frog climbs up a slope of serrated, spear-shaped leaves, until she arrives at a funnel of water concealed in the center of the bromeliad. Sensing the parent's arrival, the newly hatched larva begins to swim purposefully in a tight circle, with repeated interruptions of bobbing and sinking. The mother promptly turns about and lowers down her vent, until it breaks through the surface of the water. The tadpole, its body rigid and vibrating, aligns its head to the mother's cloaca. This is the offspring's way of begging its mother for food, and the ritualistic performance stimulates her to capitulate. She responds by plopping an unfertilized egg into the cone of shallow water. The tadpole swims up to the egg, voraciously rips through its jelly capsule and then sucks out the fatty yolk. The mother will leave an additional egg or two, and then move on to her next offspring. Throughout the tadpoles' lengthy metamorphosis, their dedicated mother will provide them with many dozens of fresh and nutritious ova. Personally, I am always humbled by this example of parental investment. We tend to regard a process where a female organism physiologically manufactures sustenance, such as breastmilk, for her offspring as a uniquely mammalian experience. But here we have what some might consider a "primitive" or "evolutionarily conservative" organism, doing exactly the same thing as the more sophisticated life-forms. The female strawberry poison dart frog sustains her offspring by producing nourishment in her body and surrendering to them valuable eggs, the manufacture of which must be vary taxing on her well-being, yet she does so nonetheless.

Not far from where the maternal frog feeds her young, another sort of mother has been multiplying by the thousands. Nearly six weeks have passed since the Atta queen departed an overpopulated colony, driven by instinct to begin a new life as the matriarch of her own subterranean metropolis. She flew many hundreds of feet through the understory, until finally landing upon the forest floor. She beat the tremendous odds stacked against her by being successfully impregnated before digging her way to a new home beneath the soggy earth. It is here she carried the precious fungus, fostering its growth, in order to bring a new generation of leaf cutters into the world. At nearly one inch long, she is the best her species has to offer, a quintessential survivor whose ultimate success is measured by her ability to ensure that the genetic lineage unique to her kind is carried forth to the next generation.

As time passes, life within the Atta city continues to prosper. Steadily, over the past month or so, the population of Attas has increased at a dramatic rate, as new members of this hymenopteran commune fulfill their predestined roles. In the past few weeks bands of foraging Attas have begun to venture out from the dark chambers of the city and up to the world of light. They go out in search of the fodder needed to nourish the life-sustaining fungus thriving deep within the bowels of the city. Finally, the population of workers has grown so large, that they are now ready to embark on their first great expedition.

The queen tends to her fungus, which sustains the colony.

A battalion of ants, twenty thousand strong, has gathered in formation at the rim of the great grotto. Imagine a six-foot-tall anthill, filled with a network of fifteen-foot-long tunnels, and you begin to get the picture. Hundreds of Attas are now piling up at the main entrance to the underground city, while they wait for the command to march forward into the forest. The awesome Atta campaign will launch upon receiving the signal to advance, but for now the ants just wait. The impressive passageway, nearly eight inches in diameter, has been constructed by thousands of excavators for this very purpose, to allow the great contingent of foragers to enter and exit. (Little life was lost in the making of these great tunnels; if any of the diggers became stuck during construction, rescue crews would've been

The Atta soldier is protected by the puny minimas.

like you to listen to a certain musical composition that captures the moment perfectly. Go out and buy *The Planets* by Gustav Holst, and play the part called "Mars, the Bringer of War," as you continue to read.

The swathe of Attas is approximately twenty ants wide and will stretch for at least a quarter of a mile. As the ants continue flowing out of the nest, it seems that there is no end in sight. The foraging brigade of workers is made up of three very distinct castes. There are the tiny minimas, which, at one-sixteenth of an inch, are the smallest caste. Then there are the medias, about a third of an inch in size. Finally, there are the colossal soldiers, or maximas, who measure in at a whopping three-quarters of an inch in length! Despite their differences in size, no one caste is more important than the other, for all the Attas, whether tiny minimas or mega soldiers, equally serve the colony. The expanding trail of shimmering Attas flows through the forest, until it arrives at the buttress of the giant strangler fig. With only a chemical trail to lead the way, the

sent to excavate them.) Just as the sun begins to set and the haze of the understory grows golden beneath the fading light, the order to move out is given, and the great wave of Attas presses forward. The marching order is delivered in the form of a chemical message, a specific pheromone that tells the ants when to move and where to go. Now, before you read any further, this is what I want you to do: In order to really appreciate the massive scale of this campaign, I would

ATTAS, ATTACK!

On numerous occasions, while lost in the observation of an animal or a plant, I have found myself standing directly on a trail of foraging Attas. Instead of going around me, they would inevitably crawl up my shoes, onto my legs, and then attack without mercy. Usually the painful sensation of biting Attas hits all at once, and by then it's too late to avoid conflict with the ornery buggers. I will never forget one notorious encounter with Attas while I was giving a lecture to a handful of students. In the middle of spouting out some gibberish about tree frogs, an intense, fiery pain shot up both my legs. The excruciating wave was so powerful, that for a brief moment, it felt as though my heart was about to burst. If I remember correctly, my response to the attack began thus: "Okay guys, I want you to look closely at the suction cups of this particular hylid [tree frog]. What you should notice is that . . . Oh my God! Owee, owee, owee!!!!!!! Get 'em off! For the love of God, get 'em off!"

The students didn't know what to make of my hysterical fit, until a few seconds later, when they too were screaming in similar fashion. We were quick to kick off our shoes and peel away our socks, as we frantically attempted to pluck off the minute assailants. I probably had over a hundred nipping ants scattered across my squirming body. They had crawled into my socks and were biting the skin under my toenails. I also had to lose a pair of shorts in a hurry, since the Attas made their way up my legs and into my crotch! It took me nearly half an hour to get rid of them all. Often, when I attempted to pull one away from my skin, the ant's thorax would twist off, leaving behind a decapitated head that was still enthusiastically chewing away. The soldiers were the worst, because they had mandibles as big as rose thorns, and when they latched on, it felt like I was getting a piece of skin pinched off by toenail clippers.

By the way, there is a fascinating fact regarding the massive mandibles of soldier ants: A few indigenous tribes in South America actually use clasping ant mandibles as sutures for closing up a wound. To do so, an individual would pick up a large soldier ant and hook each mandible through the corresponding flaps of lacerated skin. Then, the torso of the ant would be twisted free from its head, causing the jaw to contract, thus pulling the skin together. Now, unless you have a strong aversion to good old catgut, I recommend you leave the skin stitching to the docs in the ER, and let the soldier ants move on their merry way.

streaming ribbon ascends the mighty tree. All creatures, from butterflies to large lizards, scamper out of the path of the invading Attas. Although the ants have no interest in hunting insect or animal prey, if they come across a misguided creature emanating an odor that comes across as foreign to them, they will assume that the wayward life-form is an enemy and will most likely attack. One tiny ant may not seem like much, but to be covered by them as they attack in unison is an entirely different matter, which, depending on your size and constitution, may have serious consequences. The ants will stop at nothing to get where the chemically laced trail tells them to venture.

The line of ants climbs up the knobby twist of bark with little effort, with all of them, regardless of size or caste, marching side by side in the collective ascension along the strangler's massive trunk. A troop of eleven capuchin monkeys romps through the branches of the strangler as the ants pass on by. Capuchins (*Cebus capucinus*) are the very same organ-grinding monkeys we see in movies. Mind you, they are much more content leading a wild and free existence, as opposed to being dressed up like overstuffed bellboys, peddling for nickels. Capuchins are nearly twice the size of squirrel monkeys. The light tan fur over much of the capuchin's body is shaggy and thick, and it sports a dark furry cap. The face is, for the most part, hairless, and the middle of the upper lip appears cleft. The troop lingers in the crown of the strangler for just a bit, but most of the figs have either been eaten or fallen to the ground. The few figs still clinging to the tree are mostly rotten, so the troop of monkeys moves on to try its luck elsewhere.

As they sling across a bridge of braided lianas connected to a neighboring emergent, the agile primates come across a small *Boa constrictor*. The Boa is on the prowl for prey, but at just fifteen inches in length, the month-old snake is much too small to tangle with a capuchin. Not only is the Boa out of his league, his life may be in jeopardy, should the capuchins feel at

Capuchins are named after the rounded cap of fur on the top of their heads, which resembles the tonsure of a Capuchin monk.

pent, but the last one to follow notices the Boa. The capuchin curls up his lips in a menacing grin, exposing his nasty-looking canines to the snake. The monkey jumps up and down on the vines in agitation, but the snake just withdraws further into the crevice, until it is well out of reach. Realizing that there is little he can do, the capuchin scampers after the rest of his kin, and the entire troop soon disappears into the canopy. Had the Boa been older, wiser, and bigger, he would have taken advantage of his excellent camouflage and patiently waited until the little monkey had passed. At the right moment, he would have lunged out and grabbed a hold of it. He would have coiled around the helpless monkey, squeezing tighter and tighter each time the animal exhaled, until he finally asphyxiated it. Once the monkey was lifeless, the hungry Boa would have swallowed it whole. But that scenario remains just a dream to be enacted once the Boa grows up.

all threatened. The snake pulls himself into a small cavity between two of the twisted vines and then nervously waits for the monkeys to pass. The first ten monkeys amble and swing over the cable-like vines without paying any heed to the ser-

Meanwhile, two tiny frogs sit nearby the great strangler, watching the progres-

Boa constrictors kill their prey by suffocating it.

geous nonetheless. Unlike the red bodies and blue legs of their parents, these brand-new creatures are maroon in color, and it will be many months before they take on the size and color of their adult parents.

Beneath the dappled glow of sunset, the glistening froglets sparkle like amethyst crystals. They are squatting down in a crook, where the branch meets the tree, patiently waiting for the procession of Attas to pass. Then, one of the froglets sneaks up to the line of Attas and gulps down one of the minimas. The tiny ant won't go down without a fight, and bites into the froglet's tender lip. The youngster spits out the minima as quickly as he swallowed her. But the froglet is still determined to make a meal of the ant, so he hops forward once again, and then chomps down on the minima, this time swallowing the ant headfirst. The ant wriggles for just a few moments within the froglet's cramped gut but soon expires. Upon witnessing the success of her sibling, the other froglet also tries the role of a predator as she creeps toward the trail

sion of the leaf cutters; in less than a minute the Attas have advanced a quarter of the way up the tree. The teeny amphibians are the newly formed strawberry poison dart frogs that have just emerged from the dark and wet sanctuary of a bromeliad. At just over a quarter of an inch in length, the froglets are hardly visible to the naked eye, but they are gorof streaming ants and picks off another minima. The froglets avoid being overtaken by the river of Attas by carefully maneuvering along the edge of streaming ants, and after a few more minimas each, the froglets go their separate ways.

The Attas, on the other hand, stick together as they flow up the trunk of the strangler. Upon reaching the canopy, the Attas disperse throughout the branches. Minimas scamper closely behind medias and maximas, as they all head out in search of fresh fodder. After arriving at a newly formed leaf, a media ant shuffles across its shiny surface and then punctures the leaf with one of its serrated mandibles. With both mandibles slicing methodically back and forth, the ant scissors out a section of the leaf a quarter of an inch in diameter. The media is careful not to drop the segment while hauling it up to the stem. After hoisting the leaf segment straight up, like an unfurled sheet of sailcloth, the ant begins her long descent from the strangler fig tree. A nearby minima is quick to crawl over to the departing media, and climb up the larger ant's back, until she is teetering on top of the leaf. The minima will now take on the role of a soldier as she protects both the leaf and the ant beneath.

Within five minutes, thousands of ants of all castes have positioned themselves throughout the dense blanket of foliage. Some minimas are helping medias to pull back recently cut leaf segments, while many of the maximas cut and haul monstrous pieces of leaves with little effort. There is the occasional tug-of-war between two ants, each coveting a single section of tender leaf, which neither Atta is willing to give up. Of course, there are a number of sorry ants, who exhaust a great amount of time and energy cutting out a piece of leaf, only to have it slip from their grasp. Even worse, there is an occasional ant that not only drops a section of leaf but also falls down with it to the forest floor. After each ant secures her own piece of leaf, she promptly retreats to the main formation and then follows her exiting sisters (all the workers are female) down the tree and back to the city. Some begin the journey home with only a piece of leaf, while others may be carting along one or two minimas as well. Fresh troops arrive just as the first wave of Attas march home. As the retreating number of ants begins to build up, there are now two distinct streams of Attas, those that are moving toward the strangler and those that are returning home. They pass each other by the thousand, but no one ant stops to investigate another; instead, the two rivers flow freely in opposite directions.

As the returning brigade reaches the forest floor, a swarm of flies begins to

---

The fungus is the fuel on which the great Atta society runs, and without it, all who dwell within the earthen walls of this metropolis would quickly perish.

---

swoop down at them. They are a species of insect that belongs to a parasitic family of flies, called Phorids. The devious intent of these flies is to deposit eggs along the necks of the larger ants. Upon hatching, a fly larva will eat its way into the ant's body, eventually causing death. Since many of the medias and maximas have their mouths filled with leaves, they are practically defenseless against the attacking flies. That's where the minimas come in. As the flies ruthlessly dive-bomb the larger ants, the minimas bravely defend their sisters by sparring with the flies. In many cases, the tiny but tough ants are successful at driving off their attackers.

Finally the first wave of ants arrives at the Atta city, where they pass on thousands of pieces of leaves to residential minimas, who then prepare the cargo for transport deep into the city. In order to prevent the introduction of any contaminant that might kill the fungus, the leaf pieces are thoroughly cleaned. (In fact, Attas can detect the presence of fungicides—those same things we might use commercially—and weed them out.) After carrying the harvested leaves to the fungus gardens in the heart of the metropolis, the gardener minimas begin to chew up the leaves into a fine pulp, to which they add secretions of saliva and feces. They do not eat the leaves. When the mixture of macerated leaves is complete, the gardeners then carefully infuse bits of fungus onto the medium. If successfully cultivated, the fungus fragments will soon grow into a spongy, bread-like mass. The fungus is the fuel on which the great Atta society runs, and without it, all who dwell within the earthen walls of this metropolis would quickly perish.

With luck and lots of hard work, the Atta city will continue to prosper and grow. If the Atta ants within the collective remain industrious, then in just a few years their colony may grow nearly twenty feet deep into the earth and spread over a hundred feet wide! But long before the metropolis expands to such a monstrous size, the community of Attas will produce a legion of virgin queens and throngs of sex-hungry males. When the timing is right, they will fly out from the colony and into the forest to carry out the mission of spreading their kind throughout the forested frontier. Each queen will depart with a treasured lump of fungus tucked within her mouth. It

may not seem like much, but if the odds are beaten and she is successful in her pursuit to establish a colony, then that minuscule morsel of valuable fungus will eventually give rise to over a thousand individual fungus gardens that can support a population of five million Attas. Chances are that most of the queens and all of the males will perish soon after takeoff, but it takes just one determined female of good breeding to survive and start the amazing process once again. By establishing a new colony, the novel queen will ensure that the great lineage of Attas will continue to thrive well into the future, long after the original queen who had brought her into the world has disappeared.

The impact that one Atta city can have on an ecosystem is profound. In just one year, a large community of Attas can process almost three thousand pounds of leaf matter! The entire life of the Atta ant is built around the survival of an obscure species of fungus. The Attas' ability to serve and prosper as specialists, capitalizing on a resource that is uniquely theirs to harvest, is just one of the many millions of examples of the life of one organism having intertwined with another, all within the boundaries of the rainforest ecosystem. The fig tree provides a fine instance of a keystone species, as a plethora of other life-forms depends on the stoic strangler for survival. Although we may look upon the rainforest as being in a state of harmony, the truth is that much of the wildlife living there is continuously battling to gain the upper edge. While we look upon the strangler as a gentle giant, it most certainly is not. Do not forget that this is the same tree that had overtaken another in order to take root. In the rainforest, competition is the driving force that either pushes life-forms together or pulls them apart. Ultimately, the characteristics and behaviors that a species uses for survival are the manifestations of that particular life-form's pathway through evolution. The rainforest habitat surrounding the great strangler fig is far from a peaceful garden. In truth, it is a battlefield, where the fittest organism overpowers the weakest, as the eternal struggle for survival fuels the diversification of life unique to this extraordinary ecosystem.

SURVIVAL OF THE FOOLISH

Why I do half the oddball things I do is a mystery to my parents, my wife, and me. Although it would be easy to blame Ma and Pa for all my inadequacies, I have come to believe that the influences that have constructed my persona are far more complex than one particularly bad or especially great moment from my past. I believe that our personalities are the result of an amalgamation of complex biology and environmental influences, and the fabric of our characters is woven from the bits and pieces of fortifying memories that we have been collecting since infancy. While there is much of my personality that I just don't understand, there is definitely one aspect of my character that is absolutely certain to me. My addiction to interpreting and understanding the mysteries of the natural world is a direct result of the formative experiences of my youth in the Neotropical rainforest. The specific moment—whether it was seeing my first eyelash viper, with its dew-dappled, copper-colored body dangling from the knotted tendril of a philodendron, or when I came face-to-face with a wild tapir for the very first time—is unclear to me, yet I am confident that the wildlife and ecology of the Neotropics have had a profound influence on the person I am today.

Whether you know it or not, the tropical rainforest has had a profound influence on your life as well. The quality of the human experience has been greatly enhanced from the contributions made to our species by the plants and animals that comprise a rainforest. Much of the diverse bounty of fruits, vegetables, and other plant products that we savor and depend upon has its origins in the tropics. Here is just a short list of the many cultivars that are produced commercially on large farms and plantations today but that originated as a wild plant species thriving in the tropics worldwide: yams, potatoes, peppers, tapioca, cashews, Brazil nuts, bananas, oranges, pineapples, mangos, papayas, tomatoes, sugarcane, rice, and a great variety of legumes and oils, along with various squashes and melons. There are also two very important crops originating in the Neotropical rainforest that we absolutely could not live without: coffee and chocolate!

In addition to food, rainforests provide us with timber (teak and mahogany trees, for example) and gooey tree saps that are used to make everything from the original rubber tire (rubber tree) to chewing gum (chicle tree). Many of the chemical compounds produced by a plethora of plants, insects, and vertebrates have also found their way into our lives in the form of medicines that we use every day. Now, I'm not just talking about some high-end skin moisturizer that you get at an overpriced, froufrou boutique that comes wadded up in "authentic bark" wrapping and costs twenty bucks an ounce. I'm referring to basic and revolutionary medicines that we all use to enhance the quality of our health, or in some cases, keep us alive (for instance, consider the rosy periwinkle that's used in the fight against childhood leukemia). Roughly forty percent of the medicines we use to combat disease and cure ailments originated in global rainforests, even though science has only examined less than one percent of all rainforest plants for their medicinal benefits. Many of these chemical compounds serve as natural insecticides in plant tissue, and once taxonomists isolate the phytochemicals and determine what they do, they can produce synthetic versions without further harm to the delicate rainforest. Today we are successfully fighting hundreds of diseases, from arthritis to cancer, as a result of the pharmaceutical warehouse contained within this ecosystem.

Humans are not the only species to benefit from this productive ecosystem, being that nearly half of all wildlife living on Earth depends upon tropical rainforests as habitat. What I find to be most distressing is that even though human beings are aware of the great importance of tropical rainforests with regard to biodiversity, medicinal contributions, atmospheric oxygen production, and global thermoregulation, we have failed to ade-

quately protect this precious and highly sensitive ecosystem from destruction. More than three thousand acres of rainforest are destroyed every hour throughout the tropical world, which means that a mass of insects, animals, and plants the size of the United Kingdom is permanently scraped off the planet every year! There is a very real possibility that when the Nickelodeon generation of today reaches adulthood, there may not be viable tracts of pristine tropical rainforest left on Earth. Even Costa Rica, a country that is often looked upon as a model for conservation, has only thirty percent of its original rainforest remaining.

There are several contributors to the destruction of tropical rainforests; the major ones include homesteading, agriculture, cattle ranching, timber harvesting, and mineral extraction. With all this said, we still have a chance to save much of our planet's remaining rainforest. To do this we need to use more sustainable methods when harvesting the bounty of natural resources unique to tropical rainforests. I'm not suggesting that we shouldn't use rainforests to our benefit, but I am saying that we must be wiser in how we go about collecting their resources. We need to lock up large tracts of pristine rainforest in wildlife sanctuaries, national parks, and ecological reserves. Most important, we need to involve in these strategies the human communities that live in or near tropical rainforests and depend on them for their survival. With alternative livelihood resource possibilities, these communities can survive in a manner that is sustainable so that there will be plenty of tropical rainforest around for future generations to enjoy, explore, and thrive upon.

Clearly, the subject of tropical rainforest conservation is very complicated, and it's difficult for me to do it justice with just a few concluding paragraphs. There is certainly much more we could discuss, but it's time for us to move on. If you would like to get on board the conservation train, I highly encourage you to investigate the plethora of both large and small non-governmental organizations from around the world that are making a world-class effort toward protecting tropical rainforests. In addition to the national and international groups, such as the Nature Conservancy and Conservation International, you can get involved in grassroots groups that are locally and regionally based, such as the Monteverde Institute and the Amazon Conservation Team.

THE LLANOS
OF VENEZUELA

I will never forget the moment when I discovered my very first snake. I was six years old, and while rummaging through a neatly stacked woodpile in the back of the house belonging to my Uncle Dean and Aunt Loretta, my eyes set upon the strangest, most wonderful creature that I had ever seen. It was a long and slender serpent with a boldly checkered pattern of greenish brown flecks along either side of its body and a golden ribbon running directly down the center of its spine. But just as I reached out to grab it, the crafty serpent swiftly slid away from my outstretched hand and down through the catacomb of stacked timber. The near instantaneous disappearance of the snake sent me into a tizzy as I desperately flung away one split log after another, until finally there were only two logs left unturned. With trembling hands, I reached down and rolled the first log towards my feet, revealing a layer of moist black earth. As my clumsy fingers probed through the soil like a front-end loader, pill bugs were nervously rolling up their segmented bodies as slimy earthworms slid deeper into the soggy soil. There were white bundles of newly formed roots along with the flimsy patterns of structural venation that had once supported maple and oak leaves, which were now nothing more than indistinguishable clumps of decaying detritus. There was the spiral of an abandoned snail shell, a film of fine silk that had been recently spun by some sort of tiny caterpillar, and a pinecone that had grown black and mushy with age. There were all these wonderful little treasures that, under normal circumstances, I would have found intriguing to no end. I impatiently brushed them aside as I searched, however, for there was another mission at hand: to find the mysterious serpent that had escaped my grasp.

So there I was with one more log left to overturn, and as I carefully lifted the crumbling edge of rotten wood, my eyes gazed upon the serpent once again, but this time I would not provide him with an opportunity to escape. Without hesitation, my arm spontaneously lashed out before my brain had signaled it to, and in a matter of seconds, my hand clasped the snake just as it was about squirm off. My heart was beating faster than it ever had before as my legs began to tremble until both knees were knocking together. My discovery of the garter snake had sent a warm, exciting gush of energy surging throughout my six-year-old body. Looking down upon the flailing serpent, I felt absolutely euphoric and just then, something clicked inside me, as if my discovery of the snake had stimulated a hardwiring in my brain that would forever bind me to serpents. Then, just as I had latched onto the garter snake, it decided to latch onto me. I couldn't believe what I was feeling

and observing: The snake was actually chewing on my arm, and although I was terrified, I was also elated. Upon my running into the house, my mother and aunt immediately started to squeal from the tops of their lungs, as only disturbed female kin can do, which of course got the waterworks going on my end as well. My aunt then barked out, "Get rid of it, for gosh sakes! Get rid of it!" I responded with, "No!" That's when everyone went silent until my aunt spoke out once again, "What do you mean 'no'? Why not?" As the tears continued to stream down my face while bubbles of wet booger mucus pathetically gurgled at my nostrils, I answered back through an exaggerated and convulsing huff, "Because I love it!"

From then on, after that fateful encounter with the garter snake in the woodpile, not so much as ten minutes has passed without me thinking about snakes. While in school, my teachers would yell out, as they frequently did up till high school graduation, "Jeff Corwin, quit daydreaming!" Chances are that I was dreaming about snakes. I had been hooked on serpents, and then before I knew it, the addiction quickly spread to lizards, turtles, crocodiles, frogs, and salamanders, along with anything else that was amphibian or reptile in origin, or what we in "the biz" commonly refer to as herps (short for herpetological critters). During spring and summer months while growing up, I spent every available moment bumbling around local swamps, bogs, ponds, and meadows in search of these elusive creatures. My poor dad had been delegated by my mom to cart me around to all the regional herp meetings and conferences. I collected herp books like they were Marvel comics, and of course a number of the creatures resided in terrariums alongside my bed. I knew that someday I would work with herps and other creatures, but I never thought my passion for wildlife would lead me to the career that I have today. My encounter with the garter snake at such a young age had caused me to imprint these creatures on my brain, and who knows? Had it been a baseball or a guitar, maybe I'd be doing something different.

I have had the good fortune to witness and work with most of the snakes that have been lingering on my wish list since early childhood. In Borneo, Bali, and Thailand I have come across my fair share of king cobras. There have, of course, been encounters with pythons, from reticulated and Burmese to African rock. I have seen the critically endangered San Francisco garter snake scoot past my path along grassy dunes of Año Nuevo State Reserve, and the colorful flying snake of Southeast Asia has glided past my brow. I have seen long-nosed, hooked-nosed, patch-nosed, shovel-nosed, and hognose snakes of the American Southwest, while mambas, both green and black, along with many cobras spitting and not, have engaged me in Africa's southeast. In Australia everything from death adders to tiger snakes have dangled from my snake hook, while in Madagascar the elusive twig-nosed snake has slithered across my view. All of these snakes are spectacular creatures, and many of the ones that I have not mentioned are equally so. With that said, there is one great serpent, a monster in its own

Like an iceberg, it's difficult to determine just how much of this anaconda lies in wait beneath the murky water.

right, that has served as the backbone of myth and legend from one generation to the next.

This serpent is so powerful that the mere mention of its name can extinguish the bravado of the most hardened explorer, yet many indigenous communities in its habitat revere the snake as a god of virility, life, and renewal. It is a serpent of such astounding might that Spanish explorers from centuries past referred to this mega-reptile as *matatoro*, or "bull

killer." With a potential length of thirty feet (there are historical accounts of it reaching forty feet!), it is the longest species of snake inhabiting the New World. With regard to mass, this colossal serpent can attain a weight of more than five hundred pounds while having a girth nearly as thick as a telephone pole; it is simply the fattest and heaviest species of serpent on the entire planet. As a predator, it has been known to swallow everything from turtles to crocodilians! There are even confirmed accounts of this giant snake killing and then swallowing an adult jaguar! Now, if you were to offer three wishes to a herpetologist, I would be willing to wager that one of those wishes would be to witness firsthand a large individual of this species out in the wild. So just who is this mysterious snake? Well, it's name originates from the Tamil word *anaikolra*, which means "elephant killer," but you know the massive serpent simply as anaconda. I have had the chance to observe and work with many anacondas throughout South America, from Guyana to Paraguay. Now, while the yellow ana-

HEY NEAT—AN ANACONDA!

I saw my first green anaconda when I was twenty-two, while traveling by dugout canoe down the Aguarico River in northeastern Ecuador. I remember looking at an unusually stout vine that had been strewn over a substantial tree limb, arching a few feet over the surface of the water. Upon realizing that it was no vine but a thigh-thick anaconda that was two-and-a-half times longer than myself, I practically fell back into the canoe. I had been traveling with a family from the Cofan tribe for three days as they were taking me to a remote lake deep in the rainforest. Now, when I saw the anaconda and gestured to them that we should paddle over to the snake and attempt to capture it, they all looked at me as if I were delusional from dengue fever. After they had made it very clear to me that if something were to go awry with the snake, then I would be on my own, we carefully floated over to the slumbering serpent. Slowly we slid the boat under the fat snake, and just as I began to reach up to grab it, the anaconda began to rapidly slip off the tree and into the water. It seemed as though his legless mass was endless as he continued to rapidly slide into the black, tannin-rich water. Soon, there were only a few feet of snake left before it was about to disappear into the water, and that's when I marshaled what little nerve I had before finally reaching out and grabbing onto the anaconda by the last eight inches of its tail.

Everybody in the canoe had started to shout in nervous excitement, including myself. I was holding on to the very end of the thirteen-foot snake, which was thrashing about beneath the water, much of it invisible to our eyes. The sensation I had while attempting to secure the anaconda was no different than when I had encountered that garter snake sixteen years earlier. I had broken out in a cold sweat with all limbs shivering with exhilaration at the thought of the massive creature surging beneath our canoe. Then, with great trepidation, I began to pull the snake into the canoe, one foot at a time. It was like trying to control a fire hose that had been cranked up to full steam, since the serpent swayed back and forth beneath the water as I attempted to hold on to it at the other end in the stern of the canoe. At one point, the snake's head started to crawl into the bow of the teetering vessel, which sent everybody from the front screaming towards the back. After a few careful yanks, the anaconda's head had slid back into the river.

Eventually, after ten or eleven heave-hos, I was down to the last few feet of anaconda, but here's the catch: I was so close to securing the serpent, yet I was unable to see his head under-

(continued on page 234)

HEY NEAT—AN ANACONDA! —CONT'D

water. Now, if I had just pulled the remaining section of anaconda into the canoe without securing his head, I would not have been able to control it. So, if I was going to capture and control the beast, I would have to calculate where his head was underwater, based on the positioning of his neck within my grasp, and then I would need to release my left hand from its grip of the snake's neck. Finally, I would need to plunge my hand into the water with hopes that my aim was spot-on. If I was off by just an inch, my hand could end up inside the anaconda's mouth, which was wider than the hand I was reaching in with. The Cofan family that I had been tagging along with stared at me in absolute silence, with mouths and eyes wide, as I prepared to plunge my hand into the water. It took me a minute or two to psyche myself up until I finally just went for it. Beneath the water, my finger could detect the scales of what I was greatly hoping to be the back of the anaconda's jaw. Then, while holding my breath with eyes wincing in preparation for stabbing pain, I closed my grip around the snake. Upon hauling my hand out of the water, I discovered that to my relief, I had grabbed on to the snake safely and securely with all fingers intact. After a few minutes of taking the snake's weight (about eighty pounds) and length, I shot off a couple of slides and then set him free. I will never forget that moment for the rest of my life. When I am stuck in an endless line at the DMV or I am sandwiched between two screaming babies, one of which projectile-vomits some curdled formula onto my new shirt while on a transcontinental flight, I reflect on that exciting moment as a nice piece of brain candy to get me through.

conda (*Eunectes notaeus*) of southern South America attains a decent length of up to twelve feet, its cousin, the green anaconda (*Eunectes murinus*) of central and northern South America, grows to be absolutely monstrous.

THE SETTING OF OUR STORY

For our final adventure, I want to take you to a starkly different place where perhaps you would not expect to find a giant green anaconda. While the steamy jungles and twisting black rivers of the Amazon basin are often thought of as being the heart of anaconda country, I know a region in South America that has no resemblance to a rainforest ecosystem but has more in common with the prairies of the Midwest, the Everglades of southern Florida, or even the southeast African savannah. Yet, it is a haven for green anacondas. In fact, some of the grandest anacondas that I have ever had the privilege of observing were witnessed right here. So, instead of meandering down the Aguarico in Ecuador, or maybe the flood forests outside of Manaus along the headwaters of the Amazon, or through the gallery forest of Guyana, we will head out across the rolling grasslands of the Llanos in the heart of Venezuela. Some of the best adventures I have ever had in South America have been in the Llanos (pronounced *ya-nos*, meaning "plains"). Not only is this vast grassland ideal for anacondas but also it is perfect for observing a plethora of other unusual creatures, many of which are on the menu for the gigantic serpents.

The Llanos are an extensive sweep of savannah that spread out across the Orinoco River basin. It is a land of utter extremes where the habitat is either very dry or very wet, where the availability of water is often the determining factor that influences the fate of all who depend upon it. All the creatures of the Llanos are at the whimsy of seasonal rains— wildlife will either flourish or perish, depending on where it is when the rains come or depart. During the rainy season, from April to October, the thousands of rivers, creeks, and shallow water holes begin to overflow from a near-endless deluge of rain. Soon, much of the prairie landscape of the Llanos is transformed from extensive fields of withered grass, grown brown from months of desiccation, into a glassy sea of flooded grassland where often just the tips of billions of blades of tall grass pierce the water's surface. Scattered throughout the flooded Llanos are small hamlets of densely packed vegetation, which become valuable plots of terra firma for much of the wildlife looking to stay dry.

During the dry season, which occurs from November to March, the land becomes dangerously parched as most of the water holes and rivulets all but dry up, leaving behind a mosaic of chalky mud where wildlife can be entombed within the baking earth. Many creatures, such as fish, turtles, caiman, and anaconda, that become trapped in the baking mud can perish, leaving behind desiccated mummies cemented in dense earth. The water holes and rivers that contain water throughout the dry season are invaded by desperate wildlife seeking hydration and relief from the merciless sun. Shrinking pools of stagnant water are jam-packed with electric eels, piranha, rays, and other fish, all of which struggle to survive in the hot, oxygen-poor liquid. Herons, egrets, storks, and other species of waterfowl crowd together like a container crammed tight with cotton swabs. There are birds of prey, like black-shouldered hawks, caracaras, and black-headed vultures, which have an endless buffet of trapped, dying, or dead wildlife to feast upon. Swarms of turtles cluster together thicker than stones in a river, as spectacled caimans inundate the scene. The concentration of wildlife in what little precious water remains is excruciatingly profound.

Slithering through this dynamic ecosystem of contrasting seasonality is the greatest reptilian predator inhabiting the Neotropics, a resilient and impressive serpent that is very much a living leviathan. I encountered this very special green anaconda during an expedition to the Llanos in the spring of 2003. She is by far the stoutest, heaviest, and most impressive anaconda that I have ever experienced while in the field. At nearly sixteen feet in length, she is certainly not the longest anaconda that has ever lived, but her length is not what impressed me so. What I found to be so extraordinary about this anaconda was her overwhelming girth. She was almost as wide as a telephone pole while weighing a whopping two hundred and fifty pounds! It almost seemed as though she was unnaturally grand for her length. Any other green anaconda typically weighing in at her bulging load would probably be a twenty-footer. This anaconda is an absolute monster in her own right; in fact, that's what we had affectionately come to know her as: Monstra. She is a flawless serpent of great determination and brawn as she thrives in the severe terrain of the Llanos. With Monstra as our guide through the Llanos, we will explore the vast wilderness from her level, in our attempt to understand how the diverse wildlife living here endures the infinite, daily challenges to survival.

Our journey through the Llanos begins at the tail end of the dry season, as the hardy creatures that have persisted through the relentless five months of almost no rain are now eagerly awaiting restoration, as the rejuvenating rains of the wet season will soon pour down from the heavens and replenish the parched earth once again. Like a great phoenix blazing over the sun-scorched Llanos, the mighty king vulture (*Sarcoramphus papa*) soars effortlessly on a hot breeze while peering down at the landscape beneath her. Volplaning with wings spread wide, she is intensely scanning the savannah for a carcass to feast upon. The king vulture's

Behold: Monstra!

six-foot wingspan and weight of nearly nine pounds makes her the largest of all Neotropical vultures. The only characteristic more impressive than the king vulture's massive size is her appearance—she is absolutely stunning! Much of her breast, body, and shoulders is pearl white, while the primary feathers jetting from her powerful wings and the tail feathers fanning out from her rump are as black as onyx. What I find to be the vulture's most striking features are the vibrant colors of her neck and head. The velvety soft skin enveloping her neck has a black collar at the base but then turns pumpkin orange when it reaches her chin. On either side of her black face are wrinkly skin-tabs, which are suspended beneath an intense pair of blue eyes that are as bright as Brazilian topaz. Her intimidating beak is vibrant orange, as is the purse of soft flesh dangling above it.

Tracing across the expanse of grass is the vulture's shadow, which soon begins to grow sharper as she commences to spiral downward. Her eyes have spotted a brown clump that appears to be rather promising, and as she continues her descent, her keen vision confirms that indeed there is a festering corpse below. With wings stretched wide and feet reaching forward, the king vulture smoothly glides down onto a patch of trampled sod. After a few determined hops, she bounces directly on top of the goat-sized carcass, which has mummified after a week of

The king vulture is a real looker.

roasting beneath the intense equatorial sun. There are a few remaining patches of brown fur matted across the creature's rigid hide, which stretches across a substantial body. In life, the animal must have weighed a solid one hundred pounds or more. At first glance, the cadaver, which is now deformed from a week of bloating and decomposition, may have been a deer. The identity of the mysterious mammal is revealed when we examine the upper and lower incisors that are sticking out of the creature's mouth. The maw of the beast has been awkwardly twisted open due to the pressure of fetid gases that have been erupting from the putrefying innards of its body. As the stinking gas purges and leaks from either end, the bone-white teeth have continued to buck out from its mouth. Each upper incisor is nearly two inches long and an inch wide, while the lower ones aren't all that much smaller. The sun-bleached incisors resemble beaver teeth but are at least twice as big. The beaver is, of course, the largest rodent in North America, but the species of this pathetic corpse is indeed the world's largest rodent, the capybara (*Hydrochaeris hydrochaeris*).

With a few twists of her sharp beak, the king vulture whittles at a protruding lump of hide until she punctures the thick, leathery skin. As she pierces the liquefied flesh underneath, a burst of warm, stinking gas hisses out of the wound like air leaking from a balloon. If you were to get a whiff of the moist discharge of rancid gas as it blustered across your face,

you would most certainly begin to gag involuntarily until finally puking, but the king vulture takes no offense. She is quick to rip open a sizeable gash that is wide enough for her to stick her head into, which she promptly does now that the intense aroma wafting around her ornate face has stimulated her appetite. Not far from where the dead rodent lies, there is a herd of about thirty capybaras, which calmly wander past the corpse without the slightest bit of interest. The group consists of a large, one-hundred-and-forty-pound dominant male, four subordinate males, four females, and roughly twenty-one

The dry season is unforgiving of those who are unfit.

We might think capybaras look precious, but to an anaconda they look delicious!

young. They click and whistle back and forth to each other as they move past the depression of gray earth that had once been a thriving water hole, alive with many creatures, before finally drying up.

The last bit of water finally evaporated over a month ago, leaving behind a crumbling bed of caked earth, where we find the body of a desiccated fish that appears to be melted into the mud. The empty eye sockets of the fish stare up

from the dried muck and its mouth gapes wide while baring angry teeth, as if it had protested inevitable death to the bitter end. Even though the fish perished weeks ago, its skull still expresses a grimacing scowl of the suffering it had endured. As the sun radiated down on the water hole for weeks on end, the water around the fish had slowly evaporated to oblivion until eventually the fish was left gasping for wet breath. After succumbing to the choking heat, the dead fish settled into the surrounding mud, which began to harden around its dehydrating body until finally both fish and mud had fused together as one. Looking down at the dried fish, it seems as though it's a rare fossil of some ancient species that perished millions of years ago. But when you glance beyond the fish and across the crackled bed of compacted silt, you discover hundreds of other fish that suffered a similar fate. While many of the air-breathing vertebrates were able to escape the rapidly dwindling pool that eventually became a deathtrap for fish, not all were so fortunate. In addition to the dead capybara, there are dozens of empty turtle shells lodged in the solidified muck.

The herd of capybaras stomps off through the grass and over a mound of raised earth until it reaches a small lagoon on the other side. The aquatic creatures residing in this lagoon are rather fortunate, being that this oval-shaped pond contains water throughout the entire year; now at its driest state, however, the small body of water seems to contain more mud that water. This is why location is everything in the Llanos. It was just by sheer luck that the floodwaters of the previous rainy season had not carried these creatures to the shallower water hole, where many other critters faced their grim demise. The lagoon is no more than a few acres in size, yet it is now home to hundreds of life-forms.

There are a number of large birds patrolling the water's edge, including the enormous jabiru stork (*Jabiru mycteria*). With a height of five feet and a wingspan of eight feet, the jabiru is the largest wading bird in all of the Americas. Its plumage is entirely snow white, while its extraordinarily long neck is grayish black with a loose sack of membranous skin that flutters and inflates like the legs of pantyhose filled with the heated air from a blow-dryer. How do I know that an inflated tube of pantyhose resembles the puffed-up neck of a jabiru, you ask? Well, on many occasions I have seen jabiru storks cooling themselves by inflating their necks with refreshing air. As the soft wrinkly skin wrapping around their yard-long necks repeatedly bloats and deflates, a stream of cooling air continues to flow

This fish obviously missed the memo that the dry season had arrived.

in and out. When I observe this behavior, I am reminded of the time when I slipped a leg of my mother's pantyhose over her blow-dryer, which I then set on high with full heat. The only really obvious difference between the neck-skin of a jabiru and my mother's pantyhose is that the jabiru neck doesn't catch on fire and melt. Hey, give me a break—if they don't want a ten-year-old boy messing with women's pantyhose, then why the heck do they package them in giant plastic eggs?

The jabiru wades along the edge of the water hole with much of his enormous, ten-inch-long bill submerged beneath the surface. Like a spring-loaded trap, the bill slices through water while remaining open, but when it detects the presence of a fish, frog, snake, or even a small turtle, the bill quickly snaps shut. Upon grasping his prey, the jabiru stork simply throws back his head and then gobbles it down.

On this particular day, the stork is snacking on hatchling caimans. The small water hole is filled with dozens of these spectacled caimans (*Caiman crocodilus*), a moderately sized alligator-like crocodilian that successfully survives in the highly competitive and volatile environment of the Llanos. At around a foot in length, some of the caimans are just yearlings, while the numerous six- and seven-footers have been around for a number of years. There is even one spectacled caiman that is a solid eight feet long; he is certainly a crocodilian with a fair bit of history and has lived in the lagoon through good times and bad for nearly fifteen years.

The juvenile and hatchling caimans

The jabiru stork is one of the largest flying birds in all of the Americas. It is both rare and endangered.

The spectacled caiman gets its name from its appearance—it looks like it's sporting a pair of specs!

display an earthy pattern of greenish-brown blotches across their rubbery hides, which serve as ideal camouflage for blending in with the duckweed, water hyacinth, and tall grass growing along the perimeter of the lagoon. The adult caimans have uniformly drab hides that are grayish brown in color. When stalking prey through the murky water, just their eyes and nostrils are visible, while the remainder of their bodies melts with the surrounding water. The drably colored hide of adult spectacled caimans is a perfect match against the muddy banks of rivers or water holes when they are out basking beneath the sun, as they often do during the hours of mid-morning and late afternoon. Thick and bony scales called scutes, which run across the surface of their backs, function as an added layer of armor. The caimans are equipped with an arsenal of intertwining, ice pick–sharp teeth that are ideal for grabbing onto fish, turtles, wading birds, and young capybaras. In between their nicely rounded orbits, which are strategically positioned at the top of their heads, is an oval-shaped crest of raised dermis. Its rounded configuration resembles the frame of an old pair of reading spectacles, hence their name.

When the capybaras arrive at the muddy lagoon, they carefully scan the perimeter for predators and when the coast is clear, they wade into the water. Capybaras are superb swimmers, and they will spend much of the day cruising through the turbid water to escape the relentless heat of midday or to forage for succulent aquatic plants, like water hyacinth. Hanging out in the water is also a great way to escape biting flies and mosquitoes while simultaneously dislodging unwanted ectoparasites such as ticks. Capybaras are equipped with webbed digits for swimming, and as with crocodilians, their eyes are situated at the top of their heads so they can keep an eye out, so to speak, for any predators lurking about as they swim. Capybaras are excellent divers and can plunge underwater with ease; they swim completely submerged for a minute or two before having to come up for a breath. Although wallowing in the cool waters of the Llanos may be soothing for the body—and provides the capybaras with lazy access to an everlasting salad of succulent vegetation to graze on—it is

not without risk. Hidden beneath a floating raft of hyacinth or beneath the opaque water is a multitude of stealthy predators, all of which are eager to dine upon capybara.

While the dominant and subordinate males and three female capybaras flounder in the brown water, the twenty-one terrier-sized offspring hang out beneath the shade of a tree. Keeping a watchful eye over the brood, a vigilant capybara is staying alert for the first sign of danger. Multiple litters of capybara pups are often kept together in an extended collective nursery, which is monitored by one or two adult females. The tree above them shoots up twenty feet to the crown. The branches radiating up and around the crown form a natural hammock, where presently a South America tamandua (*Tamandua tetradactyla*) has chosen to take a nap. He slumbers there, actually snoring away, sheltered by the foliage above and around him. He is curled up nice and comfy with his funnel-like muzzle tucked between his forearms. The differences between him and his Central

The south American tamandua is also called a collared anteater.

American counterpart, *Tamandua mexicana*, are quite subtle, although *T. tetradactyla* is uniformly tan without the dark brown saddle exhibited by his Costa Rican cousin. As he contentedly sleeps, he occasionally twitches with slight little jerks of his claws or tics of an eyelid. Because of his small brain, many scientists would probably say the movements are just reflexes, but what if these little jolts are actually the physical manifestation of a

dream? Now, I am not attempting to anthropomorphize the tamandua, but just because he has a tiny brain with a rather paltry cerebral cortex, is he not still entitled to dream? If he were dreaming, then I imagine the fantasy unfolding in his conservative subconscious would have something to do with termites.

Above the sleeping tamandua is a pair of courting rufescent tiger-herons (*Tigrisoma lineatum*). The tiger-heron is a beautiful species of wading bird with ruddy, chestnut-colored plumage enveloping its head, neck, and breast. Cutting across the primary plumage of its wings is an intense pattern of white and black stripes, hence the name of tiger-heron. The bird's bill is bright yellow while its legs are dull green. Tiger-herons hunt frogs, fish, and small snakes while patrolling the water's edge. Upon spotting prey, the heron will lock up its body until just the right moment, and then wham! The bird shoots out its neck and spears the prey with its spike-like bill. At the present moment, though, it appears that these enamored herons have little interest in hunting. Gently, they

A little on the shy side, these rufescent tiger-herons become more active during dusk or early night.

entangle around each other's necks as they chatter their bills, with wings fluttering outward in rapturous delight. They are oblivious to what's going on down at the tree's buttress, where another fascinating creature forages along the surface roots, just behind the capybara nursery. About the size of a six-ounce can of soup, it is a rather small animal, but it is no less interesting.

At first glance the scaly, helmet-like shell enveloping his back suggests that he is perhaps some type of reptile, but the fine hairs bristling out from around his thighs and underbelly confirm that he is definitely a mammal. If you want to find the nearest living relative of this unusual little beast, then look no further than the napping tamandua in the tree crown above. As with the arboreal anteater, this tank-like critter rummaging through the brittle soil is a Xenarthran. More specifically, the diminutive creature is an eight-banded armadillo (*Dasypus sabanicola*), who is on the hunt for worms, grubs, and small insects that are buried deep in the tightly packed soil. He is small enough to fit in a human hand and weighs less than half a pound, yet when it comes to excavating for a meal, he is ferocious! He enthusiastically sniffs the soil with his narrow beak, and when his sensitive snout detects a tasty invertebrate, he swiftly begins to dig. After the long claws hanging off his forearms have ripped through the tough soil until finally reaching the squirming morsel, the pint-sized armadillo then gobbles it up. I remember the first time I saw one of these adorable armadillos, and of course, the first thing that came to my mind was a miniaturized stegosaurus. The plated armor of rubbery hide, which forms the armadillo's shell, is divided up into sections. Wrapped around both the shoulders and rump are the largest plates, while stacked in between them on both sides of the armadillo's body are up to eight narrow bands of hide that can stretch and contract like the ribs of an accordion.

As the armadillo continues his frantic hunt for prey, his ears detect a rustling of leaves from behind. He freezes up as he nervously takes a sniff with his snout pointed up in the air. His little heart is beating dangerously fast, and just when he is about to spring over the flailing roots and make a mad dash toward his burrow, a long, sickle-shaped beak spears into the leaves alongside his trembling body. The assault jettisons the armadillo two feet up in the air as he attempts to escape capture, and when he plunks back down on the earth, he hits the ground running. His legs were actually spinning before he had even landed, and his speedy exodus sends him sprinting across a hundred feet of grassland before he plunges into a hole that is just wide enough for him to squeeze

The eight-banded armadillo lives only in the Llanos.

The buff-necked ibis roots for toads and insects, as well as lizards.

is drab-brown in color, while at the top of her scalp is a rusty crown of feathers. Jetting out from her naked black face is a long, slightly curved bill. The base of each wing is soft black with a whitish-gray patch of plumage along the upper part. Supporting her odd shape is a pink pair of somewhat gangly, knob-kneed legs. The truth is that the buff-necked ibis had no interest in the tiny armadillo but, like the flighty Xenarthran, was just foraging for some grub. She continues to stab at the leaf litter around the tree with her bill, and when she finds a small lizard, the ibis is quick to extract the helpless reptile from the cover of a tangled clump of roots. With one flip, the lizard is tossed into the air, then slides down her bill until finally she chokes it down. As the buff-necked ibis continues to stalk her way from the tree toward the rim of dried mud along the lagoon, she yaps out a terrified squawk and then hastily bolts into flight.

through. He continues to scramble down his narrow, subterranean tunnel for a distance of three-and-a-half feet before he finally comes to a stop and attempts to catch his breath. He will stay there, huddled in the blackness of his den until the terror has passed and he is feeling adventurous once again. Back at the tree, the great beaked predator stalking among the buttress roots is nothing more than a buff-necked ibis (*Theristicus caudatus*).

She is a rather comically built bird standing just under three feet in height. The plumage on her head, neck, and chest

Stretched out across the grass from where the buff-necked ibis had just fretfully flown is Monstra, the colossal green anaconda. Slowly, the great snake has been slithering from one dried up water hole to another until finally arriving here, at the lagoon where a nice bath awaits her. Soon, she is sliding across the mud and into the shallow water, where she quickly disappears beneath the murky liquid. With the exception of the buff-necked ibis, Monstra has managed to slip into the water without notice from the other creatures gathered at the lagoon. As the caimans levitate from one side of the pond to the next and the capybaras swim, frolic, eat, and sleep, they are all completely oblivious to the arrival of the massive reptile that is now silently swimming among them. After a minute beneath the water, Monstra's head floats to the top while the remainder of her sixteen-foot-long body remains submerged. It is extraordinary just how huge her head is. From nostrils to nape of neck, Monstra's head is ten inches long, while the width of her head across the widest stretch of her cranium is six inches! Some of the scales on Monstra's head are as large as my fingernails, while the largest scales on her torso are bigger than my thumbnails. Out from the front

Monstra takes one last breath before submerging.

of her gently bobbing head flickers a forked tongue that is two inches long and a quarter of an inch wide. As her tongue probes the surface of the water, she soon tastes the presence of prey. After a few more flickers, her head sinks beneath the milky gray water. Once submerged, Monstra effortlessly slithers through the water like a giant eel, as the length of her spine unravels from side to side, causing her to silently propel forward.

The capybara meets his match.

The capybaras continue to wallow away the day, with little concern for their surroundings, unaware that a deadly predator is fast approaching. One of the subordinate males has wandered over to a lush patch of water hyacinth, where he begins to greedily feast. As his long incisors rip at the vegetation, a gigantic, S-shaped pattern of bubbles begins to effervesce at the surface of the water directly behind him. Then, while he tugs and chews on the floating fodder, a powerful force smashes into him from underneath the water, propelling him a yard into the air. While the giant rodent bursts out of the water, Monstra's mouth is revealed as she has latched tightly onto the capybara's shoulder. The noise of the attack along with the horrible squeal coming from the capybara's mouth, sends the rest of his herd dashing out of the lagoon as fast as their legs can push them. Then the dominant male blurts out a loud, sneeze-like huff, which serves as a universal alarm to get out of the water and rally at the grass. A number of the female capybaras dash over to the nursery, where they quickly push the pups back from the edge of the lagoon. Meanwhile, Monstra has wrapped her giant body around the doomed capybara nearly as quickly as she grabbed onto it. The capybara struggles for freedom, but within seconds the force of two hundred and fifty pounds of anaconda rapidly tighten around the rodent's body, as Monstra begins to constrict her prey.

The capybara throws back his head and winces from the blinding pain ripping though his body as his rib cage begins to collapse under the crushing folds of Monstra's deadly embrace. There is the ghastly sound of gurgling breath, wheezing involuntarily out of his lungs as the anaconda unrelentingly tightens around the capybara's torso. Bones continue to bend and snap until the pressure building up in the capybara's body grows so powerful that his entrails start to prolapse out his anus while his eyes begin bugging out wildly

from their sockets. The doomed capybara flat-lines within two minutes while ensnared within Monstra's crushing grasp; the entire execution, from capture to constriction, took place in just over five minutes. Now that the capybara has expired, Monstra releases her grip and then, with her flickering tongue, tickles her way to the top of the rodent's lifeless head. In a matter of a minute, she wraps her mouth around his football-sized head, and soon Monstra's lips are swathing over the length of the capybara's substantial body, from head to tail. With each stretching gulp, Monstra's jaws spread wider as the capybara is pulled deeper inside her until finally her lips are pursing closer together over a rapidly disappearing rump.

Now that she has swallowed her prey, she twists and slides her jaws back and forth until they finally settle back after the arduous stretch. The one-hundred-and-twenty-pound bulge that passed through her mouth is now being piped down her neck until settling as a less obvious lump within the widest part of her girth. Now that she has eaten, she will need to rest for a day or two while digestion, which may last for weeks, takes place. So, she slowly slithers over to the tree where the tamandua still sleeps, coils up within the outstretched buttress, and then tranquilly fades off. For a typical anaconda, a capybara represents a significant meal that can keep the snake satisfied for more than a month. The situation is vastly different for Monstra, being that she is in desperate need of energy that will be used to fuel her body as she begins the long journey toward life's greatest endeavor, which is, of course, motherhood.

FROM LAGOON TO RIVER

Not far from the lagoon where Monstra is fast asleep, there is a ribbon of overhanging branches with strips of forest growing along each side. There are two bands of vegetation growing parallel to each other, each one a few hundred feet wide and thick with densely entangled vines, shrubs, and pole trees. Where the two rows neighbor each other, they are connected by a bridge of interlocking branches from corresponding emergents, which weave together to form a dense strip of canopy. Beneath this canopy is a narrow tributary, which at its widest point is just fifteen feet across. The water flows slowly down this long and slender river, as there isn't all that much water passing through it. As we meander down this river we can hear the whistles, cackles, screeches, and cahcahs coming from hundreds of different bird species. While swerving around a gentle bend in the river, we come across an astonishing sight. As we stare down at the water, we can hardly accept the image that our eyes are transmitting to our brains. Just in this one section of river, covering an area that is, at most, sixty feet long and twelve feet wide, we witness a gathering of tens of thousands of river turtles (*Podocnemis viogli*). As we carefully flow through the shifting raft of turtles, a few hundred sink beneath the water only to reemerge a few yards away.

And New Yorkers think their rush hour is bad. Though we don't know why they flood the river like teens at Woodstock II, we do know that river turtles are omnivorous, meaning they eat anything—especially if it's found in the water!

I will never forget the moment when I witnessed this spectacular phenomenon. I remember staring with amazement as thousands of brown carapaces swarmed alongside my canoe as their heads, which seemed curious about my presence, would rotate toward the dugout like tiny animated periscopes. Perhaps just as thrilling as this great gathering of turtles is the reason why they do it, which, till this day, is not understood. In a minute or two we pass the swarm of river turtles and come across another cluster of creatures, which are not turtles at all but a waterlogged flock of about thirty Neotropic cormorants (*Phalacrocorax brasilianus*).

The slick birds are black as crude oil, and the sun reflecting off the water glistens against their backlit bodies as if they had been washed over with godly light. The cormorants continue to dive under the water one after the other, and to witness them beneath the surface of the river is a most amazing sight—the problem is the turbidity of the water. If you stuck your hand in six inches deep and looked down, you would hardly see it, never mind attempting to observe a bird that swims as fast and as skillfully as a seal. With their feet rapidly rolling and kicking, the adeptly aquatic birds maneuver with great dexterity and speed while pursuing schools of small fish in the murky water. When the cormorants bobble up to the surface, beads of repelling water are quick to cascade off of their glossy plumage and back into the river.

There is one creature, however, that the cormorants swim past with great urgency, for she too is an excellent swimmer but she has an appetite that is not satisfied by schools of tiny fish. Basking on top of the riverbank is an absolutely massive Orinoco crocodile (*Crocodylus intermedius*). The gigantic crocodilian is fourteen feet long and weighs well over a thousand pounds. Her hide has a lovely olive tint with greenish gray blotches scattered along her sides and back. The head of the Orinoco croc-

odile bulges out from her muscular neck, spreading out wide at first but then tapering to a slender snout.

Orinoco crocodiles are powerful predators, hunting a variety of prey, including fish, capybaras, waterfowl, anacondas, and terrestrial mammals, like deer, that are caught while venturing to the river to drink or swim. For just over two months, this one has remained close to the riverbank due to the precious clutch of fifty eggs that she deposited there. It was during the height of the dry season when she hauled herself out of the water and began to excavate a cavity in the compacted sand left to dry when the waters receded. Over the course of an evening she laid her eggs into the cavity and then covered them back up. She has been patiently waiting for them to hatch all this time, while vigilantly guarding the nest from predators, like tegu lizards and black-headed vultures. If any creature should dare approach her nest from either water or land, she will charge after them and attack with vengeance.

Finally the moment has arrived when

The Orinoco crocodile gets its common name from its habitat—the freshwater Orinoco River in the Llanos.

deep from within the nest a fragile call, which sounds similar to a gulping swallow, begins to desperately chirp outward. Upon hearing the call, the croc begins to excavate her nest. As she digs, the calling grows louder and more desperate, which causes her to dig even faster. Finally she sweeps away the last layer of sandy soil before reaching in and grasping one of the eggs within her mighty jaws. Then, her monstrous jowls begin to close around the egg containing the fragile hatchling, and as the jagged teeth of the upper and lower jaws begin to weave shut, the eggshell trapped within starts to crack until it finally collapses beneath the pressure.

This mighty croc mom is no cannibal with family, and she has no intention of gorging upon the offspring that she has been standing by for nearly seventy days. She continues to excavate the eggs from the nest, and although she does snatch them up with her nearly three-foot-long muzzle and is indeed chewing on them, she does so very gently. Her objective is to free the offspring that have been calling to her. After spending hours freeing the twenty-five baby crocs that have managed to survive the incubation process, she then escorts them to a nursery area in a small alcove of gentle water. Amazingly, the moment of liberation for her offspring has been timed to coincide with the oncoming rains of the wet season. The mother may stay with her offspring for up to three years, investing her energy in them, in order to secure a future generation of Orinoco crocodiles. Tragically, despite the extraordinary investment and quality of parental care that a mother Orinoco crocodile provides for her offspring, this species is in a terrible state. As a result of hunting (for their skins), perse-

cution, and habitat loss, the Orinoco crocodile is now a critically endangered species. Presently, there could be as few as three hundred Orinoco crocodiles surviving in the wild, and there is a genuine possibility that this valuable species may be extinct in the very near future.

Not far from where the crocodile has been steadily importing her hatchlings, in a narrow inlet of stagnant water, a small twig is barely breaking through the surface of the water. Then, the tip of the twig dilates, allowing for a stream of fresh air to flow inward. After the twig has filled with air, it sinks beneath the water. Following the twig beneath the water, we discover that it is not a mere splinter of branch but is a snorkel belonging to the most bizarre turtle to ever inhabit the planet. The alien-like reptile is none other than the mata mata turtle (*Chelus fimbriatus*). Although the narrow twig-like snorkel is only an inch in length, it is attached to quite a monster of a turtle. The neck and head of the mata mata turtle stretch out more than a foot and a half in length from its shell. The neck is so long that in cannot be retracted within the mata mata's shell; instead, it must rest along the side of its body. The head of the mata mata is remarkably fantastic. Essentially, it is designed to resemble a nondescript leaf that has begun to decompose while underwater. The shape of the head is triangular, with pointed extensions of rubbery flesh tweaking out from either jaw. The chin and lateral part of the neck are studded with fleshy tubercles, and if you look at the mouth, it seems as though it's smiling. The snorkel at the tip of its muzzle allows the turtle to respire without revealing itself to predators, though mata mata turtles have very few enemies, being that they are excellently camouflaged and they produce a foul-smelling and -tasting substance from glands along their shells.

Speaking of shells, the mata mata has the weirdest one of them all; it looks as

In the Bizarro World, the mata mata turtle would be the norm.

mata sits at the bottom of the river resembling a pile of rotting vegetation, and when a fish, small frog, or other minute critter approaches, the turtle extends its limber neck and then, when the prey least expects it, violently sucks up the hapless critter into its smiling chops faster than a Shop-Vac sucking up a feather. Okay, maybe not that fast, but pretty darn close.

Not even twelve feet above the mata mata's head, balancing on a sinewy branch, is a winged predator, a creature who is eager to extract a wiggling sample from the endless bounty of aquatic prey swimming in the brown water below. But there is little concern for the mata mata because the stealthy raptor is a black-collared hawk (*Busarellus nigricollis*), a bird with a dietary interest that is pescivorous in nature—in fact, she's often referred to as the fishing buzzard. As hawks go, she has a rather ordinary build with wide wings that stretch not much more than sixteen inches from either side of her ribcage. Although her bulk is far from monstrous, she possesses a beauty that more than compensates for whatever she

though it has been beaten with a rubber mallet. While the mata mata's head resembles a rotting leaf, its carapace is a dead ringer for a rotten log. I can't think of another living turtle, or many other herps for that matter, that displays such exquisite camouflage as the mata mata does. If the mata mata has such a foul stench, then what's with all the camouflage? Well, this turtle's masterful ability to blend in has more to do with hunting than with escaping. Mata matas are opportunistic predators that will often wait for the food to come to them, and when it does, they ambush it. Basically, a mata lacks in size. The wispy plumage fluttering about her body has a lovely cinnamon-auburn hue, while a distinct collar of black chocolate hugs her lower neck and shoulders. Perched beneath her body are two very solid, slate blue legs with an arsenal of barbed talons fanning out from each foot. As she looks down at the water with a severe glare, the black-collared hawk spots a viable target worthy of a hunt. Then, with eyes focused intently on the shifting shape hovering an inch or two beneath a wavering ribbon of turbid water, she takes flight.

Unfurling from the ridge of narrow bark, all six forward-reaching talons twinge up from the branch until the two solitary rear talons of each foot, anchored into the wood, instantly release. Quickly, she takes to a warm swirl of air that carries her away from the branch and down toward the river. As she hovers briefly and then plummets, her talons unfold from beneath her tail and then stretch forward beneath her breast with toes spread widely apart. In a matter of seconds, her talons slice through the water with a thundering slap as they

hook into the spine of a fish that had been lingering too near the water's surface. The fish's panicked attempt to retreat toward the murky deep is instantly thwarted as its body is violently jerked from the cloudy water and into the glare of hot and blinding sunlight. Despite the fish's desperate efforts to flip out from the barbarous grip of the hawk's gaff-like talons, it rapidly ascends from the familiar flow of riparian habitat into the rasping garrote of gill-drying air. Its opportunity to escape and survive swiftly falls away with the retracting river beneath it, and now the fish, which is gasping for breath, is but seconds away from inevitable death.

The levitation from the river comes to an abrupt end when the fish is sandwiched between the coil of grappling talons and the awkward crook of an overhanging branch. The sensation of brittle and dry bark, along with the throbbing pierce of impaling talons, is a first for the fish. The strange sensations of gravity, air, and pain are foreign to the fish's rudimentary neurological system, and despite the novelty of its suffering, the fish's defensive response is automatic. Shuddering with ferocious determination, the fish's jaws are wildly gnashing with jagged teeth clamping out gulps of air as it attempts to carve out a chunk from the predator's body. The teeth are as sharp as flint arrowheads and can easily sheer through gristly flesh, but unfortunately for the fish, its head is pinned firmly to the branch; thus, it is powerless to grab hold of the bird with its powerful jaws.

Looking down at the fish flailing within the grip of its knotted talons, the hawk's head wavers for a bit and then reaches down. In a matter of seconds, just after the hawk hooks her beak deep into the fish's brain, the piranha's body is flaccidly drooping over the branch. The fish's jaws lock open just a second or two after its eye bursts beneath the pressure of an impaling beak, which quickly digs deeply into the skull, mashing the piranha's tiny brain to gummy pulp. The hawk then peels back the flesh from the fish's reddish belly, until the silvery skin along the piranha's side is stripped away from its oval-

The black-collared hawk, also known as a collared fishing hawk, enjoys her conspicuous perch—from where she can divebomb her prey.

shaped body. Now that the fish's grayish pink muscle is exposed, the hawk is quick to tear shreds of savory flesh from the underling frame of needle-like bones. Within minutes, all that remains of the piranha is a bloody smear and a few translucent scales that have been ground into the bark. The black-collared hawk swipes its beak over the branch a few times to clean it of any adhering fish pulp, and then flies off in search of yet another fish.

Approximately a mile downriver is a peculiar slide of well-worn mud shooting down a steep slope of riverbank. Hidden under a shelf of sinewy roots from an overturned tree is a dark cavern of excavated earth. The entrance to the den is just above the muddy slope that slides down to the river. There is an intense musky smell coming from the cave, and then the wafting stench is followed by a hair-raising howl. The loud, freakish call has a sinus-like timbre to it, giving it an ethereal quality. Soon there are more weird cries coming from the cave, until suddenly, four brown bodies, shiny and slick, shoot down the slide and into the water. The surface of the water is still for only a few seconds before the creatures burst out and onto the riverbank one by one. They are enormous, five-foot-long otters, weighing between sixty and seventy pounds each. Their heads and necks are as wide as the nape of a Doberman pincher. Their brown fur is slick, almost like a sea lion's coat, and the webbed digits on each paw spread as wide as my hands. The two-and-a-half-foot-long muscular tail is about as thick as my forearm, and when the animal is swimming, it provides the creature with excellent balance. The most intimidating characteristic of all is the face. The large dark eyes are somewhat foggy, and they appear to sink beneath a rim of wrinkled brow along the animal's forehead. The muzzle is stout and wide, like a pit bull, and the canine teeth are large enough to wrap around your kneecap. It is perhaps the most powerful of all freshwater mammalian predators inhabiting the Americas, and it is the largest otter on the planet, the giant river otter (*Pteronura brasiliensis*).

Giant river otters are intelligent and cunning predators that can be quite ferocious when they need to be. They are commonly called river wolves, a name which probably originated from their canine-like appearance along with their gre-

The giant river otter is one of the most endangered mammals living in South America, sought after for its pelt and dying as a result of deforestation and human encroachment on the wild.

garious nature. Now, the otters that just slid out of the den are members of a tightly bonded group called a holt, and when this holt hits the river feeling hungry and mischievous, nothing is off-limits. They begin their spirited adventure by diving down and rustling up some fresh piranhas, which are instantly crunched up into tasty mouthfuls of scales and macerated fish flesh. One of the otters comes up with a river turtle, which he promptly lets go only to recapture it once again. Soon the holt grows weary of the turtle and wimpy piranhas, so the otters decide to head downriver in search of sport and prey. I can't think of a more formidable mammalian predator than a holt of giant otters. While fish serve as the main staple of the giant river otter's diet, this hunter has been known to prey on many other creatures. A seasoned holt with lots of hunting experience can easily kill a caiman or large anaconda! Giant river otters are extremely adaptive, but with less than five thousand of them left in the wild, they are also one of the most endangered mammals living in South America. The giant river otter is facing extinction because of habitat loss and persecution. To lose the giant river otter from the Amazon would be like losing the wolf in North America or the lion in Africa. Giant river otters are pinnacle predators that are as much a part of the Amazon as any other creature, and their extinction would have a devastating effect on the ecology of the region.

With body stretched across a berm of hardened mud, a male anaconda lies beneath the sun, warming his mass before heading out through the dense thicket of forest and across the Llanos. Unlike Monstra, he is much more petite in build, as male anacondas usually are when compared to females' great mass. While Monstra and this satellite male are probably similar in age, she is nearly double his weight and a third larger in length. Just as he is about to slither off, an intense ruckus of shrilling and twittering giant otters grows louder as the holt approaches. At first he senses nothing; after all, he has no external ears, so auditory reception is lacking, to say the least. The male anaconda is far from helpless, though, and soon he senses the presence of the otters. First he detects the vibration of pattering feet scampering up the berm, then there is a shifting light from shadowing creatures attempting to sneak around him without notice, and of course there is the molecular taste upon the Jacobson's organ against the roof of the mouth. Instantly he knows he is in trouble and that he is just a few seconds from being ripped apart. As the holt scampers up the bank toward the snake, the anaconda is quick to slither into his hole along the base of the berm. The otters arrive to discover that he has slithered off, but in fact he has entered one chamber just to come out another one on the opposite side of the berm. Soon, the holt moves, but so does the anaconda. He is now quickly slithering his way across the narrow band of forest and will be upon the grassland in no time at all.

(continued on page 268)

MAN: THE OTHER WHITE MEAT

I can't think of a South American mammal that I respect more than the giant river otter. Although I would never vilify these extraordinary beasts, and I recognize their important place as South America's pinnacle predator among riparian creatures, nevertheless, they inspire in me a most unmistakable hair-raising chill whenever I am gifted with the opportunity to witness them in all their wild glory. Part of the thrill comes from the sheer rarity of seeing them alive as precocious creatures ruling over their watery domain. The other reason, though, erupts from the part of my brain that acknowledges their supremacy as the greatest of all mustelid predators. Although kismet has kindly kept me out of the diverse smorgasbord frequently terrorized by the giant river otter, I have, however, witnessed the river wolf and heard his baleful bawl as he mercilessly pursues prey, and I can tell you this: Pound for pound, he is indeed South America's greatest predator. What the jaguar is to the jungle, and the harpy eagle is to the canopy, the river otter is to the mighty rivers and tributaries that it haunts.

My first experience with the giant river otter came several years ago while attempting to film, for my first series, a particularly rambunctious individual inhabiting an overly crowded wildlife rehab center in northern Venezuela. The creature occupied a substantial paddock consisting of a naturally formed pond of at least an acre in size, along with an additional acre of jungle and overgrown meadow. At the time, we had been attempting to film the otters in the wild—with little success—and felt that this rare opportunity to get up close and personal with this individual otter would afford us the luxury of some pretty radical close-ups. Before riding seven hours in a stifling van to the wildlife center, the facility's residential veterinarian had assured us that this particular otter was most cooperative and would be an absolute breeze with regard to filming. Upon arrival, however, it became quite clear that this five-foot-long, forty-five-pound individual had only one interest: to make mincemeat out of any creature to get within fifty feet of it. The veterinarian seemed to be quite taken aback by the otter's rather aggressive demeanor and assured us that he had never seen the beast behave so rudely. Let me tell you, I wish I had a dollar for every time someone told me either, "You should have been here yesterday . . ." or "Wow, he's never done that before . . . ."

Our big mistake came when we took the vet for his word when he uttered, "Trust me. He just hava bad mood a little now. Pepe is gonna be nice when you go in. He like to play. . . . People he like very much!" "Yeah right, maybe for dinner," our sound guy, John, whispered under his breath.

This is the point where we should have called it a bust, packed up the van, and headed back to Caracas. Any normal, God-fearing crew would have done exactly that, but if you've watched me on the tube, then you know that common sense and I go together like Marilyn Manson and the Pope. My response to the vet's enthusiastic assurance was simply, "I don't know about you guys, but I trust 'im!" To which Pierce, the cameraman, asked, "Who do you trust—the vet or the otter?" Eventually we decided that we would sneak into the expansive enclosure while the vet distracted Pepe with a bucket full of fish, and once we were positioned along the shoreline, Pepe would go on with life as usual while never even knowing we were there. In theory, this sounded like a brilliant idea, but in reality, what happened next was something entirely different.

So, there we were, huddled behind a log waiting for Pepe the giant river otter to meander by. Just as I was about to deliver a few otter facts to the camera, a terrified voice hollered out from beyond the paddock, "Oh me holy God! Yous gotta run! Pepe . . . he coming quick, and he angry pissed!" Anxiously we all looked to the water for Pepe, but in truth we weren't really all that nervous. After all, we were a seasoned crew that had been charged by bull elephants and had swum with bull sharks. We had seen more king cobras and crocodiles than you could shake a stick at, so what did we have to fear from an otter with a little attitude? The truth is: plenty! With camera rolling and us waiting for Pepe to make his debut, the cantankerous otter had decided to forego the lengthy swim past the camera and instead made a beeline through the tall grass directly toward us. Do you remember the scene in *Jurassic Park*, when the velociraptors, hidden from view, cut through the waving field of grass just before they yanked down their victims, one by one? Well, that's what comes to my mind when I reflect upon what happened that afternoon.

With tenacious drive and nimble delivery, the pugnacious Pepe had managed to snake his way to us through the grass within seconds of the veterinarian's pathetic yelping. We did not even see him until he was but a few yards from where we were standing. I wish I could explain the exact sound of the high-pitched shrill of bleating otter in mid-squeal. If you were to combine the shriek of a cat as its tail is being stepped on and the screech of fingernails scraping down a chalkboard, you still would not even be close to what a ticked off giant river otter sounds like. The otter broke through the wall of grass and perched up to chest-level, as we all gaped at him with terrified awe.

Listen, I'm no wimp. I have served as a chew toy for leopards and lions, and on more than one occasion, I have re-boarded a plane to complete a journey after that very same aircraft had had to make an emergency landing, so when I tell you that this otter had gumption and he had the hairs on the back of our necks standing up in "I see dead people" mode, I really mean it! At first,

(continued on page 266)

MAN: THE OTHER WHITE MEAT—CONT'D

the otter just stood there staring at us for a while, burring out its menacing howl. My only response was to call out to the otter with a confident, but friendly, "Hey there, handsome, look at you . . . You're a big fella, aren't ya? Shshshsh . . . Come on now, buddy, settle down . . . You must smell my cat at home. . . ." This is when his squeals grew more agitated, as the crew and I were within seconds of breaking into utter panic. Then, just as the otter's howl increased in intensity, I decided to go into Beast Master Control Mode. "Hey there, big guy . . . Settle down . . . I said S-E-T-T-L-E D-O-W-N!" This is the point when the otter began to move in on us. Again, though, I attempted to build a bridge of reason with the creature. "Hey-yay-yay, Y-A-Y! I said no, NO! Stop . . . or you're not gonna get . . ." Then came the moment when all hell broke loose, as we were all about to rudely discover just what a great predacious powerhouse the giant river otter truly is.

The first one to run was Chip, the field producer. I never saw a man run so fast in my entire life. He dashed off quicker than a kid running after a fleeting ice-cream truck. My first response was to yell out, "Chip, stop running, you're just making him chase you!" But I soon realized that the psychotic otter was gaining on the poor lad, so I then yelled out, "Dear God, man! Run . . . Run as fast as you can!" It was tragically pathetic to see Chip attempting to outrun the rapidly approaching river otter. You see, Chip wore this floppy Gilligan-style hat, baggy khakis, and a plaid shirt, which he buttoned tightly around his wrists. So, when I witnessed Chip's mad dash from the lissome otter, with his arms flailing wildly from his trunk as his legs bumbled and heaved over the high grass, the only thing I could think of was the scene from *The Wizard of Oz*, when the Scarecrow, played by the limber Ray Bolger, is being chased by the flying monkeys. The rogue otter tackled him to the earth just like when the Scarecrow collapsed upon the forest floor after being pummeled by one of those nasty winged primates. (Chip, however, fared much better than the Scarecrow. If you recall, the Scarecrow ended up being dismembered by the flying monkeys as they ripped him in half and pulled out all his straw.) Chip was lucky to keep all his guts intact, although he did sustain a puncture wound to his Achilles tendon. The otter's decision to leave poor Chip alone came about when he discovered an even bigger and better target: the cameraman.

We all stood there frozen as the giant otter zoomed in on the rest of us. Then, we heard the panicked call of the vet as he jumped the fence and moved in to provide us with assistance. His strategy was to attempt to sweet talk Pepe away from us. *"Hola Pepe. . . . Tranquilo, mi amigo. . . . ¿Qué es tu problema?"* Apparently Pepe possessed little interest in heeding the calming commands of his master, made even more evident when the otter promptly slinked his way over to Pierce. Seconds later, Pepe had climbed up Pierce's leg before wrapping his pit-bullish jowls around his groin! Never in my life have I seen a person grow as pasty-white as Pierce did while his family jewels were being muzzled within the bone-breaking jaws of a bipolar giant river otter.

I am ashamed to say that my first response was to nervously giggle. Now, in my defense, the otter had yet to rip out Pierce's genitals, and I honestly believed that he would not. My anxious laughter was more on the order of a failure to recognize the gravity of the situation, but when I looked over at the wide-eyed vet who was now standing next to us, his terrified expression was enough to squash my smirk mighty fast. The seriousness of the situation was made even more severe when the veterinarian mumbled, "Not funny, this. . . . My God . . . very bad! Last year, Pepe get angry bad with my helper, who get kneecap bite off and how you say . . . l-e-g-g-a-m-i-n-t-s ripped bad! He must go to Brazil for operation to fix!"

As Pepe's mouth enveloped Pierce's privates, he continued to squeal out his agitated growl. Listening to the otter's freakish wail, we all just stood there rather helpless, waiting for the creature to bite down. In the end, after some calm coaxing, along with a freshly caught fish that we had enticingly dangled back and forth, the otter eventually pulled back from Pierce. In the end, the otter was more interested in gobbling down some succulent fish than mutilating Pierce's manpurse. As Pepe scoffed down the fish, we all sprinted toward the exit of the paddock as fast as our legs could carry us. Thankfully, the only medical treatment needed was a tetanus shot for Chip, and lucky for Pierce, he left the wildlife facility fully intact.

Since that first encounter, I have had the chance to see the giant river otter wild and free in places like Brazil, Guyana, and of course, the Llanos of Venezuela. I even witnessed these creatures brazenly move in on the anaconda I had been working with in Brazil's Pantanal region—I remember screaming at the otters in an attempt to keep them at bay while I nervously stuffed the ten-foot serpent into a narrow burrow, well out of harm's way. I have had the great joy of having a lively holt of six otters serenade me while meandering downriver, and I have witnessed the extraordinary gentleness and affection that parenting otters shower upon their offspring. The adventurous spirit of these otters embodies the very region this species inhabits, and if these majestic creatures are no longer allowed to thrive along the remote South American tributaries that now serve as their final refuge, their loss will have an immeasurable impact on this ecosystem. If the impending extinction of the giant river otter is not brought to an immediate halt, the inherent purity of the pristine wilderness still intact deep within the South American frontier will forever be tainted beyond recovery.

HERE COME
THE RAINS AGAIN

Finally, after many weeks with not so much as a drop of moisture touching the earth, it begins. First there is the soft rumbling from a distant sky, and then the blue overhead begins to blacken as a cool wind washes over the landscape. Then, just after a crackling ribbon of white-and-orange lightning blasts across the brooding clouds, a black sheet of rain begins to pour down from the heavens. Soon, the streak of rain falling off in the distance begins to spread across the landscape, saturating the parched earth. The rain spatters against a dry clump of water hyacinth, where sleeping underneath is another male anaconda. He has been estivating there for a number of weeks, coiled up in an almost trance-like state, waiting for the rains to soften the baked earth around him. As the water trickles down through the dried leaves above the slumbering snake, the leaves begin to crackle until finally softening from the infusion of water.

The anaconda's tongue flickers as he begins to stir, then his head hesitantly pokes out from the bundle of vegetation and into the gray, wet light. Hanging from his face are a few white ticks that have gorged themselves on snake blood. The snake has been a good host for the ticks. They are now grotesquely corpulent with their skin stretched to near busting as their pathetic little legs stick out uselessly from their sides, unable to even touch the ground, never mind help the parasites to crawl. Their plump shape makes them appear to be more legume than tick, as they resemble freshly shucked lima beans ready for the boil. As with the snake along

Lima bean-sized ticks snack on a sleepy anaconda.

the riverbank who evaded the holt of otters, this anaconda is driven to slither out
from the shadows of his refuge and head
out across the grassland.

Close to where the reviving anaconda
stirs is another reptile, although he is not
a snake. Hunting through the crumpled
matter of a dried-up wash is South
America's version of the monitor, a hearty
and large lizard called a tegu (*Tupinambis
nigropunctatus*). As the three-foot-long
lizard forages through the debris in search
of any small creature or scrap of carrion
that he can find with his chemically sensitive tongue, another forked tongue has
detected him. The tegu scrapes back the
leaves with his clawed hand and then
probes the opened patch with his pointed
muzzle as his inquisitive tongue con-
stantly flickers. He'll eat just about anything—rodents (alive or dead!), insects, or
fruit. His markings of black and yellow
flecks are uniform across his long, smooth,
shiny body. The tegu hears something
rustling beneath the litter of dried grass
and foliage in front of him, so he rushes
over to investigate. When the tegu moves,

The tegu has no idea he's on today's menu.

he does so with both head and body
carried straight, level to the ground. He
quickly dashes over to the other side of
the wash only to find nothing.

As he frantically searches for whatever it was that had crackled in the dried
vegetation, the lizard is oblivious to the
nine-foot anaconda sneaking up on him
from behind. With ticks still hanging from
his face, the anaconda lashes out and grabs
the tegu. The lizard never saw it coming,
as the snake zealously wraps himself
around the tegu in a matter of seconds.

Taunting the anaconda only gets . . .   . . . the tegu eaten!

Unable to escape the serpent's deadly spiral, the lizard is soon crushed to death. After unwinding his coils, the anaconda swallows the tegu with little effort, and soon the lizard has vanished within the serpent's cylindrical mass. The snake does not linger around waiting for digestion to take place; instead he moves on, for he is on a mission that will take him across a stretch of savannah in search of the ultimate mate.

The fresh rainwater cleanses all it touches, as the grassland is infused with life-sustaining water and many creatures are beginning to reanimate once again. The rain has washed over Monstra, re-

viving her from nearly two days of rest beneath the tree. She begins to slither off as well, but not nearly as swiftly as the slender males, which are paltry in size when compared to her great mass. As she crawls out from the base of the tree, Monstra heads toward the neighboring lagoon where she eventually slides back in once again. For weeks while crawling across the land, Monstra has been leaving behind microscopic traces of pheromones wherever she travels. Any male anacondas within eyeshot of where she has been have keenly honed in on her intriguing scent and are now fast approaching. Monstra, on the other hand, will wait for their arrival in the comfort of the lagoon, which is slowly rising as the rain keeps falling.

It is amazing to me just how fast the land of the Llanos can be replenished with the arrival of the rains at the onset of the wet season. The change in the Llanos from a parched and dusty scrap of earth to a lush and productive landscape happens at an astonishingly fast rate once the rains have settled. Rivers and water holes begin to fill within days instead of weeks. Just a few hours of solid rain can fill a small depression, transforming it into an inviting pool where wildlife can flourish. When the water rises up from rivers and water holes, banks will overflow as the water travels in every direction like a liquid sheet. Soon the entire Llanos will be flooded beneath a layer of water, broken only where there are tall trees or mounds of higher ground. The congested flocks of birds will disperse, as will caimans and fish, now that these creatures have an endless, watery expanse to explore and hunt. Of course, the concentration of wildlife around remnant water holes during the dry season makes life easier for predators looking to go directly to the source, but overall, the dispersal of wildlife across the Llanos allows for productive areas, which have been overly burdened by residing wildlife, to lie fallow until rejuvenated once again.

Two weeks have passed since the arrival of the rainy season, and the impact that the water has had on the land is profound. Although not completely flooded, many of the water holes are overflowing, and the prairie has transformed from a dusty expanse of dry, brown grass into a lush landscape where the grass now grows green and tall. Thousands of capybaras are littered across the grassland as they grow fat from the endless bounty of nutritious fodder. Beyond their herds, loping across the horizon, is a very strange beast. At first glance from a distance, the animal resembles a German shepherd, but a closer look reveals that he is not even remotely canine-like in shape or behavior. With a length of five feet and a weight of seventy pounds he is quite a large animal. The narrow, funnel-shaped muzzle instantly tells us that he is an anteater, but his build

(continued on page 276)

THE HORSE LISPERER

Beyond serving as a haven for wildlife, the Llanos grassland is cattle country. In fact, driving cattle across the endless expanse of rugged terrain is about all a person can do to eke out a livelihood here. The Llanos can be as tough on the human inhabitants as it is on the creatures, yet people do manage to scrape out a humble existence, and they do so by raising a resilient breed of livestock called Brahman cattle. Unlike the sullen and softly constituted cows of, let's say Vermont, Brahman cattle are a much more hardy breed of bovine, capable of surviving the hostility of a contrary landscape where blistering temperatures, devastating droughts, and relentless floods comprise the everyday existence of life in the Llanos. The robust cattle ranching community is made up of the Llaneros, and their ability to carve out a niche in the severe environment of the Llanos is nothing short of miraculous. It can be quite a sight to witness a team of four or five horse-mounted Llaneros driving a river of cattle across the red blaze of sunset, with a thousand trampling hooves kicking up a cloud of amber dust.

The image of a cowboy rambling across the prairie on horseback alongside an endless throng of cattle, all against a backdrop of big sky and sweeping prairie, is a scene that often connotes the western United States. In truth, the rugged livelihood of the cattle rancher is as much a part of the cultural heritage of a number of South American countries as it is in North America. From the Llanos of Venezuela to the Chaco of Paraguay, the ranching tradition has passed, virtually unchanged, from one generation to the next. When I am exploring the savannahs of South America, I often reside in a remote ranch where life seems to pleasantly dawdle by without the overwhelming distractions of rush-hour traffic, television, telemarketers, and in some cases, electricity. Of course, I'm not actually driving the cattle, and lord knows I am not up at dawn mucking any manure or branding any backsides. I am usually just sucking up air, space, and food, while often getting in the way of the individuals who are working hard—and of course, with me there, working that much harder. Now, if I had to actually get up at four in the morning and sweat for thirteen hours under a tropical sun while trying to earn a living driving cattle and pounding in fences, well then, perhaps I would not find the ranching life to be so idyllic. But, as an occasional visitor who shows up for overflowing plates of hearty grub at the ringing of every bell and who passes the day by looking for caimans and anacondas while occasionally breaking up the monotony with a little horseback riding, I find the ranching lifestyle to be quite pleasing for the spirit.

I do recall one moment, while residing at a remote ranch in the grasslands of southwestern Brazil, that proved to be the most memorable. Like the Llanos, the Brazilian prairie of the Pantanal is complete with anacondas (albeit the shorter, yellow species *Eunectes notaeus*), capybaras, and caiman (*Caiman yacare*, as opposed to *C. crocodilus* of the Llanos). My film crew and I were on a mission to document the wildlife living in the Pantanal, which, as with the creatures of the Llanos, face many challenges of heat, aridity, and flooding. The rustic ranch that had served as our home base while working in the Pantanal was frequented by a herd of semi-wild horses that would make a pass through the grounds of the ranch at around two-thirty or three o'clock in the morning. The herd of approximately sixty horses would amble on in and graze for half an hour or so before moving on.

Late one night, after a long day of filming as well as an equally long night of caparinas (a de-

(continued on page 274)

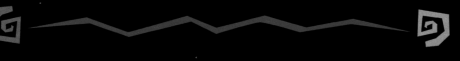

THE HORSE LISPERER—CONT'D

licious but potent Brazilian libation consisting of fresh lime juice, sugar, ice, and liberal doses of a regional sugarcane liquor called cachaca), my colleague, Pierce, and I were engaging in a most interesting conversation. While sitting back on the ranch steps, gazing out at the weary blackness of pre-morning light, the arrival of the horses, along with the brain-numbing cachaca flowing through our veins, had greatly influenced the animated dialogue playing out between us. The topic of babbling banter was essentially this: How did prehistoric man come to domesticate the horse?

Apparently our lively conversation had aroused the interest of the remaining crew members, and soon all of us were arguing on the most plausible theory behind the fusion of hominids and horses. After an hour of arguing, we finally came to the conclusion that the only way to solve this mystery was to attempt to reenact what might have transpired between man and horse six thousand years ago. In order to test our theory we would need horses and a caveman. Now, horses we had, but what about a test subject to represent primitive man? The crew decided that the best example of an extant hominid who would make an ideal caveman would be none other than myself. Thus, the challenge had been presented to me. My objective: to sneak up on one of the horses and try to ride it, perhaps as our ancestors had done thousands of years before. In order to keep things authentic we decided on two conditions: 1) There could be no talking, under the assumption that language had not yet developed (although in reality, the first people to domesticate the horse were probably speaking to each other). 2) With the exception of a rudimentary loincloth, I would have to be naked and shoeless (again, another potential misconception, seeing as whoever had domesticated the horse had probably been eating their flesh and wearing their hides long before they figured out how to ride them). So there I was, barefoot and bare-assed, sneaking up onto a herd of sleepy horses, with only a pitiful hand towel fluttering between my privates and a swarm of blood-ravenous mosquitoes.

I approached the horses with all the authenticity I could muster, making sure to throw in lots of grunting and snorting. I ambled over with legs bowed and shoulders wobbly, making sure to include the occasional knuckle drag and animated side-striding that chimpanzees seem to do. I snuck up to the shifting herd while attempting to do my very best imitation of the furry cavemen from the film *2001: A Space Odyssey*, or the sooty caveboy Cha-Ka from the TV series *Land of the Lost*. I

took on the challenge with a great sense of purpose, and while I was earnest in my endeavor to be a caveman, I have now begun to question the sincerity of my colleagues. Although much of that evening remains but a blur, I do recall a great deal of heckling and snickering coming from the shadows as I began to squeeze past a wall of bumper-to-bumper horse rumps.

Despite the lack of support and integrity from my crew, I had managed to infiltrate the herd, and now it was time for me to select a horse worthy of conquest. Carefully, with head sunk low and arm dangling beneath an overly humped shoulder (think Marty Feldman from *Young Frankenstein*), I selected a fine and sturdy mare that I would attempt to mount. Without aid of stirrups and saddle or reigns, I grabbed onto the tangled mane running down her neck and then hobbled up onto the horse's back. She whinnied with disapproval and bucked a bit in her attempt to throw me from her back, but I was not going to let go, especially with a contemptuous audience mocking my every move. This was no longer an experiment; a brief blush of sobriety had convinced me that if I was to avoid complete and utter humiliation, I would have to stay on the horse, a fact which became even more clear to me upon discovering that my makeshift loincloth was covering a pile of horse crap on the ground next to me. To my credit, I did manage to stay on the mare, and I even figured out how to steer her. By gently covering both of her eyes with my hands she would walk in a straight line; and if I wanted her to go left I would uncover her left eye, and vice versa. Eventually I just moved with the herd, traveling where they wanted to go. A couple hours later the herd looped back to the ranch where I discovered the crew along with the ranch owner, scowling with concern, upon my return. Despite their request for me to dismount and come back in, I defiantly waved off their plea and continued to move on with the horses.

It was at around five o'clock in the morning when I woke up naked and grimy on a muddy pile of overgrown sod with no horse in sight. Slowly, I groveled around in the mire of my humility until finally coming to my feet. How ironic, I thought, standing there bare and filthy, with my skin covered by hundreds of mosquito welts, resembling a distant ancestor taking to terra firma upon a bipedal stance for the very first time. I can't recall how long I had wallowed on the wet earth, but when I looked back at where I had lain, I had left behind an impression in the muddy turf—my own version of a fossil. While I had been scraped up from chest to toe and was worn weary from the idiotic trek, I managed to find my way back to the ranch with both a pounding headache and a great memory of being a caveman for a day.

is dramatically different from that of the tamandua. The fur covering his body is long and luxuriant; a thick mane running down his spine increases in length as it reaches the tail. Resembling the hairs of a massive paintbrush, the tail has a bizarrely bushy shape to it. Although much of his pelage is gray, the anteater has a triangular-shaped patch of black and white streaks along both sides of his body. The limbs of this anteater are equally unique, as he ambles forward on his knuckles with the long claws of his forearms curled up against his palm and wrists. This creature is perhaps the world's strangest anteater, and while the tamandua is designed for the challenges of an arboreal life, the giant anteater (*Myrmecophaga tridactyla*) carves out a livelihood on solid ground.

The giant anteater continues to lope across the grassland at a steady pace, but occasionally he gallops in short spurts when the wind hits him wrong or he spooks from odd smells picked up by his highly sensitive olfactory system. He stops momentarily to investigate a four-foot-tall

The giant anteater is the largest anteater on Earth.

termite mound, which erupts from the earth like a volcano in the making. With a few swipes of his three-and-a-half-inch-long claws, the giant anteater cuts his way into the dark interior, jams his muzzle in, and then begins to feast. He hangs there for ten minutes, leaning against the nest with his rear feet firmly on the ground. While his forelimbs cling to the top of the mound, he gorges on as many termites as he can siphon up his narrow snout. Eventually, he retracts his long and sticky tongue into his throat, as he drops back down on all fours and then wanders off toward a small lagoon. When he arrives at the brimming body of water, he goes to the edge to lap up a mouthful of water and then retreats to the comforting shade of a nearby tree.

As he settles himself against the shaded buttress, he hears the raspy chatter coming from a pair of nesting tiger-herons above, but soon they quiet down as well. After a stretch or two, the giant anteater pulls up his forearms and then buries his snout between them as he tucks in his back legs close to his stomach. Finally, he folds his enormous tail up and over until it covers his entire body from snout to rump. To look at him now with his massive body blanketed by the bristly, gray fur of his tail, he appears to be nothing more than a pile of withered vegetation. Although he never noticed, just inches from

Mud crusted over Casanova's face as he waited to woo Monstra.

where he drank at the edge of the lagoon was Monstra, but she had no interest in preying upon the anteater, for she is heavily engrossed in another activity.

For weeks she has lain there, much of her body submerged beneath mud and water. Monstra has moved only slightly as the days passed her by, while her gigantic body has slowly been coiling up into a massive knot. Next to her entangled body appears to be a branch encrusted with mud, but then the branch moves slightly as if drawing a breath. The branch is in fact the nine-foot anaconda, the same in-

Due to her massive size, we can clearly identify Monstra. If the puny males were her size, the mating ball would crush her. Another theory as to why male anacondas are so much smaller than females is that the males can easily identify who the female is and breed with her.

dividual who had eaten the tegu. The male has been beside Monstra for many days, both of them in a trance-like state as he writhes his cloaca close to her in his attempt to copulate with her. He has been there for so long and has been so still, the mud has hardened across his face and head; even his eyes have been crusted over, yet he does not move in risk of losing his position to pass his sperm on to her. If he were to slither around in an attempt to gain comfort, he could lose his position, for he is not the only male anaconda that is rubbing up against Monstra.

There are as many as four other males that have joined her at the lagoon, all of them with one intention: to be the first to breed with her. Coiled around the base of her tail is the same tick-covered anaconda that had been basking along the river weeks earlier, and after picking up her trail while slithering across the savannah, he arrived at the lagoon soon after, seeking a chance to breed with her. There are other anacondas just like these two, each with their own life experience of how they found their way to Monstra. Looking down upon the squirming orgy, it's almost impossible to visually separate one male anaconda from the next, being that all seem to have joined as one in their efforts to copulate with her. Anaconda mating balls may contain as many as ten males, all of which are competing for access to one female. This elaborate courtship may last as long as a month, but eventually, after the female has been inseminated, the breeding ball will begin to unravel as all the snakes go their separate ways.

SIX MONTHS LATER

Six months have passed since Monstra was entangled within the anaconda orgy, and the lagoon that had swollen beyond her banks and across the grassland is now not much more than a muddy wallow where a warm and viscous pool of stagnant water has been left behind. Just a month ago there were still generous downpours of rain occurring daily, but now the rainfall has become so infrequent that the once soft and verdant grass has faded to a brittle and paper-bag brown. When the rain does come, its arrival is but a fleeting tease barely spackling the parching earth. The residential creatures trapped within the warm liquid of the former lagoon are struggling to survive as a halo of dead and dying fish has begun to cake around the perimeter of the rapidly shrinking pool. The hot breeze whistling through the tufts of suffering grass is stifled by the constant drone of flies, which enthusiastically cloud around the stinking fish corpses. Once again, flocks of scarlet ibis, egrets, herons, and spoonbills are crowding the water hole as many of their other prospects for water and food scattered throughout the Llanos have all but dried up. The slurry of brown water continuously bubbles and bobs like pooling lava as hundreds of piranhas, catfish, snakeheads, eels, and peacock bass desperately gasp for breath. Caimans of all sizes cruise back and forth as a dozen capybaras wallow about in an attempt to stay as cool as possible. The living conditions are bleak at best, but the truth is that in a matter of a few more weeks, life here in the Llanos will be even more unbearable.

Just a few yards from the watery pit, nestled beneath an upturned shelf of densely tangled plant matter, is a pathetic coil of anaconda. Although the serpent is very long, her girth is not much thicker than the ribcage riddled down the length of each side of her wasting torso. The bony ridge of spinal column running down her back protrudes beyond the corresponding strips of backstrap muscle until it pushes up her skin like a tightly drawn line holding a triangle of tent canvas. As for the snake's dermis, its hue is dull and gray. The skin is loose about her body and seems to wrinkle and hang within the curvatures of her coils. The poor creature is infested with an expressway of mites roaming around and underneath her scales as they feed on

sloughing skin and on the tiny corpuscles of blood flowing through her epidermis. She is also inundated with white ticks, some of which have ballooned to the size of grapes. The emaciated serpent is none other than Monstra, who lays there coiled and weak, representing but a mere shadow of her former self. She is no longer the fattest snake in all the land, as she has been transformed into a nearly sixteen-foot-long bony wrack, draped within a loose tent of skin that has lost much of its luster of just a few months ago. She has not eaten in more than half a year, and her weight has plummeted from two hundred and fifty pounds at her prime to a measly one hundred and fifty. Her dramatic weight loss is not only the result of her exhausting fast but also of the squirming wad of creatures within her body that have been steadily drawing upon her energy reserves like wax seeping up a candlewick.

She has barely moved in the last six months, and when she has, it was only to reposition her body in and out of the warming glare of the burning sun. Monstra's body is now serving as a living incubator, and most of her energy is being directed to the sixty babies growing inside her. While Monstra grows weaker, her offspring grow stronger as they greedily extract from her dwindling reserve of life-force. The task of carrying a great load of developing anacondas is so taxing on the mother's body, females are capable of reproducing only once every three or four years. Prior to pregnancy, a female anaconda must gorge on great quantities of prey in order to build up the fat reserves needed to sustain herself and her developing offspring during the gravid period. It is extremely rare for an anaconda to take food while she is pregnant, and the long period of fasting will often ravage her body. For Monstra, the journey from copulation to the final stages of gravidity has been long and arduous, but she is finally ready to give birth.

Slowly, her coiled mass begins to unravel until she has stretched herself out from the shadows of the damp pocket that has formed beneath the matted layer of desiccated water hyacinth and grass. A cramping spasm begins to well up inside her as a twitching wave of jolting scales dances across her drooping skin along the last third of her body length. Slowly, she lifts her neck a few inches off the earth and wheezes in a deep breath of air. Then, the very tip of her stubby tail begins to rise. From deep within Monstra's body is the muted sound of gurgling fluid, which comes just seconds before the cloaca beneath her tail begins to dilate and the soft, pinkish gray wall of tissue inside bulges outward. Then, the tiny, cat's claw–sized spurs on either side of her cloaca protract, just as a spurt of yellowish fluid, thick and slightly bloody, comes squirting out. Again, Monstra draws in another labored breath as a second wave of cramping flows down her body. More fluid rushes out, and then with one forceful push, a stream of translucent sacks begins to spurt out of her cloaca. The slimy, membranous sacks are thin and vascular as they shoot out of Monstra's cloaca single file. Upon hitting the grass, each sack writhes and twists until finally rupturing. Soon after a burst of clear, sappy liquid dribbles out of each sack, a shimmering snake head, about thumb-thick, hesitantly sticks out. After a few hesitant flicks of the tongue, a perfectly formed anaconda almost two feet in length, nearly identical to Monstra in shape and coloration, emerges from its gelatinous sack. Again, Monstra draws in another great breath as the muscles around her lower abdomen contract, and then with one final push the last dozen or so neonates remaining inside her squirt out from the soft darkness and onto the plains of the Llanos.

A few of Monstra's neonates have not emerged from their sacks, victims of natural selection. The remaining cluster of newly born anacondas, however, is alive and thriving. Soon, they shall all be free of their amniotic sacks and will linger only briefly before melting into their surrounding habitat. Monstra makes no attempt to connect with the offspring that she has just given birth to. True, her great physiological investment comes to an abrupt end now that the clutch of sixty offspring have passed out of her body. Alas, there is another reason why she fails

to react. The inhalation of air needed to push the last of her offspring out, which now slowly leaks from her nostrils, has indeed turned out to be the last breath she will ever take. In the end, pregnancy and labor were too much for Monstra to bear, as the energy needed to sustain her life has passed on to her offspring. Monstra lays there, forever still, with no knowledge or recognition of her great sacrifice made for the betterment of her species.

– FIN –

All right, now dry your eyes and quit sniffling. Monstra isn't really dead—at least she wasn't the last time I saw her, which was about a month prior to finishing this book. As far as I know she is alive and well, eating lots of plump capybaras! I bet you never thought you could have such strong feelings for a big old serpent like Monstra. The truth is, until we see the biological commonalities that we share with other life-forms, it is often hard for us to feel any empathy for them. Of course you know that anacondas and other species of serpents are organismic, being made of flesh and blood. Yet, many people fail to realize that snakes are highly evolved vertebrates complete with heart, lungs, and other diverse organs, along with an array of relatively complex behaviors. Snakes can feel anger and will defend themselves out of fear of death. Many species of snakes exhibit intense and extremely ritualistic sexual behavior as if directly pulled from the pages of the *Kama Sutra*. The investment that anacondas make towards reproduction is incredible, from lengthy courtship and copulation, to the physiological sacrifices of a grueling pregnancy. Although the level of consciousness with regard to an individual snake's ability to recognize its life experience is not fully understood, that does not mean that a snake is an emotionally blank automaton.

I believe that feelings like passion, anger, jealousy, contentment, fear, and despair are not uniquely human. We often make the mistake of using the ability to generate emotional response as a characteristic for defining what it is to be human, but perhaps emotions are universally primordial traits, which many creatures exhibit in an effort to enhance survival. Perhaps our ability to generate emotional responses to stimuli is what we in fact share with other animals as opposed to what makes us unique. I don't think I am being anthropomorphic—this isn't about whether we have a soul or if all dogs, and anacondas for that matter, go to heaven—I just believe that emotions are tools used by many life-forms for survival. For example, all life uses fear to recognize and escape a dangerous situation, while emotions of passion are designed to draw creatures together in order to instigate reproduction. Love is an emotion that will cause one creature to care for and protect another, while hate and greed are visceral responses brought on by issues of territoriality. Okay, maybe "human" love doesn't exist among anacondas, but what about canines, primates, and cetaceans (whales, porpoises, dolphins)? Did Koko the gorilla feel love for the kitten she cared for and sadness after it had perished? What about when a dog, on his own accord, jumps into a river to save a drowning kid—does

he do it out of instinct or because he connects to the gravity of life and death?

I bring all this up because I believe that we so frequently vilify snakes—and many other organisms, for that matter—because we look upon them as being lesser creatures, which of course makes it easy for us to dismiss their presence or even worse, eliminate it. Because the Llanos is such an inhospitable place for humans and is void of many of the valuable minerals possessed by other ecosystems, it does not face the pressure of unsustainable development as much as other habitats do. The Llanos is of course impacted by the presence of man, but this impact is, for the most part, minimal. As for the anacondas of the Llanos, the greatest danger comes from the humans that fear and loathe them. By understanding the important role that these serpents play within the ecology of the Llanos and by recognizing them as more than just primitive tubes of flesh, we can develop respect and empathy for these misunderstood, magnificent giants. Because anacondas are so deeply rooted in the ecology of the Llanos, if we choose to protect them, many other species will benefit as well. If you would like to learn more about the conservation and ecology of the Llanos prairie of Venezuela, I would encourage you to contact any one of these very important organizations: Venezuela's Cinaruco-Capanaparo National Park, the Center for Environmental Research and Conservation, *Centro de Ecología* (Center for Ecology), Provita, and eco-ranches like *Estación Biológica El Frío* (El Frio Biological Station). Keep in mind that these are but just a small sample of the many non-governmental organizations working to protect the Llanos.

CONSULTED RESEARCH*

SONORAN DESERT OF ARIZONA

Anderson, E. 1987. A critical review and annotated bibliography of literature on the bobcat. Special Report Number 62, Colorado Division of Wildlife.

Animal Diversity Web of the University of Michigan's Museum of Zoology at http://animaldiversity.ummz.umich.edu.

Averill-Murray, R.C., A.P. Woodman, and J.M. Howland. 2002. Population ecology of the Sonoran desert tortoise in Arizona. pp. 109–134 in Van Devender, T.R., ed. *The Sonoran Desert Tortoise: the Natural History, Biology, and Conservation.* University of Arizona Press and the Arizona-Sonora Desert Museum, Tucson.

Averill-Murray, R.C., and C.M. Klug. 2000. Reproduction in Sonoran desert tortoises: 1999 progress report. Proceedings of the Desert Tortoise Council Symposium 1999: 31–34.

Bailey, S.J., C.R. Schwalbe, and C.H. Lowe. 1995. Hibernaculum use by a population of desert tortoises (*Gopherus agassizii*) in the Sonoran desert. *Journal of Herpetology* 29(3): 361–369.

Bailey, T.N. 1974. Social organization in a bobcat population. *Journal of Wildlife Management* 38: 435–446.

Barrett, S.L., and J.H. Humphrey. 1986. Agonistic interactions between *Gopherus agassizii* (Testudinidae) and *Heloderma suspectum* (Helodermatidae). *Southwestern Naturalist* 31: 261–263.

Beal, K.G. 1978. Immature Cooper's Hawk attempts to capture Roadrunner. Bull. *Okla. Ornithol. Soc.* 11: 31.

Beal, K.G., and L.D. Gillam. 1979. On the function of prey beating by Roadrunners. *Condor* 81: 85–87.

Beck, D.D. 1990. Ecology and behavior of the Gila Monster in southwestern Utah. *Journal of Herpetology* 24: 54–68.

Bednarz, J.C. 1987. Pair and group reproductive success, polyandry, and cooperative breeding in Harris' Hawks. *Auk* 104: 393–404.

———. 1988a. A comparative study of the breeding ecology of Harris' and Swainson's Hawks in southeastern New Mexico. *Condor* 90: 311–323.

———. 1988b. Cooperative hunting in Harris' Hawks (*Parabuteo unicinctus*). *Science* 239: 1525–1527.

———. 1995. Harris' Hawk. *The Birds of North America*, No. 146.

Bent, A.C. 1938. Life histories of North American birds of prey. U.S. National Museum Bulletin No. 170.

———. 1939. Life histories of North American woodpeckers. U.S. Natl. Mus. Spec. Bull. 3.

Bilger, W.J. 1974. Seasonal movements and activity patterns of the collared peccary. *Journal of Mammalogy* 55: 851–855.

Bleich, V.C. 1975. Roadrunner predation on ground squirrels in California. *Auk* 92: 147–149.

Bock, C.E., and J.H. Bock. 1979. Relationships of the collared peccary to sacaton grasslands. *Journal of Wildlife Management* 43: 813–816.

Bogert, C.M., and R.M. Del Campo. 1956. The Gila Monster and its allies: the relationships, habitats, and behavior of the lizards of the family helodermatidae. Bulletin of the American Museum of Natural History 109(1).

Bouskila, A. 1993. Predation risk and competition in a community of rodents and snakes. Dissertation. University of California, Davis.

———. 1995. Interactions between predation risk and competition: a field study of kangaroo rats. *Ecology* 76(1): 165–178.

Brannon, J.D. 1980. The reproductive ecology of a Texas Harris' Hawk (*Parabuteo unicinctus harrisi*) population. Master's thesis, University of Texas, Austin.

Brenowitz, G.L. 1978. Gila Woodpecker agonistic behavior. *Auk* 95: 49–58.

Brown, D.E. 1989. *Arizona game birds*. University of Arizona Press, Tucson.

Brown, D.E., J.C. Hagelin, M. Taylor, and J. Galloway. 1998. Gambel's Quail. *The Birds of North America*, No. 321.

Brown, J.S. 1989. Desert rodent community structure: a test of four mechanisms of coexistence. *Ecological Monographs* 59: 1–20.

Brown, J.H., and D.W. Davidson. 1977. Competition between seed-eating rodents and ants in desert ecosystems. *Science* 196: 880–882.

Bryant, H.C. 1916. Habits and food of the Roadrunner in California. University of California Publ. Zool. 17:21–58.

Burger, J., and M. Gochfeld. 1992. Effect of group size on vigilance in the coati, *Nasua narica*, in Costa Rica. *Animal Behaviour* 44: 1053–1057.

*Some books and articles have been used in chapters other than that in which they are noted here.

Ceballos, G., T.H. Fleming, C. Chavez, and J. Nassar. 1997. Population dynamics of *Leptonycteris curasoae* (Chiroptera: Phyllostomidae) in Jalisco, Mexico. *Journal of Mammalogy* 78: 1220–1230.

Codenotti, T.L. and F. Alvarez. 1997. Cooperative breeding between males in the Greater Rhea, *Rhea Americana*. *Ibis* 139: 568–571.

———. 1998. Adoption of unrelated young by Greater Rheas. *Journal of Field Ornithology* 69(1): 58–65.

Collins, J.T. 1985. *Natural Kansas*. University Press of Kansas, Lawrence.

Coombs, E.M. 1977. Implications of behavior and physiology on the desert tortoise (*Gopherus agassazii*) concerning their declining populations in southwestern Utah, with inferences on related desert ecotherms. Report to U.S. Bureau of Land Management, St. George, Utah.

Coulombe, H.N. 1971. Behavior and population ecology of the Burrowing Owl, *Speotyto cunicularia*, in the Imperial Valley of California. *Condor* 73: 162–176.

Daly, M., M. Wilson, P.R. Behrends, and L.F. Jacobs. 1990. Characteristics of kangaroo rats, *Dipodomys merriami*, associated with differential predation risk. *Animal Behavior* 40: 380–389.

Davidson, D.W., R.S. Inouye, and J.H. Brown. 1984. Granivory in a desert ecosystem: experimental evidence for indirect facilitation of ants by rodents. *Ecology* 65(6): 1780–1786.

Dawson, J.W. 1988. The cooperative breeding system of the Harris' Hawk in Arizona. Master's thesis, University of Arizona, Tucson.

Dawson, J.W., and R.W. Mannan. 1989. A comparison of two methods of estimating breeding group size in Harris' Hawks. *Auk* 106: 480–483.

———. 1991. The role of territoriality in the social organization of Harris' Hawks. *Auk* 108: 661–672.

Day, G.I. 1985. Javelina research and management in Arizona. Phoenix: Arizona Game and Fish Department.

Djawdan, M. 1993. Locomotor performance of bipedal and quadrupedal heteromyid rodents. *Functional Ecology* 7: 195–202.

Djawdan, M. and T. Garland Jr. 1988. Maximal running speeds of bipedal and quadrupedal heteromyid rodents. *Journal of Mammalogy* 69: 765–772.

Dunning, J.G., Jr. 1984. Body weights of 686 species of North American birds. *West. Bird Banding Association Monographs* 1: 1–38.

Dunson, W.A., M.K. Dunson, and R.D. Ohmart. 1976. Evidence for the presence of nasal salt glands in the Roadrunner and Coturnix Quail. *Journal of Experimental Zoology* 198: 209–216.

Eddy, T.A. 1961. Food and feeding patterns of the collared peccary in southern Arizona. *Journal of Wildlife Management* 25: 248–257.

Edwards, H.H., and G.D. Schnell. 2000. Gila Woodpecker, *Melanerpes uropygialis*. The Birds of North America, No. 532.

Eichholz, M.W., and W.D. Koenig. 1992. Gopher snake attraction to birds' nests. *The Southwestern Naturalist* 37(3): 293–298.

Elder, J.B. 1956. Watering patterns of some desert game animals. *Journal of Wildlife Management* 20: 368–378.

Ellis, D.H., J.C. Bednarz, D.G. Smith, and S.P. Flemming. 1993. Social foraging classes in raptorial birds. *Bioscience* 43: 14–20.

Ettershank, G. 1971. Some aspects of the ecology and nest microclimatology of the meat ant, *Iridomyrmex purpureus* (Sm.). Proceedings of the Royal Society of Australia 84: 137–151.

Fleming, T.H., M.D. Tuttle, and M.A. Horner. 1996. Pollination biology and the relative importance of nocturnal and diurnal pollinators in three species of Sonoran desert columnar cacti. *The Southwestern Naturalist* 41(3): 257–269.

Gallizioli, S., and P.M. Webb. 1958. The influence of hunting upon quail populations. Fed. Aid Proj. W-78-R. Arizona Game and Fish Department.

Germano, D. 1992. Longevity and age-size relationships of populations of desert tortoises. *Copeia* 1992: 367–374.

Gilman, M.F. 1915. Woodpeckers of the Arizona lowlands. *Condor* 76: 184–197.

Glover, F.A. 1953. Summer foods of the Burrowing owl. *Condor* 55:275.

Gompper, M.E. 1996. Sociality and asociality in white-nosed coatis (*Nasua narica*): foraging costs and benefits. *Behavioral Ecology* 7: 254–263.

———. 1997. Genetic relatedness, coalitions and social behavior of white–nosed coatis, *Nasua narica*. Animal Behaviour 53: 781–797.

González, J.A. 1996. Breeding biology of the Jabiru in the southern llanos Venezuela. Wilson Bulletin 108(3): 524–534.

Gorsuch, D.M. 1934. Life history of the Gambel Quail in Arizona. University of Arizona Bulletin 2: 1–89.

Green, G.A. 1983. Ecology of breeding Burrowing Owls in Columbia basin, Oregon. M.Sc. thesis, Oregon State University, Corvallis.

Hall, H.T., and J.D. Newson. 1976. Summer home ranges and movement of bobcats in bottomland hardwoods of southern Louisiana. Proc. Annu. Conf. Southeast. Assoc. Fish and Wildlife Agencies. 30: 422–436.

Hass, C.C., and D. Valenzuela. 2002. Ant-predator benefits of group living in white-nosed coatis (*Nasua narica*). *Behav. Ecol. Sociobiology* 51: 570–578.

Haug, E.A. 1985. Observations on the breeding ecology of Burrowing owls in Saskatchewan. M. Sc. thesis, University of Saskatchewan, Saskatoon.

Haug, E.A., B.A. Millsap, and M.S. Martell. 1993. Burrowing owl. *The Birds of North America*, No. 61.

Hensley, M.M. 1954. Ecological relations of the breeding bird population of the desert biome in Arizona. *Ecological Monographs* 24(2): 185–208.

———. 1959. Notes on the nesting of selected species of the breeding bird population of the Sonoran Desert. Wilson Bulletin 71: 86–92.

Hoffmeister, D.F. 1986. Mammals of Arizona. The University of Arizona Press and the Arizona Game and Fish Department.

Hohman, J.P., and R.D. Ohmart. 1980. Ecology of the desert tortoise on the Beaver Dam Slope, Arizona. Report to U.S. Bureau of Land Management, St. George, Utah.

Horner, M.A., T.H. Fleming, and C.T. Sahley. 1998. Foraging behaviour and energetics of a nectar-feeding bat, *Leptonycteris curasoae* (Chiroptera: Phyllostomidae). *Journal of Zoological Society of London* 244: 575–586.

Howe, S., D.L. Kilgore, Jr., and C. Colby. 1987. Respiratory gas concentrations and temperatures within nest cavities of the Northern Flicker (*Colaptes auratus*). *Canadian Journal of Zoology* 65: 1541–1547.

Howell, D.J. 1974. Acoustic behavior and feeding in glossophagine bats. *Journal of Mammalogy* 55: 293–308.

———. 1979. Flock foraging in nectar–feeding bats: advantages to the bats and to the host plants. *American Naturalist* 114: 23–49.

Howell, D.J., and B.S. Roth. 1981. Sexual reproduction in agaves: the benefits of bats; the cost of semelparous advertising. *Ecology* 62(1): 1–7.

Hughes, J.M. 1996. Greater Roadrunner. *The Birds of North America*, No. 244.

Hungerford, C.R. 1962. Adaptations shown in selection of food by Gambel's quail. *Condor* 64(3): 213–219.

Inouye, R.W., G.S. Byers, and J.H. Brown. 1982. Effects of predation and competition on survivorship, fecundity, and community structure of desert annuals. *Ecology* 61: 1344–1351.

Jennings, W.S., and J.T. Harris. 1953. The collared peccary in Texas. F.A. Report Series No. 12. Texas Game and Fish Commission, Austin.

Johnsgard, P.A. 1973. *Grouse and quails of North America*. University of Nebraska Press, Lincoln.

Jones, J.H., and N.S. Smith. 1979. Bobcat density and prey selection in central Arizona. *Journal of Wildlife Management* 43: 666–672.

Jones, K.B. 1983. Movement patterns and foraging ecology of Gila Monsters (*Heloderma suspectum* Cope) in northwestern Arizona. *Herpetologica* 39: 247–253.

Jones, M.L. 1977. Record keeping and longevity of felids in captivity. Pages 132–138 in R.L. Eaton, ed. *The world's cats: Vol. III*. Carnivore Research Institute, Seattle.

Jorgensen, C.D., and S.D. Porter. 1982. Foraging behavior of *Pogonomyrmex owyheei* in southeast Idaho. *Environmental Entomology* 11: 381–384.

Kaufmann, J.H. 1962. Ecology and social behavior of the coati, *Nasua narica*, on Barro Colorado Island, Panama. University of California Publ. Zool. 60: 95–222.

Kaufman, K. 1996. *Lives of North American birds*. Houghton Mifflin Company, Boston, MA.

Kavanau, J.L., and J. Ramos. 1970. Roadrunners: activity of captive individuals. *Science*: 780–782.

Kerpez, T.A., and N.S. Smith. 1990. Competition between European Starlings and native woodpeckers for nest cavities in saguaros. *Auk* 107: 367–375.

Kitchings, J.T., and J.D. Story. 1984. Movement and dispersal of bobcats in Tennessee. *Journal of Wildlife Management* 48: 957–961.

Klug, C.M., and R.C. Averill–Murray. 1999. Reproduction in Sonoran desert tortoises: a progress report. Proceedings of the Desert Tortoise Council Symposium 1997–1998: 59–62.

Konrad, P.M., and D.S. Gilmer. 1984. Observations on the nesting ecology of Burrowing Owls in central North Dakota. *Prairie Naturalist* 16: 129–130.

Kotler, B.P. 1984. Risk of predation and the structure of desert communities. *Ecology* 65: 689–701.

Kotler, B.P., J.S. Brown, R.J. Smith, and W.O Wirtz II. 1988. The effects of morphology and body size on rates of owl predation on desert rodents. *Oikos* 53: 145–152.

Korol, J.J., and R.L. Hutto. 1984. Factors affecting nest site location in Gila Woodpeckers. *Condor* 86: 73–78.

Knipe, T. 1957. Javelina in Arizona. Wildlife Bulletin No. 2, Arizona Game and Fish Department, Phoenix.

Lembeck, M., and G.I. Gould, Jr. 1979. Dynamics of harvested and unharvested bobcat population in California. Proc. Bobcat Res. Conf., National Wildlife Federation Sci. Tech. Ser. 6: 53–54.

Longland, W.S., and M.V. Price. 1991. Direct observations of owls and heteromyid rodents: can predation risk explain microhabitat use? *Ecology* 72: 2261–2273.

Lowe, Charles H., C.R. Schwalbe, and T.B. Johnson. 1986. The Venomous Reptiles of Arizona. Arizona Game and Fish Department, Phoenix. Ix, pp.. 115.

Macdonald, D. 1985. The encyclopedia of mammals. Facts on File Publications, New York.

MacKay, W.P. 1982. The effect of predation of western widow spiders (Araneae: Theridiidae) on harvester ants (Hymenoptera: Formicidae), *Oecologia* 53: 406–411.

Mader, W.J. 1975. Biology of the Harris' Hawk in southern Arizona. *Living Bird* 14: 59–85.

———. 1978. A comparative nesting study of Red-tailed Hawks and Harris' Hawks in southern Arizona. *Auk* 95: 327–337.

Martell, M.S. 1990. Reintroduction of Burrowing Owls into Minnesota: a feasibility study. M.Sc. thesis, University of Minnesota, Minneapolis.

Martin, B.E. 1995. Ecology of the desert tortoise (*Gopherus agassizii*) in a desert-grassland community in southern Arizona. M.S. thesis, University of Arizona, Tucson.

Martindale, S., and D. Lamm. 1984. Sexual dimorphism and parental role switching in Gila Woodpeckers. Wilson Bulletin 96: 116–121.

Maurello, M.A., J.A. Clarke, and R.S. Ackley. 2000. Signature characteristics in contact calls of the white-nosed coati. *Journal of Mammalogy* 81(2): 415–421.

Mayhew, W.W. 1965. Adaptations of the amphibian, *Scaphiopus couchi*, to desert conditions. *American Midland Naturalist* 74(1): 95–109.

McAuliffe, J.R. 1994. Landscape evolution, soil formation, and ecological patterns and processes in Sonoran desert bajadas. *Ecological Monographs* 64: 111–148.

McAuliffe, J.R., and P. Hendricks. 1988. Determinants of the vertical distribution of woodpecker nest cavities in the saguaro cactus. *Condor* 90: 791–801.

McClanahan, L. 1964. Osmotic tolerance of the muscles of two desert-inhabiting toads, *Bufo cognatus* and *Scaphiopus couchi*. *Comparative Biochemistry and Physiology* 12: 501–508.

Meinzer, W. 1993. *The Roadrunner.* Texas Tech University Press, Lubbock.

Munger, J.C. 1984. Long-term yield from harvester ant colonies: implications for horned lizard foraging strategies. *Ecology* 65: 1077–1086.

Murray, R.C. 1996. Reproduction in a population of the desert tortoise, *Gopherus agassizii*, in the Sonoran desert. *Herpetological Natural History* 4: 83–88.

Nabhan, G.P. and T. H. Fleming. 1993. The conservation of new world mutualisms. *Conservation Biology* 7(3): 457–459.

Nagy, K.A., and P.A. Medica. 1986. Physiological ecology of desert tortoises in southern Nevada. *Herpetologica* 42: 73–92.

Nagy, K.A., B.T. Henen, and D.B. Vyas. 1998. Nutritional quality of native and introduced food plants of wild desert tortoises. *Journal of Herpetology* 32: 260–267.

Naples, V.L. 1999. Morphology, evolution, and function of feeding in the giant anteater (*Myrmecophaga tridactyla*). *Journal of Zoology London* 249: 19–41.

Neal, B.J. 1959. A contribution on the life history of the collared peccary in Arizona. *American Midland Naturalist* 61: 177–190.

Newman, R.A. 1989. Developmental plasticity of *Scaphiopus couchii* tadpoles in an unpredictable environment. *Ecology* 70(6): 1775–1787.

———. 1994. Effects of changing density and food level on metamorphosis of a desert amphibian, *Scaphiopus couchii*. *Ecology* 74(4): 1085–1096.

Nunley, G.L. 1978. Present and historical bobcat population trends in New Mexico and the West. Proc. Vertebrate Pest Conference 8: 77–84.

O'Dowd, D.J., and M.E. Hay. 1980. Mutualism between harvester ants and a desert ephemeral: seed escape from rodents. *Ecology* 61(3): 531–540.

Ohmart, R.D. 1989. A timid desert creature that appears to be half bird, half reptile. *Natural History* 89: 34–40.

Osborne, D.R., and G.R. Bourne. 1977. Breeding behavior and food habits of the Wattled Jacana. *Condor* 79: 98–105.

Pemberton, J.R. 1916. Variation of the broken-wing stunt by a Roadruner. *Condor* 27:35.

Peterson, C.C. 1996. Ecological energetics of the desert tortoise (*Gopherus agassizii*): effects of rainfall and drought. *Ecology* 77: 1831–1844.

Phillips, A., J. Marshall, and G. Monson. 1964. *The birds of Arizona.* University of Arizona Press, Tucson.

Pierce, B.M., W.S. Longland, and S.H. Jenkins. 1992. Rattlesnake predation on desert rodents: microhabitat and species-specific effects on risk. *Journal of Mammalogy* 73: 859–865.

Polpis, G.A. 1991. *The ecology of desert communities.* The University of Arizona Press, Tucson, AZ.

Radcliffe, G.W., K. Esteop, T. Boyer, and D. Chizar. 1986. Stimulus control of predatory behavior in red spitting cobras (*Naja mossambiea pallida*) and prairie rattlesnakes (*Crotalus v. viridis*). *Animal Behaviour* 34: 804–814.

Rait, R.J., and R.D. Ohmart. 1966. Annual cycle of reproduction and molt in Gambel Quail of the Rio Grande Valley, southern New Mexico. *Condor* 68: 541–561.

Rand, A.L. 1941. Courtship of the Roadrunner. *Auk* 58: 57–59.

Randall, J.A. 1994. Convergences and divergences in communication and social organization of desert rodents. *Australian Journal of Zoology* 42: 404–433.

———. 1989. Neighbor recognition in a solitary mammal (*Dipodomys merriami*). *Ethology* 81: 123–133.

———. 1993. Behavioural adaptations of desert rodents (Heteromydae). *Animal Behaviour* 45: 263–287.

Randall, J.A., S.M. Hatch, and E.R. Hekkala. 1994. Interspecific variation in anti-predator behavior in sympatric species of kangaroo rat.

Randall, J.A., and C.M. Stevens. 1987. Footdrumming and other anti-predator responses in the bannertail kangaroo rat (*Dipodomys spectabilis*). *Behavioral Ecology and Sociobiology* 20: 187–194.

Redford, K. 1981. Quick-snatching anteater avoids attack. *Science News* 120: 88.

Redford, K.H., and R.M. Wetzel. 1985. *Euphractus sexcinctus. Mammalian Species.* No. 252: 1–4.

Repp, R. 1998. Wintertime observations on five species of reptiles in the Tucson area: sheltersite selection/fidelity to sheltersites/notes on behavior. Bulletin of the Chicago Herpetological Society 33: 49–56.

Reynolds, H.G. 1958. The ecology of the Merriam kangaroo rat (*Dipodomys merriami* Mearns) on the grazing lands of southern Arizona. *Ecological Monographs* 28: 111–127.

Rissing, S.W. 1981. Prey preferences in the desert horned lizards: influence of prey foraging method and aggressive behavior. *Ecology* 62: 1031–1040.

———. 1988. Seed-harvester ant association with shrubs: competition for water in the Mohave desert? *Ecology* 69(3): 809–813.

Russell, J.K. 1982. Timing of reproduction by coatis (*Nasua narica*) in relation to fluctuations in food resources. pp. 413–431 in Leigh, E.G., Jr., A.S. Rand, and D.M. Windsor, eds. *The ecology of a tropical forest: seasonal rhythms and long-term changes*. Smithsonian Institute Press, Washington D.C.

———. 1983. Altruism in coati bands: nepotism or reciprocity? pp. 263–290 in Wasser S.K. (ed.). *Social behavior of female vertebrates*. Academic Press, New York.

Schmidt, P.J., and J.O. Schmidt. 1989. Harvester ants and horned lizards predator-prey interactions. pp. 25–51 in J.O. Schmidt (ed.). *Special biotic relationships in the arid southwest*. University of New Mexico Press, Albuquerque, NM.

Schweinsburg, R.E. 1971. The home range, movements, and herd integrity of the collared peccary. *Tierpsychology* 30: 132–145.

Selander, R.K., and D.R. Giller. 1963. Species limits in the woodpecker genus *Centrus* (Aves). Bull. Am. Mus. Nat. Hist. 124: 213–273.

Sherbrooke, W.C. 1990. Predatory behavior of captive Greater Roadrunners feeding on horned lizards. Wilson Bulletin 102: 171–174.

Short, L.L. 1982. Woodpeckers of the world. Delaware Museum of Natural History Monograph Series No. 4. Greenville, DE.

Small, R.L. 1971. Interspecific competition among three species of Carnivora on the Spider Ranch, Yavapai County, Arizona. M.S. thesis, University of Arizona, Tucson.

Sowell, J. 1997. *Javelinas and other peccaries: their biology, management, and use*. The University of Arizona Press, Tucson, AZ.

———. 2001. *Desert ecology: an introduction to life in the arid southwest*. The University of Utah Press, Salt Lake City.

Sowls, L.K. 1960. Results of a banding study of Gambel's Quail in southern Arizona. *Journal of Wildlife Management* 24: 185–190.

———. 1961. Gestation period of the collared peccary. *Journal of Mammalogy* 42: 425–426.

Sperry, C.C. 1941. Food habits of the coyote. U.S. Fish and Wildlife Service, Wildlife Res. Bull. 4: 70.

Stebbins, R.C. 1985. *A Field Guide to Western Reptiles and Amphibians*. Houghton Mifflin Company, Boston, MA.

Supplee, V.C. 1983. The dynamics of collared peccary dispersion into available range. Fed. Aid in Wildland Restoration Project W-78-R. Arizona Game and Fish Department, Phoenix. 31 pp.

Sweet, S.S. 1985. Geographic variation, convergent crypsis and mimcry in gopher snakes (*Pituphis melanoleucus*) and Western rattlesnakes (*Crotalus viridis*). *Journal of Herpetology* 19: 55–67.

Tuttle, M.D. 1991. Bats—the cactus connection. *National Geographic* 179(6): 130–140.

Turkowski, F.J. 1980. Carnivora food habits and habitat use in ponderosa pine forests. U.S. Forest Service, Res. Pap., RM-215.

Thomsen, L. 1971. Behavior and ecology of Burrowing Owls on the Oakland municipal airport. *Condor* 73: 177–192.

"Tucson Update: July 2003." City of Tucson Comprehensive Planning Task Force at www.cityoftucson.org/planning/demo.htm.

Valenzuela D., and D.W. Macdonald. 2002. Home-range use by white-nosed coatis (*Nasua narica*): limited water and a test of the resource dispersion hypothesis. *Journal of the Zoological Society of London* 258: 247–256.

Vander Wall, S.B., and J.A. MacMahon. 1984. Avian distribution patterns along a Sonoran Desert bajada. *Journal of Arid Environments* 7: 59–74.

Van Devender, T.R. 2002. Natural history of the Sonoran tortoise in Arizona. pp. 3–28 in Van Devender, T.R., ed. *The Sonoran Desert Tortoise : the natural history, biology, and conservation*. University of Arizona Press and the Arizona-Sonora Desert Museum, Tucson.

Van Tyne, J., and G.M. Sutton. 1937. The birds of Brewster County, Texas. Misc. Publ. Mus. Zool. University of Michigan 37: 1–119.

Vorhies, C.T. 1933. The life histories and ecology of jack rabbits, Lepus alleni and Lepus californicus ssp., in relation to grazing in Arizona. University of Arizona Coll. Agric. Tech. Bull. 86: 455–529.

Webster, D.B. 1962. A function of the enlarged middle-cavity of the kangaroo rat *Dipodomys*. *Physiol. Zool.* 35: 248–255.

Whaley, W.H. 1986. Population ecology of the Harris' Hawk in Arizona. *Raptor Research* 20: 1–15.

Wight, J.R., and J.T. Nichols. 1966. Effects of harvester ants on production of a saltbrush community. *Journal of Wildlife Management* 19: 68–71.

Wild, P. 1986. *The Saguaro Forest*. Northland Press, Flagstaff, Arizona.

Wilkinson, G.S. and T.H. Fleming. 1996. Migration and evolution of lesser long-nosed bats, *Leptonycteris curasoae*, inferred from mitochondrial DNA. *Molecular Ecology* 5: 329–339.

Wirt, E.B., and P.A. Holm. 1997. Climatic effects on the survival and reproduction of the desert tortoise (*Gopherus agassizii*) in the Maricopa Mountains, Arizona. Report to U.S. Bureau of Land Management, Phoenix.

Woodbury, A.M., and R. Hardy. 1948. Studies of the Desert Tortoise, *Gopherus agassizii*. *Ecological Monographs* 18(2): 145–200.

Yeaton, R.I. 1978. A cyclical relationship between *Larrea tridentate* and *Opuntia leptocaulis* in the northern Chihuahuan desert. *Journal of Ecology* 66:651–56.

Young, S.P., and H.H.T. Jackson. 1951. *The Clever Coyote*. Stackpole Co., Harrisburg, Pennsylvania, and Wildlife Management Institute, Washington, D.C., 411 p.

Zarn, M. 1974. Burrowing Owl, Report No. 11. Habitat management series for unique or endangered species. Bureau of Land Management, Denver, CO.

Zervanos, S.M., and N.F. Hadley. 1973. Adaptional biology and energy relationships of the collared peccary (*Tayassu tajacu*). *Ecology* 54: 759–74.

Zimmerman, D.A. 1970. Roadrunner predation on passerine. *Condor* 72: 475–476.

Zwartjes, P.W. and S.E. Nordell. 1998. Patterns of cavity-entrance orientation by gilded flickers (*Colaptes chrysoides*) in Cardon cactus. *Auk* 115(1): 119–126.

THE SAVANNAH OF SOUTHEASTERN AFRICA

Ade, B. 1981. Wankie Observation (19th May to 28th June 1980). *Bokmakierie* 33(1):15–19

Ammann, K. 1993. Close encounters of the furred kind. *BBC Wildlife* 11(7):14–15.

Animal Diversity Web of the University of Michigan's Museum of Zoology at http://animaldiversity.ummz.umich.edu.

Anstey, S. 1992. Angola: environment status quo assessment report. Unpubl. report, IUCN, Harare.

Attwell, R.I.G. 1966. Oxpeckers and their associations with mammals in Zambia. *Puku* 4:17–48.

Bailey, R.G. 1994. Guide to the fishes of the River Nile in the Republic of the Sudan. *J. Nat. Hist.* 28:937–970.

Bell, R.H.V. 1971. A grazing ecosystem in the Serengeti. *Scientific American* 224: 86–93.

Bennet,D. 1992d. Bosc's monitor lizard. *Reptilian* 1. (2):25–27.

Berry, H.H. 1978. *Pride of Lions*. Dent, London.

———. 1981. Abnormal levels of disease and predation as limiting factors for wildebeest in the Etosha National Park. *Madoqua* 11:242–253.

———. 1991a. Namibia's seal-eating lions in danger. *Cat News* 14:10, Bougy-Villars, Switzerland.

———. 1991b. Last Skeleton Coast lions killed by farmers. *Cat News* 15:7–8. Bougy-Villars, Switzerland.

———. 1991c. Large scale commercial wildlife utilization: hunting, sightseeing, and animal production in Namibia. pp. 45–49 in Grootenhuis, J.G., S.G. Njuguna, and P.W. Kat, eds. Wildlife research for sustainable development: Proc. Conf. 22–26 April 1990. Kenya Agricultural Research Institute, Kenya Wildlife Service, and National Museums of Kenya, Nairobi.

Bertram, B.C.R. 1975a. The social system of lions. *Sci. Am.* 232:54–65.

———. 1975b. Social factors influencing reproduction in wild lions. *Journal of Zoological Society of London* 177:463–482.

———. 1976. Kin selection in lions and in evolution. pp. 281–301 in Bateson, P.P.G., and R.A. Hinde, eds. *Growing Points in Ethology*. Cambridge University Press, Cambridge.

———. 1978. *Pride of Lions*. Dent, London.

Bezuidenhout J.D., and C.J. Stutterheim. 1980 A critical evaluation of the role played by the Red-billed Oxpecker Buphagus erythrorhynchus in the biological control of ticks. *Onderstepoort J. Vet. Res.* 47:51–75

Bottriell, L.G. 1987. *King Cheetah: The Story of the Quest*. E.J. Brill, Leiden.

Bowland, A.E. 1993. The 1990/1991 cheetah photographic survey. Unpubl. report, Department of Nature Conservation, Skukuza, Kruger National Park, South Africa.

Bridgeford, P.A. 1985. Unusual diet of the lion (*Panthera leo*) in the Skeleton Coast Park. *Madoqua* 14:187–188.

Brown, L. 1971. *African Birds of Prey*. Houghton Mifflin Company, Boston, MA.

Burney, D. 1980. The effects of human activities on cheetahs (*Acinonyx jubatus Schr.*) in the Mara region of Kenya. M.S. thesis, Univ. of Nairobi, Nairobi.

Buskirk W.H. 1975 Substrate choices of oxpeckers. *Auk* 92:604–606.

Bygott, J.D., B.C.R. Bertram, and J.P. Hanby. 1979. Male lions in large coalitions gain reproductive advantages. *Nature* 282:839–841.

Cambell, K., and M. Borner. 1986. Census of predators on the Serengeti Plains, May 1986. Unpublished MS., IUCN.

Campbell, B. 1974. *The Dictionary of Birds in Color*. The Viking Press.

Caro, T.M., and D.A. Collins. 1987a. Male cheetah social organization and territoriality. *Ethology* 74:52–64.

———. 1987b. Ecological characteristics of territories of male cheetahs (*Acinonyx jubatus*). *Journal of Zoological Society of London* 211:89–105.

Caro, T.M., and M.K. Laurenson. 1990. Serengeti cheetah project. pp. 33–39 in Huish, S., and Campbell, K., eds. *Biennial report of scientific results for 1988 and 1989*. Serengeti Wildlife Research Centre, Arusha.

Caro, T.M., C.D. FitzGibbon, and M.E. Holt. 1989. Physiological costs of behavioural strategies for male cheetahs. *Anim. Behav.* 38:309–317.

Caro, T.M., M.E. Holt, C.D. FitzGibbon, M. Bush, C.M. Hawkey, and R.A. Kock. 1987. Health of adult free-living cheetahs. *Journal of Zoological Society of London* 212:573–584.

CITES fact sheet-*Loxodonta Africana* (Online), Available

Cooper, J. 1942. An exploratory study on African lions. *Comp. Psychol. Monograph* 17(7):1–48.

Cooper, R.L., and J.D. Skinner. 1979. Importance of termites in the diet if the aardwolf *Proteles cristatus* in Southern Africa. *South African Journal of Zoology* 14: 5–8.

Craig, A., and A. Weaver. 1990. The relocation of the Red-billed Oxpecker. *Bee-eater* 41(4):58–61.

Dagg, A.I., and J.B. Foster. 1976. *The Giraffe: Its Biology, Behavior, and Ecology*. Van Nostrand Reinhold, New York.

Davison, E. 1963. Introduction of Ox-peckers (*Buphagus africanus* and *B. crythorhynchus*[sic]) into McIlwaine National Park. *Ostrich* 34(3):172–173.

Deignan, H.G. 1982. Marabou. pp.. 375 in ed., *Colliers Encyclopedia* Volume 13. Macmillan Educational Company.

de Pienaar, U. 1969. Predator-prey relationships amongst the larger mammals of the Kruger National Park. *Koedoe* 12:108–176.

Dinsmore, J.J. 1997. Marabou. pp.. 190 in ed., *World Book Encyclopedia*. World Book Inc.

Donaghue, A.M., J.G. Howard, A.P. Byers, K.L. Goodrowe, M. Bush, E. Blumer, J. Lukas, J. Stover, K. Snodgrass, and D.E. Wildt. 1992. Correlation of sperm viability with gamete interaction and fertilization in vitro in the cheetah (*Acinonyx jubatus*). *Biol. Reprod.* 46:1047–1056.

Dorst, J., and P. Dandelot. 1969. *A field guide to the larger mammals of Africa*. Collins, London.

Dragesco-Joffé, A. 1993. La Vie Sauvage au Sahara. [Wildlife in the Sahara]. Delachaux et Niestlé, Lausanne (Switzerland), and Paris (in French).

Durant, S.M., T.M. Caro, D.A. Collins, R.M. Alawi, and C.D. FitzGibbon. 1988. Migration patterns of Thomson's gazelles and cheetahs on the Serengeti Plains. *Afr. J. Ecol.* 26:257–268.

Eaton, R.L. 1974. *The Cheetah*. Van Nostrand Reinhold, New York.

Eccles, D.H. 1992. FAO species identification sheets for fishery purposes. *Field guide to the freshwater fishes of Tanzania*. FAO, Rome. 145 p.

Eloff, F.C. 1973a. Lion predation in the Kalahari Gemsbok National Park. *J. Sth. Afr. Wildl.* Mgmt. Ass. 3(2):59–63.

———. 1973b. Water use by the Kalahari lion *Panthera leo vernayi*. *Koedoe* 16:149–154.

Eltringham, S.K. 1979. *The Ecology and Conservation of Large African Mammals*. The Macmillan Press Limited, New York.

Eltringam, S.K., K.B. Payne, W.R. Langbauer, Jr., C. Moss, and J. Shoshani. 1992. *Elephants, Majestic Creatures*. Rodale Press, Emmaus, PA.

Estes, R.D. 1991. *The behavior guide to African mammals: including hoofed mammals, carnivores, primates*. University of California Press, Ltd. Oxford, England.

———. 1993. *The Safari Companion*. Chelsea Green Publishing Co., Post Mills, VT.

Evermann, J.F., J.L. Heeney, M.E. Roelke, A.J. McKeirnan, and S.J. O'Brien. 1988. Biological and pathological consequences of feline infectious peritonitis virus infection in the cheetah. *Arch. Virol.* 102:155–171.

Ewer, R.F. 1973. *The Carnivores*. Cornell University Press, Ithaca, NY.

Fagotto, F. 1985. The lion in Somalia. *Mammalia* 49:587–588.

Feare, C., and A. Craig. 1998. *Starlings and Mynas*. Christopher Helm, London.

FitzGibbon, C.D. 1990. Why do hunting cheetahs prefer male gazelles? *Anim. Behav.* 40:837–845.

Fox, Michael W. 1971. *Behaviour of Wolves, Dogs, and Related Canids*. Robert E. Krieger Publishing Company, Inc, Malabar, FL.

Frame, G.W. 1977. Cheetah ecology and behaviour. pp. 74–87 in the 1976–76 Annual Report, Serengeti Research Institute, Arusha.

———. 1980. Cheetah social organization in the Serengeti ecosystem, Tanzania. Paper presented at the Animal Behavior Society, Fort Collins, CO.

———. 1981. *Swift and Enduring: Cheetahs and Wild Dogs of the Serengeti*. E.P. Dutton, New York.

———. 1984. Cheetah. pp. 40–43 in D. Macdonald, ed. *The encyclopedia of mammals*. Facts on File, New York.

———. 1992. First record of the king cheetah in West Africa. *Cat News* 17:2–3, Bougy-Villars, Switzerland.

Frame, G.W., and L.H. Frame. 1980. Cheetahs: in a race for survival. *National Geographic* May 1980:712–728.

Garland, T., Jr. 1983. The relation between maximal running speed and body mass in terrestrial mammals. *Journal of Zoological Society of London* 199:157–170.

Goddard, J. 1970. Food preferences of black rhinoceros in the Tsavo National Park. *E. Afr. Wildl.* J. 8: 145–161.

Gonyea, W.J. 1976. Adaptive differences in the body proportions of large felids. *Acta. Anat.* 96:81–96.

Gosse, J.-P. 1984. Protopteridae. p. 8–17. In Daget, J., J.-P. Gosse, and D.F.E. Thys van den Audenaerde, eds. *Check-list of the freshwater fishes of Africa (CLOFFA)*. ORSTOM, Paris and MRAC, Tervuren. Vol. 1.

Graham, A. 1966. East African Wild Life Society cheetah survey: extracts from the report by wildlife services. *E. Afr. Wildl. J.* 4:50–55.

Green, R. 1991. *Wild Cat Species of the World*. Basset, Plymouth.

Greenwood, P.H. 1966. *The Fishes of Uganda*. The Uganda Society, Kampala. 131p.

Grobler, J.H. 1980 Host selection and species preference of the Red-billed Oxpecker Buphagus erythrorhynchus in the Kruger National Park. *Koedoe* 23:89–97.

Gros, P. 1990. Global cheetah project Phase I: Cheetah status in southern Africa. Unpubl. report., Univ. of California, Davis.

Guggisberg, C.A.W. 1961. *Simba: The Life of the Lion*. Howard Timmins, Cape Town.

———. 1975. *Wild Cats of the World*. David and Charles, London.

Hamilton, P.H. 1986a. Status of the cheetah in Kenya, with reference to sub-Saharan Africa. pp. 65–76 in Miller, S. and D. Everett, eds. *Cats of the world: Biology, conservation and management*. National Wildlife Federation, Washington, D.C.

Hanby, J.P. and J.D. Bygott, J.D. 1987. Emigration of subadult lions. *Anim. Behav.* 35:161–169.

———. 1991. Lions. pp. 80–93 in Seidensticker, J., and S. Lumpkin, eds. *Great Cats*. Merehurst, London.

———. 1979. Population changes in lions and other predators. pp. 249–262 in Sinclair, A.R.E., and M. Norton-Griffiths, eds. *Serengeti: Dynamics of an Ecosystem*. University of Chicago Press, Chicago.

Hanks, J., M.S. Price, and R.W. Wrangham. 1969. Some aspects of the ecology and behavior of the defassa waterbuck (*Kobus defassa*) in Zambia. *Mammalia* 33: 473–94.

Hart B.L., L.A. Hart, and M.S. Mooring. 1990. Differential foraging of oxpeckers on Impala in comparison with sympatric antelope species. *Afr. J. Ecol.* 28(3):240–249.

Hildebrand, M. 1959. Motions of the running cheetah and horse. *J. Mammal.* 40:481–495.

———. 1961. Further studies on locomotion of the cheetah. *J. Mammal.* 42:84–91.

Hills, D.M., and R.H.N. Smithers. 1980. The king cheetah: a historical review. *Arnoldia* 9(1):1–23.

Hinton, H.E., and A.M.S. Dunn. 1967. *Mongooses: Their Natural History and Behaviour*. Oliver and Boyd Ltd., London.

Hofmann, R.R. 1973. The ruminant stomach. East African Monographs in Biology, vol. 2. East African Literature Bureau, Nairobi.

Hustler, K. 1987. Host preference of oxpeckers in the Hwange National Park, Zimbabwe. *Afr. J. Ecol.* 25(4):241–245

IUCN Environmental Law Centre. 1986. African wildlife laws. IUCN Environmental Policy and Law Occasional Paper no. 3. IUCN, Gland, Switzerland and Cambridge, UK.

Jackson, P. 1990. *Endangered Species, Elephants*. Chartwell Books, Secaucus, NJ.

Jarman, M. 1979. *Impala Social Behaviour: Territory, Hierarchy, Mating, and the Use of Space*. Verlag Paul Parey, Berlin.

Kaiser-Benz, M. 1975. Breeding the Red-billed Oxpecker (*Buphagus erythrorhynchus*) at Zurich Zoo. *Int. Zoo Yearb.* 15:120–123.

Kerley, G.I.H., M. Mason, and C. Weatherby. 1998. The role of tortoises in the thicket biome, South Africa: ranging behaviour, diet and seed dispersal. Twenty-Third Annual Meeting and Symposium of the Desert Tortoise Council.

Kingdon, J. 1977. East African Mammals: An atlas of evolution in Africa, Vol. 3(A). Carnivores. Academic Press Ins. (London) Ltd. London and New York.

———. 1979. East African Mammals: An Atlas of Evolution in Africa, Vol. 3(B) Large herbivores. Academic Press Ins. (London) Ltd. London and New York.

———. 1982. East African Mammals: An Atlas of Evolution in Africa, Vol. 3(C) Bovids. Academic Press Ins. (London) Ltd. London and New York.

Koehler, C.E., and P.R.K. Richardson. 1990. Proteles cristalus. *Mammalian Species* 353:1–6.

Kraus, D., and L. Marker-Kraus. 1991. The status of the cheetah (*Acinonyx jubatus*). Unpubl. data sheet, IUCN/SSC Cat Specialist Group, Bougy-Villars, Switzerland.

Kruuk, H. 1976. Feeding and social behavior of the striped hyena (*Hyaena vulgaris*). East African Wildlife Journal. J. 14: 91–111.

Kruuk, H. and W.A. Sands. 1972. The aardwolf (*Proteles cristatus* Sparrman 1783) as predator of termites. *East African Wildlife Journal* 10:211–227.

Labuschagne, W. 1979. [A bio-ecological and behavioural study of the cheetah, *Acinonyx jubatus jubatus* (Schreber, 1776).] M.S. thesis, University of Pretoria, Pretoria (in Afrikaans).

———. 1981. Aspects of cheetah ecology in the Kalahari Gemsbok National Park. Paper presented at Internat. Union of the Directors of Zoological Gardens, Washington D.C.

Labuschagne, W., G.W. Frame, and L.H. Frame. 1984. Cheetah male cooperation: test of a mutualism model. Paper presented at Animal Behavior Society, Cheney, Washington.

Lamprecht J. 1978. On diet, foraging behaviour, and interspecific food competition of jackals in the Serengeti National Park, East Africa. *Z. f. Säugetierkunde* 43:210–223.

Laurenson, M.K. 1992. Reproductive strategies in wild female cheetahs. Ph.D. thesis, University of Cambridge, Cambridge.

———. 1993. Early maternal behaviour of wild cheetahs: implications for captive husbandry. *Zoo Biology* 12:31–43.

Laurenson, M.K., T. Caro, and M. Borner. 1992. Female cheetah reproduction. *Nat. Geog. Res.* 8(1):64–75.

Lee, A.R. 1992. Cheetah (*Acinonyx jubatus*). Management guidelines for the welfare of zoo animals, Federation of Zoological Gardens of Great Britain and Ireland, London.

Limoges, B. 1989. Results of the national wildlife inventory and proposals for modification of the lawon hunting. Unpubl. report, Ministry of Rural Development and Agriculture, Republic of Guinea-Bissau and IUCN.

Lindburg, D.G., B.S. Durrant, S.E. Millard, and J.E. Oosterhuis. 1993. Fertility assessment of cheetah males with poor quality semen. *Zoo Biology* 12(1):97–104.

www.livingplanet.org

Lockwood, G. 1988. Oxpeckers: a success story. *Bokmakierie* 40(4):119–120

Loudon, A.S.I. 1985. Lactation and neonatal survival in mammals. *Symp. Zool. Soc. Lond.* 54: 183–207 and 183–207.

Lücker, H. 1994. Zucht des Rotschnabelmadenhackers. *Gefied. Welt.* 118:9–10.

MacPhee, R.D.E. (1994) Morphology, adaptations, and relationships of Plesiorycteropus, and a diagnosis of a new order of eutherian mammals. Bull. Am. Mus. Nat. Hist. 220.

Maddock, L. 1979. The migration and grazing succession. Pgs. 104–129 in Sinclair, A.R.E., and M. Norton-Griffiths, eds. *Serengeti: Dynamics of an Ecosystem.* University of Chicago Press, Chicago.

Makacha, S., and G.B. Schaller. 1969. Observations on lions in the Lake Manyara National Park, Tanzania. *East African Wildlife Journal* 7:99–103.

Marker, L. and S. O'Brien. 1989. Captive breeding of the cheetah (*Acinonyx jubatus*) in North American zoos (1871–1986). *Zoo Biology* 8:3–16.

Marker-Kraus, L. 1992. International Cheetah Studbook 1991. NOAHS Centre, National Zoo, Washington, D.C.

Marker-Kraus, L., and Grisham, J. 1993. Captive breeding of cheetahs in North American zoos. *Zoo Biology* 12 (1): 5–18.

Marker-Kraus, L. and Kraus, D. 1991. 1991 Annual Report. Unpubl. report, Cheetah Conservation Fund, Windhoek.

McBride, C.J. 1977. *The White Lions of Timbavati.* Paddington Press, London.

———. 1984. Age and size categories of lion prey in Chobe National Park, Botswana. Botswana Notes and Records 16:139–143.

———. 1990. *Liontide.* Jonathan Ball, Johannesburg.

McKeown, S. 1992. Joint management of species cheetah breeding programme. pp. 78–88 in Mansard, P., ed. Cats: proc. conference/workshop held at Chester Zoo on October 10, 1992 by the Ridgeway Trust for Endangered Cats and the Association of British Wild Animal Keepers. Ridgeway Trust for Endangered Cats, Hastings, East Sussex.

McLaughlin, R. 1970. Aspects of the biology of cheetahs Acinonyx jubatus (Schreber) in Nairobi National Park. M.S. thesis, University of Nairobi, Nairobi.

McVittie, R. 1979. Changes in the social behaviour of South-West African cheetah. *Madoqua* 2(3):171–184.

Melton, D.A. (1976) The biology of aardvark (*Tubulidentata-Orycteropodidae*). *Mammal Rev.* 6: 75–88.

Mengesha, Y.A. 1978. A study of oxpecker-mammal symbiosis in Ethiopia. *East Afr. Agric. Forestry J.* 43:321–326

Menotti-Raymond, M. and S.J. O'Brien. 1993. Dating the genetic bottleneck of the African cheetah. Proc. Natl. Acad. Sci. 90.

Millington, S.J. and T. Anada. 1991. Biological diversity assessment for Niger. Unpubl. report, WWF-Niger, Niamey.

Mills, M.G.L. 1984. Prey selection and feeding habits of the large carnivores in the southern Kalahari. *Koedoe* Suppl.:281–294.

———. 1990. *Kalahari Hyaenas: the Comparative Behavioural Ecology of Two Species.* Unwin Hyman, London.

Mills, M.G.L., and H.C. Biggs. 1993. Prey apportionment and related ecological relationships between large carnivores in Kruger National Park. In Dunstone, N., and M.L. Gorman, eds. Mammals as predators. Proc. Symp. Zool. Soc. Lond. 65. Clarendon, Oxford.

Mills, M.G.L., and T.M. Shenk. 1992. Predator-prey relationships: the impact of lion predation on wildebeest and zebra populations. *J. Anim. Ecol.* 61:693–702

Mills, M.G.L., P. Wolff, E.A.N. Le Riche, and I.J. Meyer. 1978. Some population characteristics of the lion *Panthera leo* in the Kalahari Gemsbok National Park. *Koedoe* 21:163–171.

Mitchell, B., J. Shenton, and J. Uys. 1965. Predation on large mammals in the Kafue National Park, Zambia. *Zool. Africana* 1:297–318.

Mizutani, F. 1993. Home range of leopards and their impact on livestock on Kenyan ranches. In Dunstone, N., and M.L.

Gorman, eds. Mammals as predators. Proc. Symp. Zool. Soc. Lond. 65. Clarendon, Oxford.

Mloszewski, M. 1983. *The Behaviour and Ecology of the African Buffalo*. Cambridge University Press, U.S.A. and Cambridge.

Moehlman, P.D. 1979. Jackal helpers and pup survival. *Nature* 277:382–383.

———. 1983. Socioecology of silver-backed and golden jackals (*Canis mesomelas, C. aureus*). In *Recent advances in the study of mammalian behavior*, Eisenberg, J., and D.G. Kleiman (eds). Special Publication #7, American Society of Mammalogists.

——— 1986. Ecology of cooperation canids. pp.. 282–302 in Rubenstein, D.I., and R.W. Wrangham, eds. *Ecological Aspects of Social Evolution*. Princeton University Press, Princeton, NJ.

Morsbach, D. 1984–1986. [The behavioural ecology and movement of cheetahs on farmland in Southwest Africa/Namibia.] Annual progress reports submitted to the Directorate of Nature Conservation and Recreation Resorts, Govt. of Namibia, Windhoek (in Afrikaans).

———. 1987. Cheetah in Namibia. *Cat News* 6:25–26, Bougy-Villars, Switzerland.

Moss, C. 1988. *Elephant Memories*. William and Morrow Company, New York.

Mundy, P. 1998. Oxpecker hybrids. *Africa: Birds & Birding* 3(4):20.

Mundy, P.J. 1992. Notes on oxpeckers. *Honeyguide* 38(3):108–112.

———. 1997. Redbilled Oxpecker. In Harrison, J.A., D.G. Allan, L.G. Underhill, M. Herremans, A.J. Tree, V. Parker, and C.J. Brown (eds) *The Atlas of Southern African Birds*. Vol. 2:482–483. BirdLife South Africa, Johannesburg.

Mundy P.J., and G. Haynes. 1996. Oxpeckers and elephants. *Ostrich* 67(2):85–87.

Myers, N. 1975. The cheetah Acinonyx jubatus in Africa. IUCN Monograph No. 4, Morges, Switzerland.

Neweklowsky, W. 1974 Beobachtungen am Rotschnabelmadenhackern, Buphagus erythrorhynchus (Stanley). *Zool. Gart.* 44:121–143.

Nowak, R.M., and J.L. Paradiso. 1983. *Walker's Mammals of the World*. Johns Hopkins University Press, Baltimore.

O'Brien, S.J., and J.F. Evermann. 1988. Interactive influence of infectious disease and genetic diversity in natural populations. *Trends Ecol. Evol.* 3(10):254–259.

O'Brien, S.J., M.E. Roelke, L. Marker, A. Newman, C.A. Winkler, D. Meltzer, L. Colly, J.F. Evermann, M. Bush, and D.E. Wildt. 1985. Genetic basis for species vulnerability in the cheetah. *Science* 227:1428–1434.

O'Brien, S.J., D.E. Wildt, and M. Bush. 1986. The cheetah in genetic peril. *Sci. Am.* 254(5):68–76.

O'Brien, S.J., D.E. Wildt, M. Bush, T.M. Caro, C. FitzGibbon, I. Aggundey, and R.E. Leakey. 1987a. East African cheetahs: Evidence for two population bottlenecks? Proc. Natl. Acad. Sci. USA 84:508–511.

O'Brien, S.J., D.E. Wildt, D. Goldman, C.R. Merril, and M. Bush. 1983. The cheetah is depauperate in genetic variation. *Science* 221:459–462.

Owens, M., and D. Owens. 1984. Kalahari lions break the rules. *Int. Wildl.* 14:4–13.

Owen-Smith, R.N. 1979. Assessing the foraging efficiency of a large herbivore, the kudu. *S. Afr. J. Wildl. Res.* 9: 102–110.

———. 1984. Rhinoceroses. In Macdonald, D.W., ed. *The Encyclopedia of Mammals*. New York, Facts on File.

Packer, C. 1986. The ecology of sociality in felids. pp. 429–451 in Rubenstein, D.I., and R.W. Wrangham, eds. *Ecological aspects of social evolution*. Princeton University Press, Princeton, NJ.

Packer, C., and A.E. Pusey. 1982. Cooperation and competition within coalitions of male lions: kin selection or game theory? *Nature* 296:740–742.

———.1983. Adaptations of female lions to infanticide by incoming males. *Am. Nat.* 121:716–728.

———. 1987. Intrasexual cooperation and the sex ratio in African lions. *Am. Nat.* 130:636–642.

Packer, C., and L. Ruttan. 1988. The evolution of cooperative hunting. *Am. Nat.* 132:159–198.

Packer, C., D.A. Gilbert, A.E. Pusey, and S.J. O'Brien. 1991a. A molecular genetic analysis of kinship and cooperation in African lions. *Nature* 351:562–565.

Packer, C., L. Herbst, A.E. Pusey, J.D. Bygott, J.P. Hanby, S.J. Cairns, and M. Borgerhoff-Mulder. 1988. Reproductive success of lions. pp. 363–383 in Clutton-Brock, T.H., ed. *Reproductive success*. University of Chicago Press, Chicago.

Packer, C., A.E. Pusey, H. Rowley, D.A. Gilbert, J. Martenson, and S.J. O'Brien. 1991b. Case study of a population bottleneck: lions of the Ngorongoro Crater. Conserv. Biol. 5(2):219–230.

Packer, C., D. Scheel, and A.E. Pusey. 1990. Why lions form groups: food is not enough. *Am. Nat.* 136:1–19.

Pellew, R.A. 1984. The feeding ecology of a selective browser, the giraffe (*Giraffa camelopardalis*). *Journal of Zoology London* 202:57–81.

Pocock, R.I. 1916. On some of the cranial and external characters of the hunting leopard or cheetah. *Ann. Mag. Nat. Hist.* 18:419–429.

———. 1927. Description of a new species of cheetah (*Acinonyx*). *Proc. Zool. Soc. London Pt.* 1:245–251.

Poll, M. 1946. Révision de la faune ichthyologique du lac Tanganika. *Ann. Mus. Congo Belge, Zool.* (1), 4(3):141–364.

Prins, H.H.T., and G.R. Iason. 1989. Dangerous lions and nonchalant buffalo. *Behaviour.* 262–296.

Pusey, A.E., and C. Packer. 1987. The evolution of sex-biased dispersal in lions. *Behaviour* 101:275–310.

Rieger, I. 1979. A review of the biology of striped hyenas, *Hyaena hyaena* (Linne, 1758). *Säugetierk Mitt.* 27: 81–95.

Rodgers, W.A. 1974. The lion (*Panthera leo*, Linn.) population of the eastern Selous Game Reserve. *E. Afr. Wildl. J.* 12:313–317.

Rogner, Manfred. 1997. Lizards vol. 2. Krieger Publishing, Malabar, FL.

Rosevear, D.R. 1974. The carnivores of West Africa. British Museum (Natural History), London.

Rowe-Rowe, D.T. 1976. Food of the black-backed jackal in nature conservation and farming areas in Natal. *East African Wildlife Journal* 14:345–348.

———. 1978. The small carnivores of Natal. *Lam-nergeyer* 25:1–48.

———. 1982. Home range and movements of black-backed jackals in an African montane region. *South African Journal of Wildlife Research* 12:79–84.

———. 1983. Black-backed jackal diet in relation to food availability in the Natal Drakensberg. *South African Journal of Wildlife Research* 13:17–23.

———. 1986. The black-backed jackal: know your problem animal. Wildlife Management Technical Guides for Farmers 15:2pp.. Natal Parks Board, Pietermaritzburg.

Rudnai, J. 1973. *The social life of the lion*. Medical and Technical Publishing, Lancaster.

———. 1974. The pattern of lion predation in Nairobi Park. *E. Afr. Wildl. J.* 12:213–225.

Ruggiero, R.G. 1991. Prey selection of the lion (*Panthera leo* L.) in the Manovo-Gounda-St. Floris National Park, Central African Republic. *Mammalia* 55:23–33.

Schaller, G.B. 1968. Hunting behaviour of the cheetah in the Serengeti National Park, Tanzania. *E. Afr. Wildl. J.* 6:95–100.

———. 1972. The Serengeti lion. University of Chicago Press, Chicago.

Scheel, D. 1993. Profitability, encounter rates, and prey choice of African lions. *Behav. Ecol.* 4:90–97.

Shoshani, J., C.A. Goldman, and J.G.M. Thewissen. 1988. Orycteropus afer. *Mammalian Species* 300: 1–8.

Simpson, C.D. 1972. An evaluation of seasonal movement in greater kudu populations in southern Africa. *Zool. Afr.* 7: 197–205.

Skinner, J.D., and R.H.N. Smithers. 1990. *The Mammals of the Southern African Subregion*, 2nd edn. University of Pretoria Press, Republic of South Africa.

Skinner, N.J. 1995. The breeding seasons of birds in Botswana 1: Passerine families. *Babbler* (Botswana) 29/30:9–23

Smithers, R.H.N. 1971. The mammals of Botswana. Mus. mem. Natl. Mus. Monum. Rhod. 4.

———. 1983. *Mammals of the Southern African Sub-Region*. University of Pretoria, Republic of South Africa.

Smuts, G.L. 1976. Population characteristics and recent history of lions in two parts of the Kruger National Park. *Koedoe* 19:153–164.

———. 1978a. Effects of population reduction on the travels and reproduction oflions in Kruger National Park. *Carnivore* 1:61–72.

———. 1978b. More sex ratio data on lions. *Carnivore* 1(2):1.

———. 1982. *Lion*. MacMillan, Johannesburg.

Smuts, G.L., J. Hanks, and I.J. Whyte. 1978. Reproduction and social organization of lions from the Kruger National Park. *Carnivore* 1(1):17–28.

Sonntag, C.F. 1925. A monograph of Orycteropus afer. 1. Anatomy except the nervous system, sense organs and hair. *Proc. Zool. Soc. Lond.* 1925: 331–438.

Spinnage, C.A. 1982. *A Territorial Antelope: the Uganda Waterbuck*. Academic Press. New York.

Stander, P.E. 1990a. Notes on foraging habits of cheetah. *S. Afr. J. Wildl. Res.* 20(4):130–132.

———. 1991. Demography of lions in the Etosha National Park. *Madoqua* 18:1–9.

———. 1992a. Foraging dynamics of lions in a semi-arid environment. *Can. J. Zool.* 70.

———. 1992b. Cooperative hunting in lions: the role of the individual. *Behav. Ecol. Sociobiol.* 29:445–454.

Stander, P.E., and S.D. Albon. 1992. Hunting success of lions in a semi-arid environment. In Dunstone, N., and M.L. Gorman, eds. *Mammals as predators*. Proc. Symp. Zool. Soc. Lond. 65. Clarendon, Oxford.

Stander, P.E., and H. Stander. 1987. Characteristics of lion roars in Etosha National Park. *Madoqua* 15:315–318.

Steele, Rodney. 1996. *Living Dragons*. Ralph Curtis Books, London.

Stuart, C.T. 1976. Diet of the black-backed jackal Canis mesomelas in the central Namib Desert, South West Africa. *Zool. Afr.* 11: 193–205.

———. 1981. Notes on the mammalian carnivores of the Cape Province, South Africa. Bontebok 1: 1–58.

———. 1991. Lion. Unpubl. data sheet, Cat Specialist Group, Bougy-Villars, Switzerland.

Stuart, C.T., and V.J. Wilson. 1988. The cats of southern Africa. Chipangali Wildlife Trust, Bulawayo.

Stutterheim, C.J. 1980. Moult cycle of the Redbilled Oxpecker in the Kruger National Park. *Ostrich* 51(2):107–112.

———. 1981a. The feeding behaviour of the Redbilled Oxpecker. *S. Afr. J. Zool.* 16(4):267–269.

———. 1981b. The movements of a population of Red-billed Oxpeckers (*Buphagus erythrorhynchus*) in the Kruger National Park. *Koedoe* 24:99–107.

———. 1982a. Breeding biology of the Redbilled Oxpecker in the Kruger National Park. *Ostrich* 53(2):79–90.

———. 1982b. Past and present ecological distribution of the Redbilled Oxpecker (*Buphagus erythrorhynchus*) in South Africa. *S. Afr. J. Zool.* 17(4):190–196.

———. 1982c. Timing of breeding of the Redbilled Oxpecker (*Buphagus erythrorhynchus*) in the Kruger National Park. *S. Afr. J. Zool.* 17(3):126–129.

Stutterheim, C.J., P.J. Mundy, and A.W. Cook. 1976. Comparisons between the two species of Oxpecker. *Bokmakierie* 28(1):12–14.

Stutterheim, C.J., and I.M. Stutterheim. 1980. Evidence of an increase in a Redbilled Oxpecker population in the Kruger National Park. *S. Afr. J. Zool.* 15(3):284.

———. 1981. A possible decline of a Redbilled Oxpecker population in the Pilansberg complex, Bophuthatswana. *Ostrich* 52(1):56–57.

Stutterheim, I.M., J.D. Bezuidenhout, and E.G.R. Elliott. 1988. Comparative feeding behaviour and food preferences of oxpeckers (*Buphagus erythrorhynchus* and *B. africanus*) in captivity. *Onderstepoort J. Vet. Res.* 55:173–179.

Stutterheim, I.M., and K. Panagis. 1985a. Roosting behaviour and host selection of oxpeckers (Aves: Buphaginae) in Moremi Wildlife Reserve, Botswana, and eastern Caprivi, South West Africa. *S. Afr. J. Zool.* 20(4):237–240.

———. 1985b. The status and distribution of oxpeckers (Aves: Passeriformes: Buphagidae) in Kavango and Caprivi, South West Africa/Namibia. *S. Afr. J. Zool.* 20(1):10–14.

Taylor, C.R., and V.J. Rowntree. 1973. Temperature regulation and heat balance in running cheetahs: a strategy for sprinters. *Amer. J. Physiol.* 224:848–851.

Taylor, C.R., C.A. Spinage, and C.P. Lyman. 1969. Water relations of the waterbuck, an East African antelope. *American Journal of Physiology* 217: 630–34.

Taylor, C.R., A. Shkolnik, R. Dmtel, D. Baharav, and A. Borut. 1974. Running in cheetahs, gazelles, and goats: energy cost and limb configuration. *Am. J. Physiol.* 227(4):848–850.

Taylor, W.A., P.A. Lindsey, and J.D. Skinner. 2002. The feeding ecology of the aardvark Orycteropus afer. *J. Arid Environs.* 50: 135–152.

Taylor, W.A., and J.D. Skinner. 2000. Associative feeding between aardwolves (*Proteles cristatus*) and aardvarks (*Orycteropus afer*). *Mammal Review* 30: 141–143.

———. 2001. Associative feeding between Anteating Chats, Myrmecocichla formicivora, and Aardvarks, Orycteropus afer. *Ostrich* 72: 199–200.

Thomas, E.M. 1990. The old way. *New Yorker*, October 15:78–110.

Tomlinson, D.N.S. 1979. The feeding behavior of waterbuck in the Lake McIlwaine Game enclosure. *Rhodesia Science News* 13:11–14.

Vakily, J.M. 1989. Les pêches dans la partie zaïroise du Lac Idi Amin: Analyse de la situation actuelle et potentiel de développement. Rapport Technique des Pêches au Zaïre. Gouvernement de la République du Zaïre, Département des Affaires Foncières, Environnement et Conservation de la Nature, et Commission des Communautés Européennes, Kinshasa/Brussels. 48 p. and Appendix.

Van Aarde, R.J., C.K. Willis, J.D. Skinner, and M.A. Haupt. 1992. Range utilisation by the aardvark, Orycteropus afer (Pallas, 1766) in the Karoo, South Africa. *J. Arid Environ.* 22: 387–394.

Van Aarde, R.J., and A. van Dyk. 1986. Inheritance of the king coat colour patterns in cheetahs Acinonyx jubatus. *J. Zool.* 209:573–578.

Van Dyk, A. 1991. *The cheetahs of DeWildt.* Stuik, Cape Town.

Van Oijen, M.J.P. 1995. Appendix I. Key to Lake Victoria fishes other than haplochromine cichlids. p. 209–300. In Witte, F., and W.L.T. van Densen, eds. *Fish stocks and fisheries of Lake Victoria. A handbook for field observations.* Samara Publishing Limited, Dyfed, Great Britain.

Van Orsdol, K.G. 1982. Ranges and food habits of lions in Rwenzori National Park, Uganda. *Symp. Zool. Soc. Lond.* 49:325–340.

———. 1984. Foraging behaviour and hunting success of lions in Queen Elizabeth National Park, Uganda. *Afr. J. Ecol.* 22:79–99.

Van Orsdol, K.G., J.P. Hanby, and J.D. Bygott. 1985. Ecological correlates of lion social organization (*Panthera leo*). *J. Zool., Lond.* 206:97–112.

Van Orsdol, K.G., and P.C. Viljoen. 1993. The effects of changes in prey availability on lion predation in a large natural ecosystem in northern Botswana. In Dunstone, N., and M.L. Gorman, eds. *Mammals as predators.* Proc. Symp. Zool. Soc. Lond. 65. Clarendon, Oxford.

Van Someren, V.D. 1951. The Red-billed Oxpecker and its relation to stock in Kenya. *East Afr. Agric. J.* 17:1–11

Watkins, B.P., and R.J. Cassidy. 1987. Evasive action taken by Waterbuck to Redbilled Oxpeckers. *Ostrich* 58(2):90

Weeks, P. 1999. Interactions between Red-billed Oxpeckers, Buphagus erythrorhynchus, and domestic cattle, Bos taurus, in Zimbabwe. *Anim. Behav.* 58(6):1253–1259

———. 2000. Red-billed oxpeckers: vampires of tick-birds? *Behav. Ecol.* 11:154–160

Wildt, D.E, J.L. Brown, M. Bush, M.A. Barone, K.A. Cooper, J. Grisham, and J.G. Howard. 1993a. Reproductive status of cheetahs (*Acinonyx jubatus*) in North American zoos: the benefits of physiological surveys for strategic planning. *Zoo Biol.* 12: 45–80.

Wildt, D.E., S.J. O'Brien, J.G. Howard, T.M. Caro, M.E. Roelke, J.L. Brown, and M. Bush. 1987a. Similarity in ejaculate-endocrine characteristics in captive versus free-ranging cheetahs of two subspecies. *Biol. Reprod.* 36:351–360.

Willis, C.K., J.D. Skinner, and H.G. Robertson. 1992. Abundance of ants and termites in the False Karoo and their importance in the diet of the aardvark, Orycteropus afer. *Afr. J. Ecol.* 30: 322–334.

Wilson, V.J. 1965. Observations on the greater kudu Tragelaphus strepsiceros from a tsetse control hunting scheme in Northern Rhodesia. *E. Afr. Wildl. J.* 3: 27–37.

Yalden, D.W., M.J. Largen, and D. Kock. 1980. Catalogue of the mammals of Ethiopia. 4. Carnivora. *Italian J. Zool.* 8:169–272.

Zimmerman, D.A., D.A. Turner, and D.J. Pearson. 1996. *Birds of Kenya and Northern Tanzania.* Princeton University Press, Princeton, NJ.

THE COSTA RICAN RAINFOREST

Ackerman, J.D. 1983. Diversity and seasonality of male euglossine bees (Hymenoptera: Apidae) in central Panama. *Ecology* 64:274–283.

———. 1989. Geographic and seasonal variation in fragrance choices and preferences in male Euglossine bees. *Biotropica* 21(4): 340–347.

Ake Assi, L. 1980. Cecropia peltata Linne (Moracees): ses origines, introduction et expansion dans l'est de la Cote d'Ivoire. Institut Fondamental d'Afrique Noire. Bulletin. Serie A. *Sciences Naturelles* 42:96–102.

Akre, R.D., and C.W. Rettenmeyer. 1966. Behavior of Staphylinidae associated with army ants (Formicidae: Ecitonini). *J. Kansas Ent. Soc.* 39: 745–82.

Alvarez-Buylla, E.R., and M. Martinez-Ramos 1992. Demography and allometry of Cecropia obtusifolia, a neotropical pioneer tree—an evaluation of the climax-pioneer paradigm for tropical rain forests. *Journal of Ecology* 80:275–290.

American Museum of Natural History. 2000. "Amazon Featherwork." Available online at www.amnh.org/exhibitions. (March 18, 2001).

Andrade, J.C. de, and J.P.P. Carauta. 1982. The Cecropia-Azteca association: a case of mutualism? *Biotropica* 14:15.

Animal Diversity Web of the University of Michigan's Museum of Zoology at http://animaldiversity.ummz.umich.edu.

Aranda, J.M. 1991. Wild mammal skin trade in Chiapas, Mexico. pp. 174–177 in Robinson, J.G., and K.H. Redford, eds. *Neotropical Wildlife Use and Conservation.* University of Chicago Press, Chicago.

Araujo, R.L. 1970. Termites of the Neotropical region. pp. 527–76 in Noirot, C., P.E. Howse, and G. Le Masne eds. *The Biology of Termites.* Academic Press, New York.

Armbruster, W.S. 1993. Within-habitat heterogeneity in baiting samples of male euglossine bees: possible causes and implications. *Biotropica* 25:122–128.

Armbruster, W.S., and K.D. McCormick. 1990. Diel foraging patterns of male euglossine bees: ecological causes and evolutionary response by plants. *Biotropica* 22(2): 160–171.

August, P.V. 1981. Fig fruit consumption and seed dispersal by *Artibeus jamaicencis* in the Llanos of Venezuela. *Reproductive Botany* 70–76.

Ayala, F.J., J.K. Wetterer, J.T. Longino, and D.L. Hartl. 1996. Molecular phylogeny of Azteca ants (Hymenoptera: Formicidae) and the colonization of Cecropia trees. *Molecular Phylogenetics and Evolution* 5:423–428.

Azevedo, F.C.C. 1996. Notes on the behavior of the margay Felis wiedii (Schinz, 1821), (Carnivora, Felidae), in the Brazilian Atlantic Forest. *Mammalia* 60:325–328.

Badger, D. 1995. *Frogs.* Voyageur Press, Stillwater, MN.

Bailey, I.W. 1922. Notes on neotropical ant-plants I. Cecropia angulata, sp. nov. *Botanical Gazette* 74:369–391.

Banazak, J., ed. 1995. *Changes in fauna of wild bees in Europe.* Pedagogical University, Bydgszcz, Poland.

Basset, Y., V. Novotny, S.E. Miller, and N.D. Springate. 1998. Assessing the impact of forest disturbance on tropical invertebrates: some comments. *Journal of Applied Ecology* 35:461–466.

Becker, P., J.S. Moure, and F.J. Peralta. 1991. More about euglossine bees in Amazonian forest fragments. *Biotropica* 23:586–591.

Beebe, W. 1925. Ecology of Kartabo. *Zoologica* 6(1):1–193.

Beletsky, L. 1998. *Costa Rica: The Ecotraveller's Wildlife Guide.* Academic Press, San Diego.

Benson, W.W. 1985. Amazon ant-plants. Pages 239–266 in Prance, G.T., and T.E. Lovejoy, eds. *Amazonia.* Pergamon, Oxford, England.

Bequaert, J. 1922. Ants of the American Museum Congo expedition. IV. Ants in their diverse relations to the plant world. Bulletin of the American Museum of Natural History 45:333–583.

Berg, C.C. 1978. Cecropiaceae, a new family of Urticales. Taxon 27:39–44.

Berish, C.W. 1986. Leaf-cutting anta (Atta cephalotes) select nitrogen-rich foarge. *American Midland Naturalist* 115(2): 268–276.

Bisbal, F.J. 1989. Distribution and habitat association of the carnivores in Venezuela. pp. 339–362 in Redford, K.H., and J.F. Eisenberg, eds. *Advances in Neotropical Mammalogy.* Sandhill Crane Press, Gainesville, FL.

Bonaccorso, F.J. 1975. Foraging and reproductive ecology of community of bats in Panama. Ph.D. diss., University of Florida.

Bot, A.N.M, C.R. Currie, A.G. Hart, and J.J. Boomsma. 2001. Waste management in leaf-cutting ants. *Ethology, Ecology, and Evolution* 13: 225–237.

Boucek, Z. 1988. Australasian Chalcidoidea, a biosystematic revision of genera of fourteen families, with a reclassification of species. CAB International, Wallingford, UK. 832 pp..

Broad, S. 1987. *The harvest of and trade in Latin American spotted cats (Felidae) and otters (Lutrinae).* Unpubl. report, World Conservation Monitoring Centre, Cambridge.

Brodie, E.D., P.K. Ducey, and E.A. Barnes. 1991. Antipredator skin secretions of some tropical salamanders (Bolitoglossa) are toxic to snake predators. *Biotropica* 23(1): 58–62.

Brokaw, N.V.L. 1987. Gap-phase regeneration of three pioneer tree species in a tropical forest. *Journal of Ecology* 75:9–19.

Bronstein, J.L. 1988. Predators of fig wasps. *Biotropica* 20(3): 215–219.

Brooke, A.P. 1994. Diet of the Fishing Bat, *Noctilio-Leporinus* (Chiroptera, Noctilionidae). *Journal of Mammalogy* 75(1):212–218.

———. 1997. Organization and foraging behaviour of the Fishing Bat, *Noctilio leporinus* (Chiroptera: Noctilionidae). *Ethology* 103(5):421–436.

Brooke, A.P., and D. Decker. 1996. Lipid Compounds in secretions of Fishing Bat, *Noctilio leporinus* (Chiroptera: Noctilionidae). *Journal of Chemical Ecology* 22:(8):1411–1428.

Brower, L.P., J.V.Z. Brower, and C.T. Collins. 1963. Experimental studies with mimicry. 7. Relative patability and Millerian mimicry among Neotropical butterflies of the subfamily Heliconiinae. *Zoologica* 48: 65–84.

Brust, D.G. 1990. Maternal brood care by *Dendrobates pumilio*: A frog that feeds its young. Ph.D. diss., Cornell University.

———. 1993. Maternal brood care by *Dendrobates pumilio*: A frog that feeds its young. *Journal of Herpetology* 27(1): 96–98.

Buchmann, S.L., and G.P. Nabhan. 1996. *The Forgotten Pollinators.* Island Press, Washington, D.C., USA.

Burger, W. 1977. Flora Costaricensis, Family #52, Moraceae. Fieldiana, *Botany* 40:94–215.

Burton, F. 1995. *The Multimedia Guide to the Non-Human Primates.* Prentice-Hall Canada Inc.

Cane, J.H., and J.A. Payne. 1993. Regional, annual, and seasonal variation in pollinator guilds: intrinsic traits of bees (Hymenoptera: Apoidea) underlie their patterns of abundance at *Vaccinium ashei* (Ericaceae). *Annals of the Entomological Society of America* 88:577–588.

Carroll, C.R. 1983. Azteca (hormiga Azteca, Azteca ants, Cecropia ants). Pages 691–693 in Janzen, D.H., ed. *Costa Rican Natural History.* University of Chicago Press, Chicago.

Carvalho, C.T. 1958. [On some mammals of southeastern Para.] *Arquivos de Zoologia* 12(5):121–132 (in Portuguese).

Chadab, R., and C.W. Rettenmeyer. 1975. Mass recruitment by army ants. *Science* 188: 1124–25.

Chapman, C.A. 1989. Spider monkey sleeping sites: use and availability. *American Journal of Primatology.* Vol.18, 53–60.

———. 1990. Ecological constraints on group size in three species of neotropical primates. *Folia Primatologica.* Vol. 55, 1–9.

Chapman, C.A. and L.J. Chapman. 1991. The foraging itinerary of spider monkeys: when to eat leaves? *Folia Primatologica.* Vol. 56, 162–166.

Chapman, C.A. and L. Lefebvre. 1990. Manipulating foraging group size: spider monkey food calls at fruiting trees. *Animal Behaviour.* Vol. 39, 891–896.

Chesser, R.T. 1995. Comparative diets of obligate ant-following birds at a site in Northern Bolivia. *Biotropica* 27(3): 382–390.

Choe, J.C., and D.L. Perlman. 1997. Social conflict and cooperation among founding queens in ants (Hymenoptera: Formicidae). pp.. 392–406 in Choe, J.C., nd J. Crespi, eds. *The evolution of social behavior in insects and arachnids.* Cambridge University Press, Cambridge, England.

Clark, D.B., and D.A. Clark. 1993. Comparative analysis of microhabitat utilization by saplings of nine tree species in neotropical rain forest. *Biotropica* 25:397–407.

Davidson, D.E., and B.L. Fisher. 1991. Symbiosis of ants with Cecropia as a function of light regime. pp. 289–309 in Huxley, C.R., and D.F. Cutler, eds. *Ant-plant interactions.* Oxford University Press, Oxford, UK.

Davidson, D.E., R.R. Snelling, and J.T. Longino. 1989. Competition among ants for myrmecophytes and the significance of plant trichomes. *Biotropica* 21: 64–73.

Davidson, D.W., R.B. Foster, R.R. Snelling, and P.W. Lozada. 1991. Variable composition of some tropical ant–plant symbioses. pp. 145–162 in Price, P.W., T.M. Lewinsohn, G.W. Fernandes, and W.W. Benson, eds. *Plant-Animal interactions: evolutionary ecology in tropical and temperate regions.* John Wiley & Sons, Inc., New York.

de Oliveira, T.G. 1998. Leopardus wiedii. *Mammalian Species* 579:1–6.

DeVries, P.J. 1983. *Heliconius hecale* (Hecale). pp. 730–731 in Janzen, D.H., ed. *Costa Rican Natural History*. The University of Chicago Press, Chicago and London.

DeVries, P.J., and J. Clark. 1987. *The butterflies of Coast Rica and their natural history: Papilionidae, Pieridae, Nymphalidae*. Princeton University Press, Princeton, NJ.

Dixson, A.F. 1987. Baculum length and copulatory behavior in primates. *American Journal of Primatology*. Vol. 13, 51–60.

Donnelly, M.A. 1987. Territoriality in the poison–dart frog *Dendrobates pumilio* (Anura: Dendrobatidae). Ph.D. diss., University of Miami.

———. 1989a. Demographic effects of reproductive resource supplementation in a terrestrial frog, *Dendrobates pumilio. Ecology* 59(3): 207–21.

———. 1989b. Effects of reproductive resource supplementations on space-use patterns in *Dendrobates pumilio. Oecologia* 81: 212–18.

———. 1989c. Reproductive phenology and age structure of *Dendrobates pumilio* in northeastern Costa Rica. *Journal of Herpetology* 23 (4): 362–67.

Donnelly, M.A., and C. Guyer. 1994. Patterns of reproduction and habitat use in an assemblage of Neotropical hylid frogs. *Oecologia* 98: 291–302.

Dressler, R.L. 1982. Biology of the orchid bees (Euglossini). *Annual Review of Ecology and Systematics* 13:373–394.

Ducey, P.K., E.D. Brodie, and E.A. Barnes. 1993. Salamander tail autotomy and snake predation: role of antipredator behavior and toxicity for three neotropical *Bolitoglossa* (Caudata: Plethodontidae). *Biotropica* 25(3): 344–349.

Ducey, P.K., D.R. Formanowicz, Jr., L. Boyet, J. Mailloux, and R.A. Nussbaum. 1993. Experimental examination of burrowing behavior in caecilians (Amphibia: Gymnophiona): effects of soil compaction on burrowing ability of four species. *Herpetologica* 49(4): 450–457.

Duellman, W.E. 1970. The hylid frogs of Middle America. Lawrence, Kansas. Museum of Natural History.

Dunlap-Pianka, H.C., L. Boggs, and L.E. Gilbert. 1977. Ovarian dynamics in heliconiine butterflies: Programmed senescence versus eternal youth. *Science* 197: 487–90.

Eidmann, H. 1945. Zur Kenntnis der Okologie von Azteca muelleri Em. (Hym. Formicidae), ein Beitrag zum Problem der Myrmecophyten. Zoologische Jahrbuecher, Abteilung fuer Systematik, Okologie und Geographie der Tiere 77:1–48, 3 tables.

Eisenberg, J.F. 1990. *Mammals of the Neotropics, Vol.1: The Northern Neotropics*. University of Chicago Press, Chicago.

Eisenberg, J.F., and K.H. Redford. 1999. *Mammals of the Neotropics, Vol 3: The Central Neotropics. Ecuador, Peru, Bolivia, Brazil*. University of Chicago Press, Chicago.

Eizirik, E., S.L. Bonatto, W.E. Johnson, P.G. Crawshaw, and J.-C. Vié, etc. 1998. Phylogeographic patterns and evolution of the mitochondrial DNA control region in two neotropical cats (Mammalia, Felidae). *Journal of Molecular Evolution* 47:613–624.

Eltz, T., W.M. Whitten, D.W. Roubik, and K.E. Linsenmair. 1999. Fragrance collection, storage, and accumulation by individual male orchid bees. *Journal of Chemical Ecology* 25:157–176.

Emery, C. 1893. Studio monografico sul genere Azteca Forel. Memorie della Royal Accademia delle Scienze dell'Istituto di Bologna (5)3:119–152.

———. 1896. Alcune forme nouve del genere Azteca For. e note biologiche. Bollettino dei Musei di Zoologia ed Anatomia comparata della R. Universita di Torino 11(230):1–7.

———. 1912. Subfam. Dolichoderinae. Genera Insectorum Fasc. 137:1–50.

Farji-Brener, A. 2001. Why are leaf-cutting ants more common in early secondary forests than in old-growth tropical forests? An evaluation of the palatable forage hypothesis. *Oikos* 92: 169–177.

Fenton, M., R. Brock, R. Paul, and M.V. Jeremy, eds. 1987. *Recent Advances in the Study of Bats*. Cambridge University Press, Cambridge, MA.

Fenton, M.B. 1985. *Communication in the Chiroptera*. Indiana University Press, Bloomington.

———. 1983. *Just Bats*. University of Toronto Press, Toronto.

Ferguson, B.G., D.H. Boucher, M. Pizzi, and C. Rivera. 1995. Recruitment and decay of a pulse of Cecropia in Nicaraguan rain forest damaged by Hurricane Joan: relation to mutualism with Azteca ants. Biotropica 27:455–460.

Fish, F.E., B. Blood, and B. Clark. 1991. Hydrodynamics of the feet of fish-catching bats-influence of the water-surface on drag and morphological design. *Journal of Experimental Zoology* 258(92):164–173.

Fleagle, J.G. 1988. *Primate Adaptation and Evolution*. Academic Press, New York.

Fleming, T.H. 1971. *Artibeus jamaicensis*: Delayed embryonic development in a Neotropical bat. *Science* 171: 402–4.

Forel, A. 1929. The social world of the ants (C.K. Ogden, Trans.). Albert and Charles Boni, New York.

Frankie, G.W., R.W. Thorp, L.E. Newstrom-Lloyd, M.A. Rizzardi, J.F. Barthell, T.L. Griswold, J.-Y. Kim, and S. Kappagoda. 1998. Monitoring solitary bees in modified wildland habitats: implications for bee ecology and conservation. *Enviromental Entomology* 27:1137–1148.

Freese, C.H. 1976. Predation on swollen-thorn acacia ants by white-faced monkeys, *Cebus capucinus*. *Biotropica* 8:278–81.

Fuller, K.S., Swift, B,. Jorgensen, A., and A. Brautigam. 1987. *Latin American wildlife trade laws, 2d edn. (rev.)*. WWF, Washington, D.C.

Ghazoul, J., and J. Hill. 2000. Impacts of selective logging on tropical forest invertebrates. In Fimbel, R.A., A. Grajal, and J.G. Robinson, editors. *Conserving wildlife in managed tropical forests*. Columbia University Press, New York, New York, *in press*.

Gilbert, L.E. 1971. Butterfly-plant coevolution: has *Passiflora adenopoda* won the selectional race with Heliconiine butterflies? *Science* 172: 585–586.

———. Pollen feeding and reproductive biology of *Heliconius* butterflies. *Proc. Nat. Acad. Sci., U.S.A.* 69: 1403–7.

———. 1975. Ecological consequences of a coeevolved mutualism between butterflies and plants. pp. 210–240 in Gilbert, L.E., and P.H. Raven eds. *Coevolution in Animals and Plants*. University of Texas Press, Austin.

———. 1976. Development of theory in the analysis of insect-plant interactions. In *Analysis of ecological systems*, ed. D.J. Horn. Ohio State University Press.

———. 1980. Food web organization and the conservation of neotropical diversity. pp. 11–33 in Soulé, M.E., and B.A. Wilcox, eds. *Conservation Biology*. Sinauer, Sunderland, MA.

Gill, Frank B. 1988. Trapline foraging by hermit hummingbirds. *Ecology* 69:1933–1942.

Ginsberg, H.S. 1983. Foraging ecology of bees in an old field. *Ecology* 64:165–175.

Goetsch, W. 1953. *The Ants*. The University of Michigan Press. Ann Arbor, Michigan.

Goldman, E.A. 1920. Mammals of Panama. *Smithsonian Misc. Coll.* 69(5):1–309.

Gotwald, W.H., Jr. *Army Ants: The Biology of Social Predation* (Cornell Series in Arthropod Biology)

Grzimek, Bernard. 1990. *Grzimek's Encyclopedia of Mammals* (Vol. 3). McGraw-Hill Publishing Company, New York.

Hart, A.G., and F.L.W. Ratnicks. 2000. Leaf caching in *Atta* leafcutting ants: discrete cache formation through positive feedback. *Animal Behaviour* 59: 587–591.

———. 2001. Task partitioning, division of labour and nest compartmentalization collectively isolate hazardous waste in the leaf-cutting ant Atta cephalotes. *Behav. Ecol. Sociobiology* 49: 387–392.

Heithaus, E.R., Fleming, T.H, and P.A. Opler. 1975. Foraging patterns and resource utilization of seven species of bats in a seasonal tropical forest. *Ecology* 56: 841–54.

Hershkovitz, P. 1977. *Living New World Monkeys (Platyrrhini) with an Introduction to Primates*, Vol 1. University of Chicago Press, Chicago.

Hilborn, R., and M. Mangel. 1997. *The ecological detective*. Princeton Monographs in Population Biology. Princeton University Press, Princeton, NJ.

Hill, J.E. and J. Smith. 1984. Bats: A Natural History. British Museum (Natural History).

Holdobler and Wilson. 1990. *The Ants*. Belknap Press of the Harvard University Press. Cambridge, MA.

Hood, C.S. and J. Jones, Jr. 1984. *Noctilio leporinus*. Mammalian Species No. 216:1–7, 6 figs.

Howard, J.J. 1987. Leafcutting ant diet selection: the role of nutrients, water, and secondary chemistry. *Ecology* 68(3): 503–515.

———. 1988. Leafcutting and diet selection: relative influence of leaf chemistry and physical features. *Ecology* 69(1): 250–260.

IUCN. 1996. "Cat Specialist Group: Species Accounts: Margay (*Leopardus wiedii*)." Available online at http://lynx.uio.no/catfolk. (November 27, 2001).

IUCN. (2002). 2002 IUCN Red List of Threatened Species. The IUCN Species Survival Commission. Retrieved from Internet 11/12/02, www.redlist.org.

Janzen, D.H. 1966. Coevolution between ants and acacias in Central America. *Evolution* 20:249–75.

———. 1967. Interaction of the bull's horn acacia (*Acacia cornigera* L.) with an ant inhabitant (*Pseudomyrmex ferruginea* F. Smith) in eastern Mexico. *Univ. Kansas Sci. Bull.* 47: 315–558.

———. 1969. Allelopathy by myrmecophytes: the ant Azteca as an allelopathic agent of Cecropia. Ecology 50:147–153.

———. 1971. Euglossine bees as long-distance pollinators of tropical plants. *Science* 171: 203–205.

———. 1973. Dissolution of mutualism between Cecropia and its Azteca ants. *Biotropica* 5:15–28.

———. 1973. Evoltion of polygynous obligate acacia-ants in western Mexico. *Journal of Animal Ecology* 42: 727–50.

———. 1974. Swollen-thorn acacias of Central America. *Smithsonian Conrtrib. Bot.* 13: 1–31.

———. 1975. *Pseudomyrmex nigropilosa*: A parasite of a mutualism. *Science* 188: 936–37.

———. 1979a. How to be fig. Annual Review of Ecology and Systematics 10:13–51.

———. 1979b. How many parents do the wasp from a fig have? *Biotropica* 11:127–29.

———. 1979c. How many babies do figs pay for babies? *Biotropica* 11:48–50.

———. 1983. *Costa Rican Natural History*. The University of Chicago Press, Chicago and London.

Janzen, D.H., G.A. Miller, J. Hackforth-Jones, C.M. Pond, K. Hooper, and D.P. Janos. 1976. Two Costa Rican bat-generated seed shadows of *Andira inermis* (Leguminosae). *Ecology* 57: 1068–75.

Janzen, D.H., P.J. DeVries, M.L. Higgins, and L.S. Kimsey. 1982. Seasonal and site variation in Costa Rican euglossine bees at chemical baits in lowland deciduous and evegreen forests. *Ecology* 63:66–74.

Jaramillo, A., and P. Burke. 1999. *New World Blackbirds: The Icterids.* Princeton University Press, Princeton, NJ.

Jimbo, S., and H.O. Schwassman. 1967. Feeding behavior and daily emergence pattern of *Artibeus jamaicensis.* Atas Simp. *Biota Amazonica* 5: 239–53.

Johns, A.D. 1986. *Effects of habitat disturbance on the rainforest wildlife in Brazilian Amazonia.* Unpubl. report, WWF–US, Washington, D.C.

Johnsgard, P.A. 1997. *The Hummingbirds of North America.* Smithsonian Institution Press, Washington, D.C.

Jolly, A. 1972. *The Evolution of Primate Behavior.* Macmillan Publishing Company, New York.

Judd, W.S., R.W. Sanders, and M.J. Donoghue. 1994. Angiosperm family pairs: preliminary phylogenetic analyses. Harvard papers in *Botany* 5:1–51.

Kays, R.W. 1999. Food preferences of kinkajous (*Potos flavus*): a frugivorous carnivore. *Journal of Mammalogy* 80(2): 589–599.

Kays, R.W., and J.L. Gittleman. 2001. The social organization of the kinkajou *Potus flavus* (Procrynida). *Journal of Zoology London* 253: 491–504.

Kinzey, W.G. 1997. *Ateles.* In Kinzey, Warren G., ed. *New World Primates: Ecology, Evolution, and Behavior.* Aldine de Gruyter, New York.

Konecny, M.J. 1989. Movement patterns and food habits of four sympatric carnivore species in Belize, Central America. pp. 243–264 in Redford, K.H., and J.F. Eisenberg, eds. *Advances in neotropical mammalogy.* Sandhill Crane Press, Gainesville, FL.

Kraucunas, Nathan. 1996. "Milwaukee Public Museum: Birds of the Rainforest." Available online at http://www.mpm.edu/research. (March 18, 2001).

Kricher, J. 1989. *A Neotropical Companion: An Introduction to the Animals, Plants and Ecosystems of the New World Tropics.*

Kunz, T.H., and C.A. Diaz. 1995. Folivory in fruit–eating bats, with new evidence from *Artibeus jamaicensis* (Chiroptera: Phyllostomidae). *Biotropica* 27(1): 106–120.

Kunz, T.H., and G.F. McCracken. 1996. Tents and harems: app.arent defence of folicage roosts by tent-making bats. *Journal of Tropical Ecology* 12: 121–137.

Lee, J.C. 1996. *The Amphibians and Reptiles of the Yucatan Peninsula.* Comstock Publishing Associates. Ithaca, NY.

Leyhausen, P. 1963. [The South American spotted cats.] *Z. Tierpsychol.* 20:627–640 (in German).

Lieberman, S.S. 1986. Ecology of the leaf litter herpetofauna of a Neotropical rain forest La Selva, Costa Rica. *Acta Zool. Mex.*, n.s. 15: 1–72.

Limerick, S. 1980. Courtship behavior and oviposition of the Poison–Arrow Frog *Dendrobates Pumilio.* Herpetologica, 36: 69–71.

Linksvayer, T.A., A.C. McCall, R.M. Jensen, C.M. Marshall, J.W. Miner, and M.J. McKone. 2002. The function of hitchhiking behavior in the Leaf-cutting Ant *Att cephalotes.* *Biotrpica* 34(1): 93–100.

Longino, J.T. 1989a. Geographic variation and community structure in an ant–plant mutualism: Azteca and Cecropia in Costa Rica. *Biotropica* 21:126–132.

———. 1989b. Taxonomy of the Cecropia–inhabiting ants in the Azteca alfari species group: evidence for two broadly sympatric species. Contributions in Science (Natural History Museum of Los Angeles County) 412:1–16.

———. 1991a. Azteca ants in Cecropia trees: taxonomy, colony structure, and behavior. pp. 271–288 in Huxley, C.R., and D. Cutler, eds. *Ant–plant interactions.* Oxford University Press, Oxford, UK.

———. 1991b. Taxonomy of the Cecropia–inhabiting Azteca ants. *Journal of Natural History* 25:1571–1602.

Lubin, Y.D. 1983. *Nasutitermes* (Hormiga Blanca, Nasute Termite, Arboreal Termite). pp. 743–745 *in* Janzen, D.H., ed. *Costa Rican Natural History.* The University of Chicago Press, Chicago and London.

Lubin, Y.D., and G.G. Montgomery. 1980. Defenses of *Nasutitermes* termites (Isoptera, Termitidae) against *Tamandua* anteaters (Edentata, Myrmecophagidae). *Biotropica* 9: 26–34.

Lubin, Y.D., O.P. Young, and G.G. Montgomery. 1977. Food resources of anteaters (Edentata: Myrmecophagidae). I. A year's census of arboreal nests of ants and termites of Barro Colorado Island, Panama Canal Zone, *Biotropica* 9: 26–34.

Macdonald, D. (ed.) 1984. *The Encyclopedia of Mammals,* Facts on File Publications, New York.

Mansard, P. 1997. Breeding and husbandry of the Margay *Leopardus wiedii yucatanica* at the Ridgeway Trust for Endangered Cats, Hastings. *International Zoo Yearbook* 35:94–100.

Mares, M.A., R.A Ojeda,. and M.P. Kosco. 1981. Observations on the distribution and ecology of the mammals of Salta Province, Argentina. *Ann. Carnegie Mus.* 50:151–206.

Matheson, A., S.L. Buchmann, C. O'Toole, P. Westrich, and I.H. Williams, eds. 1996. *The conservation of bees.* Academic Press, London.

McDade, L.A. 1992. Pollinator relationships, biogeography, and phylogenetics. *Bioscience* 42:21–26.

McVey, M.E., R.G. Zahary, D. Perry, and J. MacDougal. 1981. Territoriality and homing behavior in the Poison Dart Frog (*Dendrobates pumilio*). *Copeia,* 1: 1–8.

Meerman, J., 1994. Summary of herpetofauna distributions in Belize. Report to National Protected Areas Management Project.

Mellen, J. 1989. *Reproductive behaviour of small captive cats* (Felis ssp.). Ph.D. thesis, University of California, Davis.

Melquist, W.E. 1984. *Status survey of otters (Lutrinae) and spotted cats (Felidae) in Latin America*. Unpubl. report, University of Idaho (Moscow) and IUCN (Gland, Switzerland).

Milton, K. (1981). Estimates of reproductive parameters for free-ranging *Ateles geoffroyi*. *Primates*, 22, 574–579.

Mittermeier, R.A. (1988). Ecology and behavior of neotropical primates, 2. Washington, D.C., World Wildlife Fund.

Mondolfi, E. 1986. Notes on the biology and status of the small wild cats in Venezuela. pp. 125–146 in Miller, S.D., and D.D. Everett, eds. *Cats of the World: Biology, Conservation and Management*. National Wildlife Federation, Washington, D.C.

Montgomery, G.G. 1980a. Socio-ecology of Xenarthra (= Edentat): Parental investment by extreme K-strategists. In Eisenberg, J.F., et al., eds. *Mammalian Behavior*. Special Publication, American Society of Mammalogists.

———. 1980b. Impact of mammalian anteaters (*Cyclopes, Tamandua*) on arboreal ant populations. In Montgomery, G.G., ed. *The evolution and ecology of sloths, anteaters and armadillos (Mammalia: Xenarthra = Edentata)*. Smithsonian Institution Press, Washington, D.C.

———. 1980c. Home-range spaces, movement patterns, and foraging strategies of the four species of Neotropical anteaters. In Phillipes, R.L., and C.J. Jonkel, eds. *Proceedings of the 1975 Predator Symposium*. Montana Forest and Conservation Experiment Station, School of Forestry, University of Montana, Missoula.

———. 1983. *Heliconius hecale* (Hecale). pp. 461–463 in Janzen, D.H., ed. *Costa Rican Natural History*. The University of Chicago Press, Chicago and London.

Moore, B.P. 1964. Volatile terpens from *Nasutitermes* soldiers (Isoptera, Termitidae). *Journal of Insect Physiology* 10: 371–75.

Morrison, D.W. 1978a. Foraging ecology and energetics of the frugivorous bat *Artibeus jamaicensis*. *Ecology* 59: 716–23.

———. 1978b. Influence of habitat on the foraging distances of the fruit bat *Artibeus jamaicensis*. *Journal of Mammalogy* 59: 622–24.

———. 1978c. Lunar phobia in a Neotropical fruit bat, *Artibeus jamaicensis*. *Animal behavior* 26: 852–55.

———. 1979. Apparent male defense of tree hollows in the bat *Artibeus jamaicensis*. *Journal of Mammalogy* 60: 11–15.

———. 1983. *Artibeus jamaicensis*. pp. 449–451 in Janzen, D.H., ed. *Costa Rican Natural History*. University of Chicago Press, Chicago and London.

Mueller, F. 1876. Ueber das Haarkissen am Blattstiel der Imbauba (Cecropia), das Gemuesebeet der Imbauba–Ameise. *Jenaische Zeitschrift fur Medizin und Naturwissenschaft* 10:281–286.

———. 1880–1881. Die Imbauba und ihre Beschuetzer. *Kosmos* 8:109–116.

Natural History Museum of Los Angeles County at www.nhm.org.

New, T.R. 1998. *Invertebrate surveys for conservation*. Oxford University Press, New York.

Nowak, R.M., and J.L. Paradiso. 1983. *Walker's Mammals of the World* Vol. 1. The Johns Hopkins University Press, Baltimore and London.

Nowak, R.M. 1999. *Walker's Mammals of the World* (Sixth Edition, Volume II). The Johns Hopkins University Press, Baltimore and London.

Nowell, K., and P. Jackson. 1996. *Wild Cats: status survey and conservation action plan*. IUCN, Gland, Switzerland.

Orgeix, C.A. d', and B.L. Turner. 1995. Multiple paternity in the red-eyed treefrog *Agalychnis callidryas* (Cope). *Molecular Ecology* 4: 505–8.

Orians, Gordon H. 1985. *Blackbirds of the Americas*. University of Washington Press, Seattle, Washington.

Paintiff, J.A., and D.E. Anderson. 1980. Breeding the margay at New Orleans Zoo. *Intl. Zoo. Yearb.* 20:223–224.

Paz y Miño, G. 1988. Notas sobre la caceria y la conservacion de los felidos en la Amazonia Ecuatoriana. [Notes on the hunting and conservation of cat species in Ecuador's Amazonia]. *Fundacion Simon Bolivar Boletin Cientifico* 2(3):1–14. Quito, Ecuador (in Spanish).

Pearson, D.L., and R.L. Dressler. 1985. Two-year study of male orchid bee (Hymenoptera: Apidae: Euglossini) attraction to chemical baits in lowland south-eastern Peru. *Journal of Tropical Ecology* 1:37–54.

Perfecto, I., and J. Vandermeer. 1993. Distribution and turnover rate of a population of Atta cephalotes in a tropical rain forest in Costa Rica. *Biotropica* 25(3): 316–321.

Peruquetti, R.C. 2000. Function of fragrances collected by euglossine males (Hymenoptera: Apidae). *Entomologica Generalis* 25: 33–37.

Peruquetti, R.C., L.A.O. Campos, C.D.P. Coelho, C.V.M. Abrantes, and L.C.O. Lisboa. 1999. Abelhas Euglossini (Apidae) de àreas de Mata Atlântica: abundância, riqueza e aspectos biològios. *Revista Brasileira de Zoologia* 16:101–118.

Petersen, M.K. 1977a. Courtship and mating patterns of margays. pp. 22–35 in Eaton, R.L., ed. *The world's cats 3(3): biology, behavior and management of reproduction*. Carnivore Res. Inst., University of Washington, Seattle.

———. 1977b. Behaviour of the margay. pp. 69–76 in Eaton, R.L., ed. *The world's cats* 3(2). Carnivore Res. Inst., University of Washington, Seattle.

Petersen, M.K. and M.K. Petersen. 1978. Growth rates and other post–natal developmental changes in margays. *Carnivore* 1(1):87–92.

Phillips, D.M., J. Rasweiler, and F. Muradali. 1997. Giant, accordioned sperm acrosomes of the Greater Bulldog Bat, *Noctilio leporinus*. *Molecular Reproduction and Development* 48:(1):90–94.

Powell, A.H., and G.V.N. Powell. 1987. Population dynamics of male euglossine bees in amazonian forest fragments. *Biotropica* 19:176–179.

Prator, T., W.D. Thomas, M. Jones, and M. Dee. 1988. A twenty–year overview of selected rare carnivores in captivity. pp.. 191–229 in Dresser, B., R. Reece, and E. Maruska, eds. *5th World Conference on Breeding Endangered Species in Captivity, Cincinnati, Ohio.*

Pröhl, H. 1997. Territorial behavior of the strawberry poison-dart frog, *Dendrobates pumilio*. *Amphibia Reptilia* 18 (4): 437–42.

Pröhl, H. and W. Hödl. 1999. Parental investment, potential reproductive rates, and mating system in the strawberry dart-poison frog, *Dendrobates pumilio*. *Behav. Eco.* Sociobiology 46: 215–220.

Pröhl, H. and O. Berke. Spatial distributions of male and female strawberry poison frogs and their relation to female reproductive resources. *Oecologia* 129: 534–542.

Putz, F.E., and N.M. Holbrook. 1988. Further observations on the dissolution of mutualism between Cecropia and its ants: the Malaysian case. *Oikos* 53:121–125.

Pyburn, W.F. 1963. Observations on the life history of the tree frog, *Phyllomedus callidryas* (Cope). *Texas Journal of Science* 15(2): 155–70.

———. 1964. Breeding behavior of the leaf-frog *Phyllomedus callidryas* in southern Veracruz. *Yrbk. Amer. Phil. Soc.* 1964: 291–94.

———. 1970. Breeding behavior of the leaf-frog *Phyllomedus callidryas* and *Phyllomedusa dacnicolor* in Mexico. *Copeia* 1970 (2): 209–18.

Redford, K.H. and J.F. Eisenberg. 1992. *Mammals of the Neotropics, Vol. 2: The Southern Cone.* University of Chicago Press, Chicago.

Reilly, J.C., D.A. Ritter, and D.R. Carrier. 1997. Hydrostatic locomotion in a limbless tetrapod. *Nature* 386: 269–271.

Remsen, J.V. Jr., M. Hyde, and A. Chapman. 1993. The diets of neotropical trogons, motmots, barbets, and toucans. *Condor* 95:178–182.

Rettenmeyer, C.W. 1961. Observations on the biology and taxonomy of flies found over swarm raids of army ants. (Dipter: Tachinidae, Conopidae). University of Kansas Science Bulletin 42: 993–1066.

———. 1963. Behavioral studies of army ants. University of Kansas Science Bulletin 44: 281–465.

Rickson, F.R. 1971. Glycogen plastids in Mullerian body cells of Cecropia peltata—a higher green plant. *Science* 173:344–347.

Robinson, J. G. & Janson, C. H. 1987. *Capuchins, Squirrel Monkeys, and Atelines: Socioecological Convergence with Old World Monkeys.* pp.. 69–82. Primate Societies. The University of Chicago Press, Chicago and London.

Rosengaus, R.B., M.L. Lefebvre, and J.F.A. Traniello. 2000. Inhibition of fungal spore germination by *Nasutitermes*: evidence for a possible antiseptic role of soldier defensive secretions. *Journal of Chemical Ecology* 26(1): 21–37.

Rowe, N. 1996. *The Pictorial Guide to the Living Primates.* Pogonias Press, East Hampton, NY.

Roubik, D.W. 1983. Experimental community studies: time–series tests of competition between African and neotropical bees. *Ecology* 64:971–978.

———. 1989. *Ecology and natural history of tropical bees.* Cambridge University Press, Cambridge, MA.

———. 1992. Loose niches in tropical communities: why are there so many trees and so few bees? pp. 327–354 in Hunter, M.D., T. Ohgushi, and P.W. Price, eds. *Effects of resource distribution on animal-plant interactions.* Academic Press, San Diego, CA.

———. 1993. Tropical pollinators in the canopy and understory: field data and theory for stratum "preferences." *Journal of Insect Behavior* 6:659–673.

———. 1996a. Measuring the meaning of honey bees. pp. 163–172 in Matheson, A., S.L. Buchmann, C. O'Toole, P. Westrich, and I.H. Williams, eds. *The conservation of bees.* Academic Press, London.

———. 1996b. African honey bees as exotic pollinators in French Guiana. Pages 173–182 in Matheson, A., S.L. Buchmann, C. O'Toole, P. Westrich, and I.H. Williams, eds. *The conservation of bees.* Academic Press, London.

———. 2000. Pollination system stability in tropical America. *Conservation Biology* 14:1235–1236.

Roubik, D.W., and J.D. Ackerman. 1987. Long–term ecology of euglossine orchid-bees (Apidae: Euglossini) in Panama. *Oecologia* 73:321–333.

Roubik, D.W., and H. Wolda. 2000. Do honey bees matter? Dynamics and abundance of native bees before and after honey bee invasion. *Population Ecology, in press.*

Schnitzler, H.U., E. Kalko, I. Kaipf, and A. Grinnell. 1994. Fishing and echolocation behavior of the greater bulldog bat, *Noctilio-Leporinus*, in the field. *Behavioral Ecology and Sociobiology* 35:(5):327–345.

Schupp, E.W. 1986. Azteca protection of Cecropia: ant occupation benefits juvenile trees. *Oecologia* 70:379–385.

Scott, N.J. 1983. *Bolitoglossa subpalmata* (Escorpiones, Salamandras, Mountain Salamander). pp. 382–383 in D.H. Janzen, ed. *Costa Rican Natural History.* The University of Chicago Press, Chicago and London.

Skutch, A. 1973. *The Life of a Hummingbird*. Crown Publishers, Inc., New York.

Skutch, A.F. 1969. Life histories of Central American Birds. Pacific Coast Avifauna, no. 35. Berkeley: Cooper Ornithological Society.

———. 1996. *Orioles, Blackbirds, and Their Kin*. University of Arizona Press, Tucson.

Smythe, Nicholas. 1978. *The Natural History of the Central American Agouti* (Dasyprocta Punctata). Smithsonian Institutional Press, Washington, D.C.

Southwood, T.R.E. 1988. *Ecological methods*. Third edition. Methuen, London.

SPSS. 1997. SYSTAT 7.0 for Windows. SPSS Inc.

Stiles, F.G. 1975. Ecology, flowering phenology, and hummingbird pollination of some Costa Rican *Heliconia* species. *Ecology* 56: 285–301.

———. 1979. The ecology and evolution of a lek mating system in the long-tailed hermit hummingbird . American Ornithol. Union Monr., no. 27.

Stiles, F.G., and L.L. Wolf. 1974. A possible circannual molt rhythm in a tropical hummingbird. *American Naturalist* 108: 341–54.

Stuart, A.M. 1963. Origion of the trail in the termites *Nasutitermes corniger* (Motchulsky) and *Zootermopsis nevadensis* (Hagen), Isoptera. *Physiol. Zool.* 36: 69–84.

Studier, E.H., S. Sevick,, D. Ridley, and D. Wilson. 1994. Mineral and nitrogen concentrations in feces of some neotropical bats. *Journal of Mammalogy* 75:(3):674–680.

Sunquist, M.E., and G.G. Montgomery. 1973. Activity pattern of a translocated silky anteater (*Cyclopes didactylus*). *Journal of Mammology* 54: 782.

Swartz, M.B. 2001. Bivouac checking, a novel behavior distinguishing obligate from opportunistic species of army-ant-following birds. *Condor* 103: 629–633.

Symington, M.M. 1987. Long-distance vocal communication in *Ateles*: functional hypotheses and preliminary evidence. *International Journal of Primatology*. Vol. 8, 475.

Tello, J.L. 1986b. *The situation of the wild cats* (Felidae) *in Bolivia*. CITES Secretariat, Lausanne.

Thorne, B.L. 1980. Differences in nest architecture between the Neotropical arboreal termites *Nasutitermes corniger* and *Nasutitermes ephratae* (Isoptera: Termitadae). *Psyche* 87: 235–43.

Uhl, C., K. Clark, H. Clark, and P. Murphy. 1981. Early plant succession after cutting and burning in the upper Rio Negro region of the Amazon basin. *Journal of Ecology* 69:631–649.

Valerio, C.E. 1971. Ability of some tropical tadpoles to survive without water. *Copeia* 1971 (2): 364–65.

Van Roosmalen, M.G.M. 1985. Habitat preferences, diet, feeding strategy, and social organization of the black spider monkey (*Ateles paniscus paniscus* Linnaeus 1758) in Surinam. *Acta Amazonica*. Vol. 15 (3/4 suppl.), 1–238.

Vasconcelos, H.L., and A.B. Casimiro. 1997. Influence of Azteca alfari ants on the exploitation of Cecropia trees by a leaf-cutting ant. *Biotropica* 29:84–92.

Vaughan, C. 1983. *A report on dense forest habitat for endangered wildlife species in Costa Rica*. Unpubl. report, Univ. Nacional, Heredia.

Vogel, S. 1966. Parfümsammelnde Bienen als Bestäuber von Orchidaceen und Gloxinia. Österr. Bot. Z. 113: 302–361.

Vrkoc, J., K. Ubik, L. Dolejes, and I. Hrdy. 1972. On the chemical composition of frontal gland secretions in termites of the genus *Nasutitermes*. *Acta. Ent. Bohemoslov* 70: 74–80.

Walton, B. 1991. Catcalls. *BBC Wildlife* 9(3):198–202.

Weigel, I. 1975. Small cats and clouded leopards. pp 281–332 in Grzimek, B., ed. *Grizmek's animal life encyclopedia 12: Mammals III*. Van Nostrand Reinhold, New York.

Weygoldt, P. 1980. Complex brood care and reproductive behavior in captive poison–arrow frogs, *Dendrobates pulimio* O. Schmidt. Behavioral Ecology and Sociobiology 73: 29–32.

———. 1987. Evolution of parental care in dart poison frogs (Amphibia: Anura: Dendrobatidae). *Z. Zool. Syst. Evol.-Forsch.* 25 (1): 51–67.

Wheeler, W.M. 1942. Studies of neotropical ant–plants and their ants. Bulletin of the Museum of Comparative Zoology, Harvard 90:1–262.

Whitten, W.M., A.M. Young, and N.H. Williams. (1989) Function of glandular secretions in fragrance collection by male euglossine bees. *J. Chem. Ecol.* 15: 1285–1295.

Willis, E.O. 1972. The behavior of spotted antbirds. A.O.U. Monograph, No. 10.

———. 1977. Lista preliminar das aves da parte noroeste e áreas vizinhas da Reserva Ducke, Amazonas, Brasil. Rev. Brasil Biol. 37: 585–601.

———. 1983. Antbirds. pp. 546–547 in Janzen, D.H., ed. *Costa Rican Natural History*. University of Chicago Press, Chicago and London.

Willis, E.O., and Y. Oniki. Birds and army ants. *Annual Review of Ecology and Systematics* 9: 243–263.

Wolda, H. 1979. Fluctuations in abundance of tropical insects. *American Naturalist* 112:1017–1045.

———. 1992. Trends in abundance of tropical forest insects. *Oecologia* 89:47–52.

Wolda, H., and D.W. Roubik. 1986. Nocturnal bee abundance and seasonal bee activity in a Panamanian forest. *Ecology* 67:426–433.

Wright, S.J., C. Carrasco, O. Calderon, and S. Paton. 1999. The El Niño southern oscillation, variable fruit production, and famine in a tropical forest. *Ecology* 80:1632–1647.

Yu, D.W., and D.W. Davidson. 1997. Experimental studies of species–specificity in Cecropia–ant symbioses. Ecological monographs 67:273–294.

THE LLANOS OF VENEZUELA

Alho, C.J.R. 1986. Manejo da Fauna Silvestre. pp. 183–197 in Boock, A., ed. *Anais do 1 Simpósio sobre Recursos Naturais e Sócio-Econômicos do Pantanal.* EMBRAPA-CPAP Documento 5, Corumbá, MS.

Alvarez del Torro, M. 1972. *Los reptiles de Chiapas.* Tuxtla Guitierrez: Instituto de Historia Natural de Chiapas.

Amaral, A. do. 1977. Serpentes do Brasil. University of São Paulo.

Animal Diversity Web of the University of Michigan's Museum of Zoology at http://animaldiversity.ummz.umich.edu.

Bicca-Marques, J.C. 1992. Drinking behavior 58: 107–111.

Bicca-Marques, J.C., and C. Calegaro-Marques. 1994. Exotic plant species can serve as staple food sources for wild howler populations. *Folia Primatol* 63: 209–211.

———. 1995. Locomotion of black howlers in a habitat with discontinuos Canopo. *Folia Primatol* 64: 55–61.

Bravo, S.P., and G.E. Zunino. 2000. Germination of seeds from three species disperses by black howler monkeys (*Alouatta caraya*). *Folia Primatol* 71: 342–345.

Calegaro-Marques, C. and J.C. Bicca-Marques. 1993. Allomaternal care in the black howler monkey (*Alouatta caraya*). *Folia Primatol* 61: 104–109.

Campos, Z. 1993. Effect of habitat on survival of eggs and sex ratio of hatchlings of *Caiman crocodiles yacare* in the Pantanal, Brazil. *Journal of Herpetology* 27: 127–132.

———. 1995. Relationships between the rainfall, nesting habitat, and fecundtity of *Caiman crocodilus yacare* in the Pantanal, Brazil. *Journal of Tropical Ecology* 11(3): 351–358.

Cintra, R. 1988. Nesting ecology of the Paraguayan caiman (*Caiman yacare*) in the Brazilian Pantanal. *Journal of Herpetology* 23: 320–322.

———. 1989. Maternal care and daily pattern of behavior in a family of caimans, *Caiman yacare*, in the Brazilian Pantanal. *Journal of Herpetology* 23: 320–322.

Coutinho, M., and Z. Campos. 1996. Effect of habitat and seasonality on the densities of Caiman in southern Pantanal, Brazil. *Journal of Tropical Ecology* 12(5): 741–747.

Crawshaw, P.G. Jr., and H.B. Quigley. 1991. Jaguar spacing, activity and habitat use in a seasonally flooded environment in Brazil. *Journal of Zoology London* 223 : 357–370.

Crews, D. 2000. Reply to Shine, et al. *Animal Behaviour* 59: 6.

Crockett, C.M., and J.F. Eisenberg. 1987. Howlers: Variations in group size and demography. pp. 54–68 in Smuts, B.B., D.L. Cheney, R.M. Seyfarth, R.W. Wrangham, and T.T. Struhsaker, eds. *Primate Societies.* University of Chicago Press, Chicago.

Cunningham, E., and Birkhead, T. 1997. Female roles in perspective. *Trends in Ecology and Evolution.*

Deutsch, L.A. 1983. An encounter between a bush dog (*Speothos venaticus*) and paca (*Agouti paca*). *Journal of Mammalogy* 64: 532–533.

Dubs, B. 1992. *Birds of Southwestern Brasil.* Betrona Cerlag, Kusnacht, Switzerland.

Eigenmann, C.H., and W.R. Allen. 1942. *Fishes of western South America.* The University of Kentucky, Lexington.

Eisenberg, J.F. 1989. *Mammals of the Neotropics.* Volume 1. The Northern Neotropics. University of Chicago Press, Chicago, London.

Emmons, L.H. 1997. *Neotropical rainforest mammal: a field guide.* Second Edition. University of Chicago Press, Chicago and London.

Fittkau, E.J. 1973. Crocodiles and nutrient metabolism of Amazonian waters. *Amazoniana* 4: 103–133.

Fragoso, J.M.V. 1997. Tapir-generated seed shadows: scale-dependent patchiness in the Amazon rain forest. *Journal of Ecology* 85: 519–529.

Galetti, M., A. Keuroghlian, L. Hanada, and M.I. Morato. 2001. Frugivory and seed dispersal by the Lowland Tapir (*Tapirus terrestris*) in Southeast Brazil. *Biotropica* 33(4): 723–726.

Gardner, J.B. 1955. A ball of garter snakes. *Copeia.*

Glander, K.E. 1978. Drinking from arboreal water sources by mantled howling monkeys (*Alouatta palliata*). *Folia Primatol* 29: 206–217.

Greene, H.W., and R.W. McDiarmid. 1981. Coral snake mimicry: Does it occur? *Science* 213: 1207–12.

Guggisberg, C.A.W. 1975. *Wild cats of the world.* Taplinger Publishing Company, New York.

Heckman, C.W. 1998. *The Pantanal of Pocone: the biota and ecology in the northern section of the world's largest pristine wetland.* Kluwer Academic Publishers, Dordrecht/ Boston/London.

Herrera, E.A., and D.W. MacDonald. 1989. Resource utilization and territoriality in group-living Capybaras (*Hydrochoreus hydrochaeris*). *Journal of Animal Ecology* 58(2): 667–679.

Herzog, H.A., and Galvin, S. 1997. Common sense and the mental lives of animals: An empirical approach. In Mitchell, R.W., N.S. Thompson, and H.L. Miles, eds. *Anthropomorphism, Anecdotes, and Animals.* New York: SUNY Press, New York.

Horwich, R.H. and J. Lyon. 1990. *A Belizean Rain Forest: The Community Baboon Sanctuary*. Community Conservation Consultants.

Houston, D.C. 1984. Does the King Vulture, *Sarcoramphus papa*, use a sense of smell to locate food? Ibid 126: 67–69.

Johnson, M.D., and J.D. Gilardi. 1996. Communal roosting of the crested caracara in southern Guatemala. *Journal of Field Ornithology* 67(1): 44–47.

Kahl, M.P. 1969. Observations on the Jabiru and Maguari Storks in Argentina. *The Condor* 73: 220–229.

———. 1971. Spread-wing postures and their possible functions in the Ciconiidae. *Auk* 88: 715–722.

Konig, C. 1982. *Journal of Ornithology*. 123: 259–267.

Lang, J.W. 1989. pp. 120–121 in Ross, C.A., ed. *Crocodiles and Alligators*. Golden Press, Silverwater, NSW.

MacDonald, D.W. 1981. Dwindling resources and the social behavior of Capybaras (*Hydrochoreus hydrochaeris*) (Mammalia). *Journal of Zoology London* 194: 371–391.

MacDonald, D.W., K. Krantz, and R.T. Aplin. 1984. Behavioural, anatomical, and chemical aspects of scent marking amongst Capybaras (*Hydrochoerus hydrochaeris*) (Rodentia: Caviomorpha). *Journal of Zoology London* 202: 341–360.

Medem. 1983. *Los Crocodylia de Suramerica II Editorial Carrera*. Bogotá, Columbia.

Mores, A., and J. Ojasti. 1986. *Hydrochoerus hydrochaeris*. *Mammalian Species* 264: 1–7.

Murphy, R.M., J.S. Mariano, and F.A. Moura Duarte. 1985. Behavioral observations in Capybara colony (*Hydrochoerus hydrochaeris*). *Applied Animal Behaviour Science* 14: 89–98.

Olmos, F., R. Pardini, R.L.P. Boulhosa, R. Bürgi, and C. Morsello. 1999. Do tapirs steal food from palm seed predators or give them a lift? *Biotropica* 31(2): 375–379.

O'Shea, M.T. 1994. *Herpetological Review* 25: 124.

Pope, B. 1966. Population characteristics of howler monkeys (*Alouatta caraya*) in northern Argentina. *Am. J. Phys. Anth.* 24: 361–370.

Por, F.D. 1995. *The Pantanal of Mato Grosso (Brazil)*. Kluwer Academic Publishers, Dordrecht/Boston/London.

Ramo, C., and B. Busto. 1988. Observations at a King Vulture (*Sarcoramphus papa*) nest in Venezuela. *Auk* 105: 195–196.

Redford, K.H., and R.H. Wetzel. 1985. *Euphractus sexcintus*. *Mammalian Species*. 252: 1–4.

Rivas, J.A. 1999. The life history of the green anaconda (*Eunectes murinus*), with emphasis on its reproductive biology. Dissertation. University of Tennessee, Knoxville.

Rivas, J.A., et al. 1999. Caiman crocodiles. *Herpetological Review* 31.

Rodrigues, F.H.G., and J. Marinho-Filho. 1996. Feeding on a marsh-living herbaceous plant by Black Howler Monkeys (*Alouatta caraya*) in Central Brazil. *Folia Primatol* 65: 115–117.

Rodríguez-Estrella, R., and L. Rivera-Rodríguez. 1992. Kleptoparasitism and other interactions of crested caracara in the Cape Region, Baja California, Mexico. *Journal of Field Ornithology* 63(2): 177–180.

Rosas, F.C.W., J.A.S. Zuanon, and S.K. Carter. 1999. Feeding ecology of the Giant Otter, *Pteronura brasiliensis*. *Biotropica* 31(3): 502–506.

Roth, P. 1989. Der Hyazinthara, Anodorhynchus hyacinthinus. *Papageien* 1/89: 20–24.

Salas, L.A., and T.K. Fuller. 1996. Diet of the lowland Tapir (*Tapirus terrestris* L.) in the Tabaro River Valley, southern Venezula. *Candian Journal of Zoology* 74: 1444–1451.

Savage, J.M. 2002. *The Amphibians and Reptiles of Costa Rica*. University of Chicago Press, Chicago and London.

Schaller, G.B. 1983. Mammals and their biomass on a Brazilian ranch. *Arq. Zool. Sào Paulo* 31: 1–36.

Schaller, G.B., and P.G. Crawshaw. 1981. Social dynamics of a capybara population. *Saugetierkundliche Mitteilungen* 29:3–16.

———. 1982. Fishing behavior of the Paraguayan caiman (*Caiman crocodilus*). *Copeia* 66–72.

Sharpe, C.J., and Rodriguez, I. Caniama National Park, as found at www.thelostworld.org.

Shine, R.G. 1994. Sexual size dimorphism in snakes revisited. *Copeia*.

Sick, H. 1993. *Birds in Brazil: a natural history*. Princeton University Press, Princeton, NJ.

———. 1967. *Studies of Birds and Mammals of South America*. London, Murray, Tryon Gallery.

Strussman, C., and I. Sazima. 1993. The snake assemblage of the Pantanal at Pocone, western Brazil: faunal composition and ecological summary. Studies in Neotrop. *Fauna Environ.* 28(3): 157–168.

Tinbergen, N. 1951. *The Study of Instinct*. Oxford University Press, New York.

Wehekind. 1955. *British Journal of Herpetology* 2: 9–13.

Wilson, E.O. 2002. *The Future of Life*. Knopf, New York.